AF342162

THE GOD OF THE PASTOR

EMPIRICAL STUDIES IN THEOLOGY

EDITOR

JOHANNES A. VAN DER VEN

VOLUME IV

THE GOD OF THE PASTOR

*The Spirituality of Roman Catholic Pastors
in the Netherlands*

BY

GERARD ZUIDBERG

BRILL

LEIDEN · BOSTON · KÖLN

2001

Library of Congress Cataloging in Publication Data

Zuidberg, Gerard
  The God of the pastor : The Spirituality of Roman Catholic Pastors
in the Netherlands / by Gerard Zuidberg.
      p.   cm. — (Empirical studies in theology, ISSN 1389-1189 ; v.4)
  Includes bibliographical references and index.
  ISBN 9004117008 (alk. paper)
  1. Catholic Church—Clergy—Religious life—Netherlands 2. Priests-
-Religious life—Netherlands. 3. Spirituality—Catholic Church.
  I. Title. II. Series.

[BX1912.5 .Z85   2000
262'.142492—dc21
                                                                    00-060862
                                                                    CIP

Die Deutsche Bibliothek - CIP-Einheitsaufnahme

Zuidberg, Gerard:
The God of the pastor : The Spirituality of Roman Catholic Pastors in the
Netherlands / by Gerard Zuidberg. – Leiden ; Boston ; Köln : Brill, 2000
  (Empirical studies in theology ; Vol. 4)
  ISBN 90–04–11700–8

ISSN   1389-1189
ISBN   90 04 11700 8

CONTENTS

PART TWO

RELATION TO GOD, JESUS AND THE SPIRIT

PART THREE

FORMS OF EXPRESSING SPIRITUALITY

PART FOUR

CHURCH AND SACRAMENTS

PART FIVE

SPIRITUALITY AND MINISTRY

PART SIX

EVALUATION AND ASSESSMENT

ACKNOWLEDGEMENTS

It was a long process for me to deal productively with the variety of data that emerged during the course of my inquiry. I did not receive my education in the atmosphere or the school of empirical research. I had to learn step by step to look at my data from some distance and 'to learn how to play with it'. The process of elaborating on the data was sustained by the desire that my description would be a properly readable and manageable whole and would, at the same time, do justice to all the things I had heard during the talks with the thirty pastors who had been prepared to give interviews.

My inquiry was supervised by Prof. Dr. J.A. van der Ven who taught me the basics of the discipline of research, but above all stimulated me with his critical outlook to deal with the data yielded by the inquiry patiently and playfully.

I am also indebted to Prof. Dr. F. Haarsma, not only for encouraging me to put a lot of work into this study, but also for supplying me with some important data from existing literature dealing with ministry and spirituality. He also graciously agreed to write the afterword to this book. Above all I hope that this publication will do justice to what pastors feel and experience as their spirituality. I am aware of the fact that this is *my* inquiry and *my* processing of the material as *I* collected it by means of *my* interviews. In that sense what is said about inquiries like the present one is entirely true: the inquiry is strongly marked by, and bears the stamp of, the feelings, experience and views of a particular researcher.

I am also greatly indebted to a number of persons who read with me, to the parish and its staff who allowed me to spend time on the study next to my regular work, and in no small measure to all of the thirty pastors who were prepared to put their story into my hands.

Ton van den Ende took care in a creative manner of the final arrangement of the text and the layout.

I like to dedicate this book to my housemates Marie-José Janssen, Liesbeth and Gerard Loman on the occasion of our fourth lustrum.

INTRODUCTION

1. *The background to this publication*

This book is the result of a study into the spirituality of Catholic pastors in the Netherlands.[1] The immediate background to it was the publication of the results of a research project of the Nijmegen Institute for Studies in Empirical Theology (NISET) of the Catholic University of Nijmegen on the subject of the professionalisation of the ministry ("Professionalisering van het kerkelijk ambt", Schilderman and Visscher 1993). This research project was conducted under the auspices of the Federation of Associations of Pastoral Workers in the Netherlands, and was aimed at gaining a clear insight into the situation of pastors within the Dutch Archdiocese and into the chances of developing the professional skill required for their ministry. One part of this research project concerned the spirituality of pastors as an aspect of professional skill.

The CUN research into professionalisation

According to the basic idea of this research project, the professional or pastoral skill of pastors contains four aspects: scholarly knowledge, insight, skills and attitudes. The professional skill of pastors is related to the question of whether they have sound scientific knowledge of their field (such as the biblical and Christian traditions, systematic and practical theology, and the socio-cultural context), insight (i.e. into the structures and the goals of such knowledge), skills (e.g. the ability to conduct counselling interviews, the ability to preside in the liturgy, community building capacities) and attitudes (incorporating sincerity, evangelical orientation, collegiality and spirituality). In the Nijmegen research project spirituality is thus understood to be one of the attitudes.

---

[1] The word 'pastors' in the Dutch context stands for both ordained priests and theologically trained male/female pastoral workers.

Tendencies emerging from the Nijmegen research

In this research project a number of tendencies were revealed with respect to the meaning and content of spirituality:

– One tendency in particular was generally apparent, namely that the large majority of pastors interviewed no longer express their belief in God according to traditionally accepted practice: praying before and after meals, reciting the daily office and fasting. These traditional ways of expression are now only found among a minority. A large group of pastors appear to have abandoned traditional religious practice. There were, however, few signs of any new forms of religious expression being developed, on which we could report.

– Religious experiences are strongly related by pastors to experiences of solidarity with people, especially at important moments in life. These experiences are especially related to 'contingency-experiences', that is to say, experiences relating to critical situations, such as illness or death.

– With the majority of pastors spirituality does not appear to be a separate attitude, but aspects of spirituality are partly linked with the attitudes of sincerity and evangelical orientation. It may be concluded that pastors understand their spirituality as a way of living and working professionally in an attitude of sincerity, oriented on the gospel. Few pastors speak of spirituality as an element apart from their ministry;

– Pastors refer to the Christian tradition as an important source of spirituality and they find their discussion-partners especially among religiously-minded and committed members of the church;

– Spirituality is an important condition for pastors' being pastors in the first place, but it is also regarded as a goal of pastoral practice. It is the hope of all pastors to stimulate spirituality among their fellow-believers;

– There appears to be a connection between the traditional forms of expressing spirituality, such as praying before and after meals, reciting the daily office, fasting, etc., and certain traditional theological views concerning ministry. We are still unable to say anything about the question of the connection between modern interpretations of ministry and modern expressions of spirituality.

What is contemporary spirituality?

These findings raise a number of questions, and thus stimulate our curiosity: what does the contemporary spirituality of pastors look like? The following are of importance in this regard:

– The fact that pastors give hardly any answers to questions about modern forms of expressing spirituality, while their faith is, at the same time, expressed less and less in traditional forms, makes one wonder how contemporary spirituality is being expressed. Is it possible to gather anything about new forms of expression in more detailed personal interviews? What, for example, is the concrete content of prayer, reflection, and solidarity? There are also questions about the relation between faithful speaking about God and the way in which this is expressed in prayer, reflection and solidarity;

– What is the significance of the fact that religious experiences are strongly associated with experiences of social and existential nearness, in which, according to the Nijmegen research project, the experiences of critical moments in life in particular play an important part?

– If spirituality is mainly oriented on the Christian tradition, the question arises how pastors speak concretely about God, Jesus and the Spirit.

– In what way is spirituality part of professional skill, and what is, in particular, the significance of the finding that many pastors do not experience spirituality as a separate attitude next to sincerity and evangelical orientation? How are we to understand the fact that many pastors do not speak about spirituality as something apart from their ministry?

– The question can also be put in another way: what is the relation between professional skill and spirituality? In what sense is spirituality a condition for pastoral practice? And is it possible to say anything about the influence of spirituality on ministry and, vice versa, about the influence of the actual practice of ministry on the concrete content of spirituality?

– When the Nijmegen research project finds, for example, that univocal spiritual images of ministry are lacking, and encounters a diversity of images in which preference is given to images such as the pastor as companion, friend, sister or brother, what connections may then be discerned with the ways in which concrete content is given to spirituality?

Further study required

The idea thus arose to supplement the rough findings of the Nijmegen research project with a concrete description of the actual spiritual experience of pastors. More detailed research was opted for.

– The primary goal of the research was to gain a better understanding of the concrete content of the spirituality of pastors and its significance in the practical context of their ministry.

– A second, related goal was to gain insight into the question of whether and how the concrete content of a contemporary spirituality offers perspectives for promoting a sound, professional ministry.

2. *The concept of spirituality*

In this study the question is raised in what way pastors, living in today's culture and working in the Roman Catholic Church, give shape and content to their religiosity. In other words: what does their spirituality amount to?

In spiritual literature spirituality is defined in all sorts of ways. Spirituality is, for example, interpreted as the form in which people express their commitment to that which transcends them. From the perspective of this commitment people look at the world, other people, and themselves. That does not mean that what transcends people is necessarily apart from the world, other people, and themselves. The mystery is sometimes closer than people may suspect.

Spirituality is the perspective from which earthly reality is viewed. The way in which concrete content is given to this is different for every individual human being. People have different ways of giving shape to their view of reality according to their commitment to that which transcends them. This specific content came to be designated spirituality during the course of history.

The Titus Brandsma Institute at Nijmegen defines spirituality as "an ongoing reshaping in commitment to the Unconditional" (Waaijman 1992, 91). Here the emphasis is on the dynamic character of spirituality, in which people are constantly brought in motion through the confrontation with that which in the end does not allow itself to be defined by people and to which people themselves cannot attach any conditions. At the same time this definition indicates that spirituality has something to do with looking for, and working at, a content which becomes manifest in practical everyday life.

Related to these descriptions is the way in which J. Wissink and Th. Zweerman use three keywords to indicate what spirituality might be: Spirituality "stands for *organisation of life* (recently often indicated as lifestyle). It also stands for *orientation of life* or meaning of life ('meaning' then understood as the direction in which we assume, or hope, our destination lies). Finally the word 'spirituality' implies that essential moment of the *élan of life*: the inspiration or even passion which 'provides the electricity' for existence, i.e. makes it alive and makes it a risky enterprise" (Wissink and Zweerman 1989, 9).

These three aspects are essentially interdependent: "There is only hope for a viable and effective spirituality, when the orientation and the élan 'land' at the place where people are in fact trying to give shape to their lives: it will always be a question of our general style of living as an embodiment and profession of the emotions that drive and pervade us. The concrete content of the above-mentioned formal features of spirituality may differ according to the group concerned and it will also always bear the mark of temporality" (ibid. 9).

For the purposes of our study this description by Wissing and Zweermans is a suitable starting point. We proceed then from the view that spirituality is continually developing. It is a never-ending process of being touched and moved by, and entering into a relationship with, that which transcends people.

3. *Reflection in and on spirituality*

In our study of the significance of the spirituality of pastors we are interested in the question in what way reflection not only occurs in the experience of spirituality, but also as reflection on spirituality. In doing so, we allow ourselves to be guided by the model which Van der Ven has put forward, drawing on the work of Peirce, Dewey, West and Gelpi, in his description of "Reflective ministry" (Van der Ven 1997, 93 ff.).

Reflection in spirituality

Reflection plays a part in every concrete form of expression of spirituality. In our association with the divine we gain experiences which we process, about which we argue and which we judge and take into account in what we do and refrain from doing. In our prayers, for example, we see, we hear, we feel. We experience joy, grief, fear and anger, gratitude and disappointment. We are open to these experiences and, at the same time, by praying, we evoke these perceptions and feelings. They are not vague feelings, for we use all kinds of images in the process. They are images that we carry along in our memories: for example, images of light and dark, of direction and chaos, images of acceptance and defence, of finding a hearing and of being rejected, images of God, and images of people. These images become active once more or conjure up new, different, images. For example, images of a road, a wall, an opening or a closed circle. All these images are interconnected in a kind of network.

These images are important in that they influence our experiences, choices and actions. At the same time we can think about these images. Various reasoning processes take place within us. This happens mostly unconsciously. With regard to the reflection involved in our spirituality three processes can be distinguished:

1. Abduction, in which we reason from a part to the whole: if something is true for one, small part, then it will also be so for the whole;

2. Deduction, in which we draw a conclusion by means of a process of reasoning;

3. Induction, in which the experiences we have lead us to decide whether our conclusion was right or wrong.

An example of reflection in spirituality

We can, for example, resolve to start using the breviary once again in order to pay more attention to our daily prayer. The first few times we notice that the texts printed as readings don't really speak to us and sometimes only irritate us. They are texts which, in our opinion, are strange and offer little inspiration. Following the process of reasoning, we assume unconsciously that, if this is the case with a small part of the breviary, the whole breviary will mean little to us. We thus draw the conclusion that the prayers from the breviary are of no use to us. By trying again regularly, we discover that our conclusion was either right or wrong.

On that basis we can arrive at choices that can or can not incite us to action: we can go on praying, give up prayer, or start praying in another way. This provides us with new experiences, which in their turn influence the images we carry inside ourselves. By praying in another way, it is possible, for example, to break through the image of the closed circle and to make room for the more power-ful image of an open, passable, road.

On the basis of reflection, people do, or do not, bring themselves to act. Choices are made. Through this process the character of peo-ple who, in their everyday practice, act in certain ways rather than others, and make certain choices, is also illuminated. In doing, and reflecting in doing, people discover themselves. Sometimes acutely: *"that is how I am as a praying human being"*; sometimes less acutely: *"that is the way it mostly is"*. At the same time an inner dialogue takes place: I talk to the various aspects within myself, and in this way my self is shaped.

Van der Ven points out that each experience, each practice, con-tains reflection, the rational aspect. In fact, experience and reflection are never separated.

This is the first form of reflection: reflection in spirituality. It is an aspect of each concrete form of spirituality. Reflection can always be shown to be at work—sometimes explicitly, sometimes less explicitly.

Reflection on spirituality

A second form of reflection builds upon this. That is reflection *on* spirituality. It is the aspect of distancing ourselves from concrete experience, momentarily "freezing" our experience, so to speak, and, from a distance, trying to find an answer to the question: what has actually happened here and now? We spend some time consciously thinking over the road we have travelled thus far, asking ourselves what has occurred in our experience. Such reflection occur espe-cially when external factors begin to impact upon our actual spirit-uality, as a result of which we are challenged to look, from a distance, at the course we have taken and to weigh the latter against possi-ble new courses. It has something to do with the context in which we live and act.

The development of spirituality always takes place in a context and is therefore subject to influences from the context in which peo-ple live and work. To the context belong biography, personal iden-tity, culture and the work situation. It is through influences from, and interaction with, the context, that people continue to be confronted withnew choices. Reflection is then required in order to find a new di-rection, expressed in the renewed content of our spirituality. Such reflection, in the sense of consciously distancing oneself from direct perception and experience, may be referred to as reflection on spirituality.

For example: the development of a modern culture, in which God is increasingly experienced as hidden, may confuse us, and provoke feelings of uneasiness, insecurity and fear. Our upbringing and theological training may have been very different. This may create such a complicated situation that we start looking for ways of getting out of it. In doing so, the question presents itself of which opportunity offers the most attractive way out. Do we stick to what we have been taught, do we break new ground, do we handle texts and prayers differently, do we grow in the process or do we sustain damage, and how are we to become ourselves in the process? These considerations can lead to a decision that will determine our manner of dealing with God. We can think about this entire process from a distance and, finally, reach the conclusion that we have pondered on all this more or less adequately.

An example from pastoral practice

Here I shall define the two forms of reflection also with respect to their mutual relatedness, this time in greater detail. I shall not do this by means of experiences in spirituality, but shall choose a concrete example from pastoral practice, one I have described in a contribution to an issue of the journal *Speling*, in which different kinds of developments in the experience of virtue were discussed (Zuidberg 1996 a).

A 73-year-old woman had actively participated in the church until 20 years ago, and had felt at home in a parish liturgy, which was being renewed, and in forms of joint reflection. In the period that followed, she began to experience major difficulties with various restorative tendencies in the Dutch Roman Catholic Church, with the result that she withdrew. She now not only feels estranged from the church, but has also undergone a process as a result of which she feels and thinks less and less in religious terms. She prefers to call herself "a-religious" or "secular". She is suffering from an incurable disease and wishes to have a discussion with a pastor who "does not immediately bring up church and faith".

In our early meetings she tells her religious history and asks if I am prepared to help her bring her life to completion in an honest and authentic way.

Listening to her story about her estrangement from church and faith, I see, feel and experience a number of things within myself: I feel impotence, anger and pain because things had to go like this for her. I realise that all kinds of images emerge and intermingle within myself: images of God who wants to be humanly near, and texts from Scripture that have become dear to me. I realise that I have had the good fortune to live and work in a concrete church community in which God's human nearness could become manifest in a heart-warming manner. I experience the meetings with her as moments that affect me strongly. I am moved by her honest and convincing way of talking, and I recognise an ideal within myself of being able to live life in a similar way.

As I seek to make room for that ideal within myself, I notice that there is plenty of scope for it in our discussions. She tells about the pain in her marriage, the experience of having been constantly used by her husband, and the fact that the children she bore were unwanted. During the meetings I notice that various reasoning processes are taking place within myself. My mind tells me that perhaps a talk with the children, in order to reach closure, might be helpful. If she is honestly trying to deal with the end of her life here and now, she may perhaps also be able to do that in a final talk with her children. I suggest this to her and we agree that we shall have a go at it. She adds that she wishes the conversation with them to be honest and true to reality. All kinds of images emerge within myself: images of ideal communication, limitations, and disappointing experiences in similar talks. At the same time there is the hope, the wish, that it will succeed. The ensuing talks show that my conclusion was correct. She proves able and willing to talk to her children about her extremely difficult history in an honest manner.

A lot happens during the weekly contacts. I notice after every meeting that quite a lot happens within myself too. I feel the need, but also the obligation, to reflect in a goal-oriented manner on the course and contents of our talks. I distance myself from what has happened, keep a diary and note down especially the things I see happening on her final journey, but also within myself, what images she evokes apart from my experiences and perceptions and the way in which I respond to her. I look from a distance at what has taken place in our contacts and try to get a clear picture of it.

I notice in that reflection that now, more at a distance, by way of reasoning, I am connecting with things from my own religious history, my experiences with the church, my development in ministry, which is showing increasingly secular features, my looking for a language in which my experience of faith can be articulated. I notice that the course of our talks is strongly influenced by all that. I conclude that my belief in God has become increasingly linked with my connection with the earth, that I have frequently struggled with developments in the church and have tried to find a way of my own through them. I could give this back to her, but we could also discuss the mystic tradition, which has become dear to her and—to my surprise—to me too.

The necessity of the two forms of reflection in and on my ministry makes itself felt most in the final period of her life in which the talks with the children take place. At that moment a number of new factors emerge: the children, each with his or her own history, the wordless conflicts, and periods of both connection and estrangement. I notice that my own context strongly influences my way of supervising these talks. By reflecting on it, I discover what choices I make and with what choices I continue to be confronted during these talks. It would be no exaggeration to say in retrospect that I really "had to put myself out" or "had to go to all lengths" to remain loyal to this woman in her wish, while not disguising anything of what was going on within myself.

I can also say now that, by reflecting on this whole process, I have broadened my awareness of what knowledge, insight, skills and attitudes are available in me. And through precise reflection I gain a better insight into my spirituality. I discover that the content of this spirituality is closely related to the wish for acting truthfully and honestly in the spirit of the gospel. This wish was nurtured and frequently modified by my own religious history, but it should be added that this religious history is strongly embedded in my professional development.

Importance of reflection for spirituality

The two forms of reflection, reflection in and on spirituality, can have an important effect on spirituality, as much as on the way the ministry is carried out. By means of reflection we can gain insight into the tension between ideals and reality and, in doing so, grow in the creative manner in which we can handle this tension. The second form of reflection is the first form made explicit. In the second reflection the first is nurtured, criticised, adjusted.

We start from the assumption that it is possible to point to a continuum among pastors, which shows to what extent they develop reflection in the first and the second sense. We assume that in all pastors the first form of reflection is found, but to a far lesser degree the second form of reflection. The purpose of our study is to gain insight into the shifts on the continuum of reflection from less to more.

Two questions

Against the background of the foregoing we arrive at two questions:

1. What does the spirituality of the pastors interviewed by us look like in relation to their ministry?

2. What is the significance of reflection in and on spirituality? In our description of the various aspects of pastors' spirituality, at the end of the various sections in which spirituality is described in concrete terms, we shall inquire to what extent we find that pastors exemplify a "reflective spirituality". In doing so we are especially interested in reflection on spirituality. In our judgement, reflection on spirituality is linked to the possibilities of spirituality developing in our time.

Ministry: putting one's spirituality at people's disposal

The use of the term "reflection" also has an internal, pastoral motive: for ministry to function properly, it is imperative for pastors, apart from other aspects, to have immediate access to their spirituality and to be able to put it to people's disposal. Spirituality is then one of the resources in pastoral practice.

Bishop Ernst, using the words of Willem Berger, gave the following description of ministry: "Ministry is putting your faith at people's disposal". Faith, here, means giving concrete content to spirituality, while embedding it in the Judeo-Christian tradition. He pointed out that ministry is the skill of putting the concrete content one has given to spirituality at people's disposal in dealing with them.

For this to happen it is necessary for a pastor to have immediate access to her or his spirituality. This only becomes possible by reflecting on it, by thinking about and looking at it, walking around it, as it were, in order to see what it amounts to in concrete terms. Here we see a transition from individual spirituality to public spirituality. Pastors are supposed to experience spirituality not only for themselves. They are supposed to make their own spirituality work for the benefit of their ministry. Thus the spirituality of pastors becomes visible and verifiable.

We shall have recourse to the account of the first and second kind of reflection, so as to be able to describe how pastors have immediate access to their spirituality.

4. *The research sample*

At the beginning of this introduction, mention was made of the Nijmegen research project. This so-called survey-research, the purpose of which was to gain insight into the general features of pastors as a group, inquired after elements in traditional and modern spirituality. The answers given by the pastors were subjected to a factor-analysis: which elements in fact belong together? Only one factor emerged from this analysis, namely that factor which incorporates various elements of traditional spirituality.

According to the Nijmegen research, the modern forms of spirituality do not show any real coherence. That is a disappointing result. Disappointing, since it was assumed that it would be possible to say at least something about the more modern forms of spirituality.

On the basis of these findings we took the next step. We asked ourselves: when did traditional spirituality lose its plausibility? In what period can a thorough shift in the experience of spirituality be discerned? In our judgement it was the period sometimes referred to as the "Cultural Revolution", namely from 1965 until 1975. This period was characterised by broad social developments, such as democratisation, social criticism, different views about, and experiences of, marriage, and a radical change in religious experience, which found particular expression in the commotion brought about by the book *"Honest to God"* by J.A.T. Robinson.

This period saw great shifts in institutions for theological educational: mergers of several major seminaries and monastic training colleges, that so far had operated independently; the foundation of several theological faculties; modernisation in the curriculum of theological education and more attention to pastoral education, including work placement and supervision.

This is the reason why we were interested in that group of pastors who received their training during that period. Since theological study takes at least 5 years, we chose those pastors who studied between 1965 and 1980.

Having selected the group of pastors, we then limited the number. We restricted ourselves to 30. In choosing these 30 pastors, we looked for a proportional division of ordained and non-ordained pastors, men and women, regular and secular priests. The group of pastors who were interviewed included the first group of pastoral workers in the Roman Catholic Church in the Netherlands. It was equally important that pastors from several fields of activity would be represented: parish-ministry, ministry in institutions, and forms of social ministry.

The research could also provide insight into the possible differences in spirituality between ordained and non-ordained, female and male pastors, and pastors active in different sectors of ministry.

In the concrete selection of the pastors we made use of the registers of the seven dioceses. We looked at the year in which the pastors concerned received their first appointment in ministry. That year had to be after 1965 and before 1981.

In this way a rough division was made between a relatively "older" and a relatively "younger" group. Having selected the pastors from the registers in this way, we then looked at the distribution with respect to the present fields of activity: parish ministry, institutional ministry and social ministry, and according to the aspect of having, or not having, been ordained, and according to the place of theological training: Amsterdam, Heerlen, Nijmegen, Tilburg and Utrecht. From each training institution at least 5 pastors were chosen.

While using the registers of the various dioceses, we noticed that a number of pastoral workers in the Roermond diocese were not officially registered. We therefore looked for two more pastors, active without having been officially appointed by the bishop.

5. *Three themes in the interviews*

With respect to the method of questioning used in the interviews with the thirty pastors, during the course of 1994, three themes were chosen in consultation with J. van der Ven and Fr. Haarsma:

1. The context of spirituality. By context is meant: the life history, the growth and development of the personal identity and the

surrounding socio-cultural reality to which, among other things, the Church as institution belongs.

2. The way in which pastors speak about their relation with and to God, Jesus and the Spirit: how do they describe their faith, hope and love and how do they speak in metaphors about God, Jesus and the Spirit? How do they express what they experience as a relationship with the divine?

3. The relation between this experienced spirituality on the one hand, and ministry on the other. What can be said about the place of spirituality in the professional skill of pastors?

The list of themes employed in our interviews has been added as an appendix at the end of this publication. The order of the list was followed as closely as possible. The broad themes mentioned above constituted the three main lines of the interview. It was, however, not a fully structured interview. Several questions were followed by more detailed questions. This was done whenever I got the impression that the answers given were too vague or impersonal.

Corrections and additions

The interviews, which were all fully recorded on tape, were typed out and sent to the interviewee concerned, who was then asked for possible corrections and additions in cases where they thought the text was incomplete. All the interviewees reacted in writing, though some of them also made telephone calls that were again recorded on tape. Most reactions consisted of endorsement, concrete and practical additions (especially data, names), and—with a third of the pastors—additions as to the content of the interview. The corrections and additions were then added to the existing interview texts. Also, for one part (part II, chapter 5.3), namely as far as the description of the Spirit is concerned, I asked the pastors again, at a later date, for information in writing, because not enough information had been requested during the interviews.

6. *Research method*

I opted for a qualitative approach, in the sense that I was chiefly interested in qualitative methods of data collection by means of personal interviews, and in a qualitative analysis of this data by means of tracing relations and tendencies.

As has already been said, all the interviews were fully recorded on tape and then typed out verbatim. The material was then entered into the computer programme "Kwalitan" (Cf. Glaser and Strauss 1980; Van der Ven and Ziebertz 1993b; Van der Ven 1993–1994). This programme, according to Van der Ven, provides the two principal functions provided by all software programmes for qualitative research: the possibility of entering concepts into the scenes or content parts of the text material, as well as the possibility of interconnecting these scenes on the basis of the concepts concerned. Besides, the software programme fulfils a few additional functions, such as combining scenes on the basis of the concepts found and listing the frequencies of these concepts.

Three phases in the qualitative analysis

1. Open coding
The text is divided into scenes or separate parts according to content; each scene is then provided with concepts as keywords, and finally the scenes that contain identical or related concepts are compared to one another;
2. Axial coding
The researcher starts looking for dimensions in the list of concepts which has emerged during the process of open coding (for example, the concept of faith contains the dimension of God's omnipotence as well as the dimension of God's goodness); This is followed by a search for the connection between the various dimensions; then follows a search for the way in which, starting from the dimensions, the concepts vary among themselves, by looking at differences that are as great or small as possible; finally, starting from the dimensions, the concepts are brought in relation to one another;
3. Selective coding
In this final phase the most important concepts are selected, after which one or more key concepts are selected; finally, relations are established between the key concepts that have thus emerged, and other concepts.

In our research, this entire procedure was not followed. We restricted ourselves to the phase of "open coding" and some aspects of "axial coding" and "selective coding".

Processing the data

1. The texts were provided with keywords that, each in turn, charted a particular part of the interviews. Out of all 30 interviews a list emerged of 2300 different keywords.

2. These were compared among themselves and brought under headings, so that the list could be reduced to 160 keywords.

3. From these a selection was made, based on the various fields and the concrete content of spirituality.

In this way the final list of 36 keywords emerged. This then became the working list.

Further research into connections between keywords and tendencies provided the material for the concrete arrangement of the book. In the first place, the context of religious development. In the second place, the relation to God, Jesus and the Spirit. In the third place, the concrete experience of spirituality. In the fourth place, church and sacraments. In the fifth place, the relation between spirituality and ministry. In the sixth place, the evaluation and the postscript by Fr. Haarsma. The book is concluded with the list of themes used in the interviews, and a bibliography.

PART ONE

CONTEXT OF RELIGIOUS DEVELOPMENT

INTRODUCTION

In the general introduction it was indicated that the description of the spirituality of pastors is based on the idea that spirituality always develops in a particular context. According to this view, spirituality is not merely an inner process. Spirituality does not develop apart from, or independently of, the contexts in which pastors live and work. Therefore a number of questions were asked about the way in which pastors think about their context. These questions concerned the four aspects of a context: we could call them the four basic aspects of religious development.

All four aspects concern a relation of some sort:

1. The relation to one's own biography. The concrete point at issue here is the question of the relation between pastors and the parental environment they come from, as well as their relation to their further development in life;

2. The relation to the self or the centre of identity. How do pastors look at their own personal identity? What self-image do they have?

3. The relation to the surrounding culture, in particular the relation to the cultural development which we call secularisation;

4. The relation to the institution of the Church. This is an aspect of the cultural context, but we shall deal with this as a separate aspect, because it plays a separate role in the spirituality of pastors who work within this institution.

This first part will describe the relation of pastors to these four aspects of the context of their religious development. We shall be inquiring how the relation to this context contributes to the development of spirituality.

CHAPTER ONE

BIOGRAPHICAL ASPECTS

The saying goes: If you do not know where you come from, you do not know where you are going either. In other words: for those who have no perspective on their own history, it is difficult to work at the future. It is certain that we humans, in developing our lives, always continue to have some sort of relation to our origin, and that there is a constant flux in our view of that origin.

The question in this chapter is how the pastors interviewed look back on their past and how they are aware of its influence on the development of their spirituality. First of all, the way in which pastors look back on their childhood, and on the parental environment they grew up in, is described. This is followed by a description of whether, and in what way, there have been conflicts with the parents. Then the social position of the parental environment is described. Finally, I shall describe what views these pastors have of their further development. How do pastors look at their development?

I am aware of the fact that, in the interviews, I asked questions mainly about the relation between pastors and their parents. The relations with their brothers, sisters and other members of the family were hardly ever brought up as a subject, if at all. On the other hand, questions were asked about the significance of certain important persons during the period of education and training.

1. *Relation to parents*

In the interviews, pastors sometimes clearly revealed their pain at being questioned on their relationship with their parents. At the same time one often discerns a compassionate tone, because during the course of life, a better understanding of people's vulnerability, including that of parents, has been acquired. Some interviews bear the stamp of gratitude. These pastors had the good fortune in life of being able to develop in such a way that they can now look back gratefully on their past. In others an atmosphere of pain and sorrow can still be discerned. They feel that the damage done in their childhood is irreparable. Some pastors have completely distanced themselves from their parents.

I shall describe, successively, how some of them speak about an open and warm relationship with their parents. Others mention the lack of any real bond with their parents, how a father and/or mother dominated the scene, or how a father and/or mother was often absent. Some of them tell about an authoritarian father or mother, and finally, some look back on a relationship with vulnerable parents.

An open and warm relationship with both parents

At home there was an open and cordial atmosphere, marked by a sense of security and safety. This made an unrestrained development possible. The things one could do were encouraged and stimulated, while the things one could not do, did not have to be done. It was possible to talk about anything. This atmosphere became the basis for lasting and positive contacts. Because of the atmosphere at home, there was that sound basis of trust so essential for being able to handle further developments.

The interviews that mention this are, on the whole, marked by an open atmosphere. The pastors concerned still like to keep in touch with their parental home, insofar as the parents are still alive. They talk about their history in a quiet, relaxed, way. It is true that some of them experienced tough confrontations and moments of conflict later in life with respect to other official bodies, such as, for example, the institution of the Church. The basis of trust, however, which they had originally received from their parental environment is so strong that they are not frustrated by them.

Distance from both parents

In a few interviews the bond with the parents, whether positive or negative, is said to have been completely broken. The memory of home has faded. It evokes few images. One pastor says, typically: "I have always had the idea that I went my own way at an early age." In this interview there are indeed hardly any memories of the past. With one of them the conversation about the relation with people at home is avoided, while for another it has simply become a closed book. A third has been "homeless" since her youth, and she has had to undertake a lot in order to find a home for herself.

For this pastor, it means that she has kept on searching and working creatively in order to find some sort of shelter together with people whom she has chosen for herself. In the case of the first two, who did not maintain any contact with their parents, we also see something else: it is difficult for them to establish contacts with colleagues and friends. Perhaps their experiences in the past constitute an obstacle to making new contacts, for example with colleagues. They also speak more reservedly than the other persons interviewed about personal experiences and feelings.

Positive influence

A small number of pastors who talk about their fathers in this way, have great respect for the father. They attribute to him a strong authority because of his wisdom and his respect for people. The strong influence of the father later on became a source of conflict for some of them. In spite of the great admiration and, at times, warm respect for the father, these pastors were faced with a struggle, later in life, to break free from the pressure exerted by their dominant father.

A relatively large number speak with admiration and love about the important role of their mothers. This is partly connected to the fact that the father was absent, or was so occupied by his work that the task of bringing up the children, and the contact with the children, became entirely the mother's concern. Most of them indicate the important role of their mother, especially in her nearness, her personal attention, and the way in which she managed to provide a sense of security. One of them describes his parental home as one in which the father could not be near, whereas the mother, in spite of all the tensions caused by the father, was able to create an atmosphere of spaciousness and security. This expresses an atmosphere of trust by which a child is supported in finding his or her own way.

> *Mother was a big-hearted and caring person. She gave each of us the chance to be what we wanted to be. She did not approve of everything I did, but she did give me a free rein.*

For the majority of these pastors the mother is chiefly the stable factor in bringing up the children. She determines the home environment through her cordial and caring presence. Some pastors were brought up solely by their mother. For one or two of them this was not so fundamentally different, because the mother took care of a lot of things and was able to allow them some freedom:

> *The relationship with my mother, fortunately, has never been a problem. She allowed me my freedom and there was never any overprotective attitude. I have never had the feeling that my mother wanted to push me in a certain direction. She was a very friendly woman and we had a cordial, affectionate, relationship.*

For these pastors the mother's presence became a stable basis for their further development. Here, too, however, lie seeds for conflicts later in life. For some of them the bond with the mother could grow into a heavy pressure, leaving too little room for a growing child to choose his or her own way.

Absence of the father or mother

While for a small number of pastors the absence of the mother (through premature death) is an important fact, for a third of those interviewed the absence of the father was of importance. To a large extent his absence was due to the heavy work he had to do and to scanty wages. His life was work. For others the early death of the father was an event which had a great impact.

Most of these pastors indicate that the absence of the father at an early stage became the occasion for them to start looking more actively for their own way in life. In their development in life it is indeed possible to indicate several moments at which they learned to make choices. This is probably connected with the fact that at a rather early age they were given an important responsibility within the family.

In those interviews where it is mentioned, the absence of the mother is connected with the experience that the father had a dominant influence. For some of them the absence of the mother became a source of conflict: the early death of the mother caused a fundamental crisis of confidence, and a permanent restlessness. This restlessness continued to influence the lives of the pastors concerned for a long time.

An authoritarian father and/or mother

Some pastors who talk about the authoritarian character of the father describe it in rather mild terms: *"he meant well."* They talk about it charitably and they also say that, in spite of the authoritarianism, they have received a lot from the father. The term authoritarian is understood here as denoting a quality of someone who has authority, in this case not on formal grounds or on the basis of biblical pronouncements. These pastors did not retain any negative feelings about it. Others are most resolute in declaring that any discussion with their father was impossible. One of them, for example, describes the atmosphere in the relationship with his father as an atmosphere of silence: *"we had better not talk about it."*

In the interviews where it is mentioned, the mother's authoritarian behaviour is connected with "the moral pressure" exerted by her. One of them, for example, says: *"Mother tried to bring us up neatly and decently, which created in me an aversion to anything connected with moral virtues."* For some of them it was especially an atmosphere in which conflicts were covered with a cloak of charity. No conflict was allowed to exist. Or there was an atmosphere of fear as a result of the pressure exerted by the mother.

Father or mother as vulnerable persons

The vulnerability of the father or mother is associated either with weak health or with vulnerable qualities, such as being easily given to fear, or the constant tendency to worry too much. This caused isolation and sometimes drunkenness. The pastors who say something about this show, on the one hand, how much the atmosphere in the family suffered from it, but on the other hand, they show that they have learned how to deal with it compassionately. That is especially the case later in life, when they themselves have undergone some development.

Summary

In a number of interviews it becomes clear that pastors are able to speak with some detachment about their development, and are able to say something about the importance of the home situation for their further development.

Some pastors are able to indicate clearly what the cordial atmosphere at home has meant for them, while others indicate that they are well aware of the way in which the authoritarian father has had an influence on their further development. The same applies to all the aspects mentioned. This can be pointed out most concretely in the case of those who speak about their parents as vulnerable persons.

With others, the interviews mention either a spontaneous "living away" of the problems arising in the relationship with the people at home, or of a well-nigh unquestioned acceptance of the influence exerted by the parents.

Some of them do not feel any need during the interview to go concretely into their relationship with their parents.

2. *Conflicts with parents*

With little less than half of the pastors interviewed, sharp conflicts emerge with respect to the home situation. Something of this kind was already indicated in the foregoing. A strong influence, an authoritarian attitude, or a strong moral pressure on the part of the father and/or mother became sources of restlessness and discomfort, and led to conflicts. Sometimes the conflict was fought out in the open, or at least attempts were made to do so, but sometimes the conflict, although clearly felt, could not be raised in any way with those whom it concerned. Sometimes the conflict was dealt with, sometimes not. Sometimes the conflict was latent under everything a pastor did and said during his later development. In certain interviews one gets the impression that the pastors concerned are not so clearly aware of the effects that remain.

The conflicts are connected with the following three aspects: appreciation of physical being and the development of an inner life, in particular in the field of sexuality; appreciation of morality, that is to say in the field of expectations with respect to that which is good, right and meaningful; appreciation of religiosity and expressions of it, for example church attendance. With nearly all pastors who mention conflicts, the conflict exists with respect to several aspects simultaneously.

Conflicts in the field of physical and sexual experience

Several pastors have had to learn to distance themselves from a legalistic and often negative attitude with respect to things corporeal and sexual. Especially the women among them are explicit in speaking about this:

> *A lot of emphasis used to be laid on the negative aspects of sexuality. I myself have had to learn that as a woman I do not always have to be strong, as my*

mother was accustomed to being. It is precisely my strength to dare to feel and live my own physical identity.

This female pastor indeed gradually came to offer resistance to the role of women in the Church, especially through her study of theology. It started already with a struggle at the conclusion of her studies, when she wanted to write a thesis on the position of women in the Church. That struggle sprung from her becoming conscious of the fact that she wanted to be fully accepted as a woman. She felt completely dependent on others until she discovered that her identity no longer had to be described in merely negative terms:

Women are negatively anchored in all kinds of myths, also in the Bible and in our religious traditions. Evil is nearly always attributed to women. Perhaps that was one of the reasons for me to go deeply into the Bible. That was the direction that appealed to me most. I have had to do everything myself, though.

She points out in the interview that there is a clear connection between her struggle for full recognition in the Church on the one hand and her conflict with her mother on the other. In this way, this woman becomes aware not only of the positive meaning of her physical being and sexuality, but also of her social position and role in the Church.

A development following on this is her discovery that, as a woman, she not only represents the so-called *"soft and emotional sides"* of life, but that she is equally *"capable of handling reality in a rational way"*. In doing so, she offers resistance against the culture in which she grew up.

The point at issue in this interview is the process undergone by a woman who becomes aware of the fact that she no longer has to offer resistance against the world of men, but finds enough strength in her own "self". Resistance leads to finding one's own strength and meaning. This has enabled her to say: *"This is I, with everything that goes with it. Thus am I God's image."*

A fairly large number of other pastors speak in a similar fashion about their development, which was marked by a conflict with the mother or father with regard to the experience of things corporeal and sexual. Sometimes the conflict is discussed openly. This, however, is limited to just a few cases. Where this is the case, the basis of the relationship with the parents is a positive one. In cases where it was not possible to discuss this openly, this was due, on the one hand, to the incommunicative attitude of the mother or father, and on the other, to an uncertain, hesitant attitude toward the parents. Some pastors declare that they were unable to judge whether they could *"do this to their parents"*. Others avoid the conflict, because it was clear to them that it was impossible to discuss it. A number of pastors have come to terms with the conflict gradually.

Conflicts with respect to morality

With some, there is a strong link between their own assessment of what is right or wrong, and the ideal image of the father or mother. For example a high moral consciousness of the father was combined with a great sense of duty, strong commitment and appreciation of justice. In this way the father set high ideals for his children.

One pastor, for example, says that, despite the great regard he still has for his parents, he also has to admit, painfully, that the high ideal continued to influence him for a very long time. It took a long time for him to dare, and to be able, to free himself from the pressure which this ideal image exerted on his life. Particularly with regard to the ideal of becoming a priest, this meant choosing for a life characterised by availability and heroic sacrifice. This made him a lonely person. In his loneliness he continually longed for his mother who had already died very early on.

A female pastor says, on the subject of the high moral consciousness of her father, that for a long time she lived with the conviction that only that which is tiresome is good. This went so far that she even began to become suspicious when at a certain moment things were simply going well.

In the interviews with these two pastors it is said that the mother had died early, so that she was absent for the rest of their lives. The relationship with the father was the determining factor in their further development. In either case, there was no open and sharp conflict with the father, but the interior conflict of both pastors was growing gradually. Later in life—when they have already been active in the ministry for a number of years—both find themselves in a crisis in which it becomes a matter of finding one's "self" and henceforth actively taking responsibility for one's own life.

In some other interviews it appears that the mother has had a lot of influence on standards of decency, fear of what people will think, and notions of proper and decent behaviour. Some female pastors had great difficulty in freeing themselves from their mother's expectations.

For one of them, the strong pressure exerted by her mother on her *"virtuous life"* meant that she became increasingly averse to anything smelling of 'virtue'. Only gradually did she free herself by becoming more and more oriented on what, deep within herself, she felt to be right and just. God had no longer anything to do with what *"had to be done at all costs, but with what is good for the world. That has become something of myself."* She begins to realise that morality has nothing to do with duty or ideals, which have no connection with reality. She knows that every time she falls back again into a legalistic understanding of what is morally right, she will be encountering her mother with whom she has to take up the struggle once more.

Some pastors came to find themselves caught up in the tension between differences in the expectations cherished by their mother and their father respectively with regard to the children. The parents also had different ideas about morality. With one of them the mother allowed much more freedom than the father did, and it was the mother in particular who was attentive to opportunities for the children to develop. With respect to the father there were a lot of tensions, for he had difficulty in dealing with new things. Mother allowed more freedom and was more caring.

The pastor who is talking here had to find his own way, groping for: who am I, what can I do, how far can I go in growing up? It still determines his life nowadays, although he now finds himself in a completely different situation. With his father it was impossible to have a personal talk. There was the continual threat of a conflict. So they talked about trivial things so as to keep the atmosphere pleasant. It became more difficult, however, especially when they were alone. Things were not as they should be between father and son.

This pastor found his way by increasingly distancing himself from the compulsive character of his father and by testing his own options in open conversation with his mother. It took a long time, however, to become really free: even now he still finds himself in the process of freeing himself.

For the majority of this group of pastors the tension brought about by the pressure of the father or the mother on the experience of moral standards and values continued to play a role in their lives for a long time. This group is characterised by the fact that they are still struggling to become truly free. At the same time it is evident that a number of these pastors have gained a lot of space and creativity as a result of their struggle.

Conflicts with respect to religious experience and its expressions

Most pastors say that their youth was marked by devotional practices such as saying the rosary, praying before and after meals, the use of holy water and regular church attendance. Some regard it as a positive period. *"That whole Roman Catholic childhood is part of my experience. I thought it very beautiful".*

All interviews show that the pastors have said good-bye to this traditional pattern. With two-thirds of the pastors interviewed this took place without much ado. The overall impression is of a traditional pattern losing its meaning more or less automatically. Ritual gradually disappears as an expression of religiosity. One out of three, however, deliberately distanced themselves from it. One of them articulates this distancing as follows:

> *Piety was part of life, you joined in it automatically. I already felt estranged from my home at an early stage. I was actually glad when I went back to the seminary after the holidays again. From the time when I was twelve years old, my home situation ceased to exert any real influence on me.*

A few others state quite frankly: *"I wanted to get away from that whole, closed, Roman Catholic environment"* and *"piety and religion were a kind of escape from a rather tough existence".*

One of these pastors says that the highly traditional religious atmosphere imposed at home by his father is the reason why he can no longer bring himself to pray in his own family:

> *I find myself still in the process of freeing myself from the things I always had to do, such as, for example, obligatory church attendance.*

In his family little is now made of this.

Summary

About a third of the pastors show in the interview that the conflict with the parents has clearly had its place in the further course of their lives. This becomes apparent in the way these pastors indicate whether and how they have come to terms with the conflict. For some of them the conflict made itself felt in all of the three fields that we have indicated: the appreciation of things corporeal, the process of dealing with ethical standards and values, and religious experience.

Most pastors, looking back on the past, declare that they are no longer constrained by what has happened. Some of them show that it has remained a hard, painful spot in their lives, while others point out that this aspect of the past has become a closed issue for them. Those in the latter category know that they have not come to terms with the conflict and that it will continue to play a role, in spite of the fact that it has become a closed issue for them.

It is important for this group of pastors to be aware of the fact that they have, anyhow, developed an attitude with respect to what happened in the past. They are also accountable for it. Some of them show in the next part of the interview that they have actively looked for their own way in their physical, ethical and religious experience.

Several other pastors, too, have gradually distanced themselves from old patterns, but they have had to struggle less in order to get away from what they received at birth. Some had the good fortune of having grown up in a free, open atmosphere. They do not so much feel the need to distance themselves from what used to happen at home. Among the latter two groups of pastors there are some that show that they are clearly aware of the meaning of their experiences for the rest of their lives. They realise that a less conflictual, sometimes harmonious, development constituted an important contribution to the development of a balanced pattern of life.

3. *The environment of origin*

Environment of origin and its continuing influence

Half of the pastors interviewed come from an agrarian environment, while the other half come from various other environments. Four of them come from working class families, three from a shop-keeping families, three from the educational sector, one is the son of a therapist, another the daughter of an administrative clerk, and in one case the father had no profession. In the case of two of them the environment is still unknown.

Two pastors declare that their personal life and faith, but also their ministry, still bear the stamp of their agrarian background. One of them calls the *"agrarian soberness and realism"* aspects that now characterise his ministry. The other speaks about the *"daily dedication of the whole family in which one was entirely included"* as something of which the memory is still vivid in his mind. He thinks it quite normal that he is still dedicated to people now. This is indeed characteristic of pastors who come from a shop-keeping environment.

Half of the pastors with an agrarian background speak of a transition in their life history from a rather closed, agrarian culture to an open, urban culture. Contact with an open, urban culture meant being liberated, getting away from a narrow, closed, Roman Catholic tradition. There is room for initiatives of one's own. One is challenged to look for new answers. These pastors, however, also speak of a transition from a soft and gentle culture to a more aggressive, alienating one which sometimes displays hostile features. At the same time, for some of them this becomes an invitation to learn how to look critically at the culture they came from.

An important aspect for some is the question of language. The transition to an urbanised society challenges them to look for a new language. According to one of them, a permanent tension can be discerned between agrarian village culture and urban culture. This is expressed, for example, in the way of addressing God: *"our God"* (typical of the village community) and *"my God"* (the individualisation of urban culture).

The pastors coming from a working class environment point out that there were tough moments in their youth which have continued to influence some of them: the memory of the struggle to be accepted as an equal of others who come from a higher environment. In this process, the pain because of a lack of appreciation, for example from the side of the Church, was a lasting memory. This still continues to make itself felt with two of the four. They reject, for example, any form of patronising by any public body whatsoever, but certainly by the Church.

The pastors coming from a teacher's family bear the stamp of a strong moral upbringing and discipline. At the same time, two of the three speak gratefully of the sensitive atmosphere in which they were brought up. They retain positive memories of it.

Large or small family

Most pastors grew up in a large family. For some of them the great poverty is the characteristic feature of that background, while for others it is the cordial atmosphere. For half of the pastors the atmosphere at home was strongly determined by the work and the care for everyday existence. This was connected with the business at home (farm, shop, market gardening), or with the loss of the father or mother through illness or death. The size of the family often meant, for the daughters, that they were given a task in the care of the other children and in the housekeeping. For some, the size of the family was the reason why far too little personal attention could be given. One of the pastors says that he was constantly looking for a small place of his own, because there was too little room for so many children. This has remained characteristic for this pastor in his further development: he is still looking for a place where he can be at home. For most pastors the effect of the lack of personal attention has been that they did not get around to a richer emotional development until later in life.

On the other hand, some of them also show that right from childhood the large family has given them a feeling for plain and simple everyday reality: you will have to make do with the qualities you received by birth. Furthermore there is a strong sense of justice: to each his/her own. Some declare that as a result of the size of the family they learned what it means to associate with equals and to have allies. For some the effect of this was also that they learned how to fight for a place and position of their own: *"you simply had to"*.

Poor or rich

Several pastors experienced poverty and the marginal existence resulting from it as a tough confrontation with reality.

Three pastors tell how the position of the poor family they come from (large family, small income, marriage with somebody from a lower class) was aggravated by the gulf separating them from the rich, established people around them. The Church, in particular, played a negative role in this by rather playing up to the rich than paying serious attention to the poor. This still continues to influence these pastors as regards their position in the Church and the way in which they give content to their ministry. Attention for the lower classes is a central issue for them. This was one of the reasons for them to opt for a society-oriented ministry.

One pastor indicates how the poverty at home became a basis for *"learning how to handle poverty creatively"*. He learned how to look for possibilities of coping with existence. In his present ministry he tries to promote the autonomy of people who come from an environment that has not given them enough opportunities for development.

One or two come from a (relatively) well-to-do environment, like a large farming business, a well-patronised shop, or a teacher's family. In nearly all cases these families had a social conscience: care for others who are less well to do, while both the father and the mother took part in club life and charity work. The pastors who come from such an environment show a strong social orientation. They also point out that they have had to learn that real engagement demands critical reflection on their own position as pastors.

Summary

It is especially the pastors who are clearly aware of the positive or negative influence of the environment they come from, who are also aware of the social position they now occupy. They are aware of the factors determining their actual position, and the social choices now made by them.

The others, to be sure, do speak about their memories of the environment they come from, but they are less articulate about the way in which it now determines their social position and their choices.

4. *Further development*

When pastors speak about their subsequent life history, insofar as it influences their life and work, six aspects which determined this development can be distinguished: The encounter with certain persons who exerted a strong influence; certain places where one had one's home, where one lived and worked; theological training; social and political movements; the process of secularisation; and, finally, the development in church politics. Here, we shall discuss briefly the first four aspects. The process of secularisation and the development in church politics will be dealt with more extensively later on.

Persons who had an influence

Certain persons had a great influence on the development of values and standards. Contact with an influential person could enhance self-acceptance, where one felt supported in choices that one had made. This can also be articulated negatively. Most interviews speak about positive influences, such as that of certain teachers, supervisors, fellow pastors etc. Some interviews show how certain persons had a negative significance: by acting in a rejecting, disapproving manner, through bad co-operation, or unreliable and authoritative behaviour.

Influential persons are either people who were close to the pastors concerned, or great figures at a distance, such as leaders and innovators in the realm of politics and the Church, like Kennedy, Ghandi, Pope John XXIII, or St. Francis. Some of the pastors interviewed testify that the encounter with less remarkable figures, such as a disabled person or a confirmed invalid, has had an important influence. These concrete persons brought the pastor closer to his or her true self.

Places

Places where the interviewees have lived and worked have left important traces in their lives. In this respect the older group mention, among other things, the seminary or the monastery. For some, the boarding-school atmosphere was characterised by a morality and ascesis, which weighed down heavily upon them, especially as far as their own physical nearness and development were concerned. There was no sense of security. Others, on the other hand, had many opportunities for cultural development, which would otherwise never have got started at home. In this connection, some pastors mention the attention to liturgy and singing, as well as literature and the significance of religious instruction. Another significant place is the home environment, as is the place where they lived during their theological studies. Several of the older persons interviewed have frequently gone to new places, especially on account of the changes, and the attendant shifts, in the theological training institutes. For a number of, mostly younger, pastors, living together in a student environment in a big city was a revelation, but sometimes also a frightening experience. The transition from village to town was an important moment for several of them.

The places where pastors have worked, and gained important working experiences, have been very influential for some of them: for example, a period in a developing country became a confrontation with issues of wealth and poverty. The ways of living and believing of the poor were heart-warming because of the directness and spontaneity that characterised their life together.

Some pastors had working experience before they opted for the ministry. Others had first worked in a neighbourhood centre, in health care, or in social work or education. That is where they experienced at first hand the revolutions taking place in the caring and helping professions. Sometimes they were able to discover in these areas what the meaning of religion in a secularised environment could be.

Theological education

Theological education became an important period for several pastors. Certain teachers enabled them to discover new perspectives in the development of their faith. For some, this was an upsetting experience: faith in a certain kind of God was turned upside-down. A number of them speak about the great influence of certain teachers who were able to establish a connection between theology and spirituality. In this respect they point, especially, to the significance those teachers attached to the religious experience of students. A major role is attributed to the supervisors who helped the students integrate their theological education into an emerging pastoral practice. In this respect some indicate that the supervision at the time of the pastoral work placement was an important support in coming to terms with the moments of crisis in which one occasionally found oneself as a student. An important place is given by several interviewees to student pastors who, both in personal guidance and in various kinds of reflection and liturgy, provided the students with a framework within which they could work at their personal religious development and their growth toward important choices in life.

Social and political movements

Social and political movements were of great importance for a small number of, mainly older, pastors. These were, especially, the movements of renewal and protest of the sixties, such as the student uprisings in Paris and Berlin, the "Maagdenhuis" occupation, the rise of the movement of Christians for socialism, and the peace movement. For some, the confrontation with the position of the working class was very influential.

Perception of one's own development

A number of these and other factors, such as the significance of the process of secularisation, and the developments in church politics, will be dealt with more extensively in the chapters that follow. What is important for this section is the question whether and how the persons interviewed show some perception of their development, and whether they have immediate access to this development. The answer to this is to be found in the way in which, in the interviews, pastors reveal how they have come to terms with certain events that were of fundamental importance in their lives. It is, of course, true that development in life does not depend only on this. Far less remarkable developments also leave their traces. The history of a person's life is perhaps determined for the greater part by the most trivial and ordinary of experiences. At issue here, however, are the most fundamental experiences, for they illustrate most clearly how the persons interviewed are aware of their history.

Fundamental events that are mentioned in the interviews are to be understood as moments of crisis that challenged the pastors at times to make new choices, or at least, during a limited period, to subject their life and work to serious criticism.

The experiences that had the most fundamental impact were those that confronted the pastors with their own limitations: experiences relating to illness and health, both physically and mentally, experiences of failure and defeat, and experiences in the co-operation with colleagues. Sometimes they were tough, critical experiences, such as confrontations with inhuman violence or the death of somebody very dear to them. For others it was the experience of being rejected rather than accepted, or of being confronted with what they perceived as negative developments in the Church. In some cases it was the experience of being forced to change their position or status in life. New choices had to be made in order for them to retain their own integrity. For some, an important confrontation took place during the period of their theological education. This unsettled their belief in God unexpectedly.

Nearly all pastors (only three excluded) speak about some such fundamental event, although there are differences in the ways they speak about it and give it a place in their history.

With a number of them it is impossible to speak of a clear relation to such events. The interview runs smoothly, also when it comes to fundamental events. This may be interpreted as a sign that the pastors have come to terms with what has happened. Some of them, however, declare that there is as yet not sufficient room in their lives to enable them to look at what has happened to them detachedly. The words used in such cases suggest that *"that was simply how it happened"*, or that it did not really touch the essence of their being.

With others one concludes that they have (not yet) come to terms with these fundamental events. This is most striking in the case of developments in the Church, or conflicts with colleagues, or confrontations with oppressive situations, like poverty and exploitation. These pastors intimate that it is impossible for them to give such negative experiences a meaningful place in their lives. It is impossible for them really to come to terms with these experiences, or to integrate them. Some pastors speak with pain, others with anger, about what has happened, or is still happening. Among this group those persons stand out who are aware of an impossibility of coming to terms with events from their past.

Then there is a small group of pastors who indicate that they have not been able to come to terms with the experience of failure and defeat. Everything they relate about their lives is dominated by a sense of impotence sometimes expressed in silence, in not being able to say another word.

With a little more than a third of the pastors interviewed a clear grasp of the transitions that have been made in life can be discerned. These pastors show in the interview that they have been able properly to survey the history of their lives and to achieve some distance: they are able to look at their lives and "play" with their history. They are able to point to those moments they have come to terms with, but also those they have not. At the same time they are able to say something about the way in which certain moments of transition have been given a recognisable place in their biography.

With some of them this becomes clear in that they are able to provide a clear survey of successive events, and to indicate why these have made such an impression. They show self-knowledge. A female pastor exemplifies this in the way she puts her development against the background of a much broader social and cultural development. An example of this is the change in the perception of the position of women in society and the church, in which the specific experiences of this female pastor are given a recognisable place. In the interview with another pastor a near-complete survey is given of his personal moments of transition and therefore also of his moments of crisis. These are given a place within the wider context of cultural history. Personal growth goes together with changes in social relations, in theology, and in literature. Personal history is embedded in broader developments.

Other pastors—just over half of the thirty—give the impression that they have "carried" the developments less consciously "with them" to their life here and now. Several of them have less distance to what has happened and sometimes deal less spontaneously with it than does the first group. The following statement is a typical example: *"Life just goes the way it goes"*.

It is mostly those who give prominence to the influence of the relationship with their parents that have a clear insight into the course of their own development. The rest of the pastors emerged as people who live more spontaneously with memories of their past, or who are less clearly aware of the influence of the past.

5. *Summary of chapter 1*

In this first chapter I have described how the pastors look back on four aspects of their biography: the relationship with their parents, conflicts with their parents, the environment they come from and its social position, and finally, the meaning of moments in the further development of their lives.

With respect to all four aspects it has become clear that just over a third of those interviewed have developed a conscious relation to their biography. These pastors are aware of the influence their parents exerted, and continue to exert, of the significance of conflicts they have, or have not, been able to come to terms with, of the social position of the environment they come from, and finally, of the influence of fundamental moments in the further development of their lives. On the whole, these four aspects occur with all the pastors belonging to this group.

An important datum is the fact that some of them were able, not only to relate during the interview how they have come to terms with certain conflicts and how they look back on them now. These pastors are also able to indicate what factors play a role in the way they look back on it now. Their present situation in ministry and the way of life they have chosen influence their perception of their biography.

Others show a different picture of how one's history can be dealt with. These pastors pay less conscious attention to it, some of them deal more casually with all the things that have happened to them, and several of them point out *"that life just goes the way it goes"*. Some of them 'live away' the sharp edges; others remain silent, or are unable to say anything about it. All this does not mean that they have, or have not, come to terms with their history. Sometimes a hard spot remains, because one could not come to terms with it. What is important is the way in which one is aware of it.

CHAPTER TWO

PERSONAL IDENTITY

This chapter will describe how pastors have developed a relation with their "self". In the literature of the Titus Brandsma Institute the "self" is understood as "one's own person or one's own essence". It is one's "identity, awareness of one's own self, self-awareness" (*Waaijman* 1988, 103). In this connection, Ben van de Maas speaks of "my fundamental individuality, originality and uniqueness, the core of my person, my self" (*Van de Maas* 1972, 33). This description constitutes the basic perspective of this section of the book.

Three aspects that indicate the essential structure of the self or personal identity are described: the physical aspect, the intra-personal aspect (the relationship with one's own inner being) and the interpersonal aspect (the relationship with others). The interviews explicitly inquired into these aspects. These aspects are not exhaustive as far as the description of the relation to the self is concerned, but it seemed to us to be sufficient to restrict ourselves to three questions: how do pastors speak about their body; how do they speak about their personal strengths and weaknesses, about their possibilities and limitations, and about their male and female aspects; and how do they speak about their relationships with others?

The central question is the following: how do pastors, in their speaking about these three aspects, have a perception of their personal identity? In the description it will be inquired, again and again, how the experience of these three moments is influenced by factors like resistance against expectations, values and moral standards in the environment, and the presence of some kind of guidance or therapy.

1. *The physical aspect*

The majority of the thirty interviews show a development in which pastors have grown in their appreciation of the meaning of their body.

With just over a third the relation to the body is a very prominent aspect of their self-awareness. These pastors speak about it in a straightforward and frank manner, declaring that they have a grasp of their relation to the physical aspect. Others speak of it in more general terms. Occasionally, some hint of their appreciation of it emerges, but then in rather vague terms. Some pastors say nothing at all about the significance of their physical aspect, except in negative phrases like: *"it evokes few associations with me"* or *"I don't have anything in particular to say about it"*. With these pastors little or no awareness concerning their relation to their body emerges. At least, nothing is said about it.

In the following, we shall restrict ourselves to the group of pastors who explicitly articulate their relation to the physical aspect. A number of pastors who speak explicitly about their relation to their body indicate four different aspects of the experience. Some pay more attention to one aspect, while others emphasise another: growth in appreciation of, and the courage to deal with, the body in a positive manner; the process of becoming aware of the wholeness or oneness of spirit and body; growing sensitivity to both the vulnerable and the strong aspects of the body; and growing sensitivity to the body as expressive of the spirit. These four aspects will now be described in greater detail.

Growth in appreciation

With several pastors we read how they have grown from an anxious experience toward a positive appreciation of their body. Education and training at an early age was a major, and mostly negative, influence. Experiences of falling in love, entering into personal relationships, having male and female friends, and getting married and having children all contributed to a greater openness for the positive meaning of things corporeal.

For some of them it was a real effort to allow this growth within themselves. Others had to fight in order to gain such a positive experience. In the relation with a partner they discovered that their physical experience was limited and—as they realised afterwards—rather poor. Some of them indicate that therapy has helped them to discover that their body was entitled to attention, and that they were allowed to enjoy their body. In this group of pastors one encounters resistance against the restrictive influence of their past. It is mainly a resistance against views implying that things spiritual are supposed to be more important than things corporeal and that the need for physical experience is supposed to be something inferior.

I kept it away from me for a long time. I think I did not actually intend to fall in love. When it happened, however, I had to learn that physical love is worth quite as much as spiritual love. I was not brought up to think that way. I think my mother always impressed it upon me that in the end it is better for one to be a strong woman who has no need for this.

Others articulate the growth toward positive appreciation as something that happened to them: *"it just happened"*. They were brought up in an open atmosphere in dealing with the physical aspect, and gradually this open attention was strengthened. Touching and being touched created a sensitiveness to the power and fascination of things corporeal. This not only applies to those pastors who entered into physical relationships, but also to some of those who have remained celibate.

I find the word 'physical' a fascinating word. Increasingly I notice this by looking at myself. I like to touch people, to pat somebody on the back or give somebody a big hug.

Through his frequent personal contact with people this pastor experienced that physical contact is something natural which one can handle naturally. The fact that he is celibate does not alter the fact that he is sensitive to the physical aspect. He is one of those for whom personal contact with other people has lead to a growing appreciation of the body. He experiences this as a gift he has received.

With some, I sense a significant increase in their care and respect for the body. It boils down, then, to taking care of one's own physical health, but also paying attention to the *"integrity of the body"*. One should not handle the body carelessly. There is some hesitation with respect to possible medical interventions. This hesitation is prompted by anxiety lest the body be damaged.

Sensitivity to the wholeness of human nature: unity of spirit and body

Among the pastors who have grown in their positive appreciation of the body, the conviction prevails, as could be expected, that spirit and body complement one another, and together constitute one whole.

In my opinion, body and spirit belong together. They cannot be separated. In the togetherness of body and spirit everything comes together.

One pastor says about himself that he comes from a tradition in which things corporeal were experienced less freely and given less attention. However, through contacts with young people who handle these things far more easily and spontaneously, he has learned how to be open to the whole: spirit and body. Young people find this quite normal. He has come to feel the same about it. Another pastor indicates that attention to the 'muse-inspired' moment in her life, particularly to dance, has made her strongly aware of the integrity of her existence. Yet another lays the emphasis on sexual experience, in which a new language is heard and felt. The body speaks the language of the spirit.

All these pastors indicate that their spirituality is not only a matter of the spirit. Their body also has an important place in their religious experience. For several pastors this has become a *"great discovery in their life"*. Other pastors also indicate the physical side of spirituality, though more incidentally, but they do not speak of it as concretely as does the former group.

Growth in sensitivity to the vulnerable and strong sides of the body

Some pastors experienced personally the meaning of vulnerability and brokenness. They have a critical phase behind them as far as their physical health is concerned. One of them says that he increasingly discovers in his life that his body repeatedly shows signs of fragility as well as.

> *I feel my brokenness, I am frequently brought down to earth again. And at the same time I feel the strength of the desire to go beyond this. It is a matter of becoming whole, becoming one. My erotic side and my sexuality have a religious content. God can be experienced in erotic terms, but at the same time there is that fragility, the side of the passions, the fact that by no means everything is pure and beautiful.*

By saying this, he does not mean that physical being and sexuality as such have a negative meaning. The power of one person's physical side, however, may express itself negatively and overpoweringly toward another person. Weakness and fragility are for him characteristic facets of the experience that the body can sometimes hold him firmly in its grasp. Another pastor points out how the body speaks a language more original than the language of the spirit:

> *I do a lot with my hands, I speak with them. I have become more strongly aware of this and I have also been forced to this, for sometimes my body has already spoken before I literally speak. I have become aware of what I do with my posture, my shoulders, my way of looking. I am learning to listen to my own limitations, for example when I am getting tired.*

In sexuality a new language becomes audible and tangible, also in the vulnerable domain. The experience of corporeal existence makes pastors aware of the fact that they are ordinary, earthly beings. The experience of physical vulnerability is a recurrent sign of the contingency of their limited existence.

> *The language of love is of great importance to me. Since the moment when I said good-bye to celibate life, sexuality has been an enriching experience: the fact that you can simply turn to each other and give yourself over. This is profoundly connected with vulnerability and susceptibility, a matter of thoroughly being the person that you are.*

Sensitivity to physical being as expressive of things spiritual

The pastors who took the word in the foregoing section also consider it very important to show through their bodily posture what they do, experience and say. For some of them the posture of the body in meditation and prayer is an expression of an inner attitude; others talk of the language of the body as an expression of solidarity and the desire to be close to others.

> *I have strongly developed my bodily posture in connection with my way of meditating. I meditate with my whole body. It is then that I strongly recognise the meaning of the body.*

Somebody else has the experience that it is precisely in ministry that bodily expression can have a liberating effect. Sexual experience has the same power in a personal relationship. Sometimes the body can say something that can barely be expressed in words.

> *It used to be something distant for me. It is true that I was present in my body, but I was not really so kind to it. My relationship and my marriage made me discover a totally different dimension. It has become far easier for me to make physical contact, also in my work. And this makes it easier for people to tell their story.*

From the foregoing it becomes clear that growth in sensitivity to things corporeal is often linked to the experience of a relationship expressed physically, and to resistance against the values and standards imprinted upon one since birth or through the morality of the church.

A typical example is the experience of a female pastoral worker who relates how, as a nun, she rebelled against a conception of bodily fasting and abstinence which she found to be alienating. She experienced this as a form of suppression of her own desires. By means of conversations with a third person she discovered that it affected her belief in God. For how can you deal with God and with yourself, when you suppress that which is alive in us humans as something natural?

Summary

In just over a third of the pastors we find a strong growth in their positive appreciation of physical being. This adds to their sensitivity to the unity of spirit and body, their sensitivity to strength and vulnerability, and to the expressive possibilities of the body. For some of them this development was a quite natural and spontaneous one. Their home environment had given them a great openness and freedom that continued to exert a positive influence in the further development of their lives. Others—and these are the majority—have had to make an effort to acquire this openness and freedom in dealing with their body.

Those who are most precise in articulating their growth in the appreciation and perception of the limitations and possibilities of things corporeal are largely the same as those who were indicated in chapter 1 as the group that dealt most consciously with their biography. Those who speak less plainly, and sometimes only in general terms, about their own body are largely identical with the group of those who have developed a different, more spontaneous, or less conscious, relation to their own biography.

2. *The intrapersonal aspect*

In the interviews questions were asked about two particular aspects of self-awareness: do you have any perception of the possibilities and limitations of your personality and of its female and male sides? These two aspects, besides the physical aspect, are important for the way in which pastors look at themselves. In a following section the relation to others will be discussed.

Perception of possibilities and limitations

In just over a third of the pastors we find a clear perception of their own possibilities and limitations. With the others, this perception is less clear. With regard to some pastors the question may be asked whether they are capable of critical reflection on their own possibilities and limitations. In the case of others it is obvious that they are well on their way toward developing themselves.

Experiences in which possibilities and limitations are discovered

As a result of a personal relationship or bond with another person pastors grow toward accepting a certain dependence. They feel less constrained to tax themselves to the utmost, believing instead that they will be accepted as they are. This amounts to the discovery that autonomy is not the same as *"being able to do everything oneself and having to carry every burden alone"*. Strength can go together with surrender.

In associating with others, pastors discover that they do not have to go all the way by themselves and that at difficult moments they can draw recognition and support from friends and colleagues. A concrete example is the way in which some pastors mutually support one another with regard to the church crisis, or the way in which they dare to confide in somebody who is willing to stand by them during a personal life crisis.

In a personal relationship the views of the partners may differ considerably. As a result of this, some pastors discover what is dear to them. They will then endeavour to find out how much it is really worth to them. A pastor in a mixed marriage, for example, who takes the great differences in religious experience between his wife and himself seriously, may be confronted with the choice of having to look for places of his own for his religious experience. He has discovered what it is worth to him. In a relationship where few personal experiences can be shared pastors run the risk of overstepping their bounds in looking for sufficient affirmation in their work. This tendency is also found in some priests who lack any deeply personal bond.

With pastors who have a family, children play an important role in 'downsizing' matters and putting them into perspective, for instance as far as expressions of religiosity are concerned. Children are capable of bringing the pastor back to *"down-to-earth reality"*, for they see their father or mother at ordinary moments at home. According to some it is there, more than anywhere else, that it becomes clear *"who the pastor himself is"*.

Several interviewees mention resistance against expectations and standards arising from the home environment or imposed by the present institution of the church. As a result of this, a number of pastors increasingly discover what their autonomy is based on and where their strength lies. More or less against their will, they are forced to start looking for a basis of their own, and they become aware of the things that are dear to them. On the other hand, it is also true that their resistance springs precisely from that which they hold dear. Some of them feel seriously hurt in connection with the insights that they have had to gain themselves regarding the things they consider valuable and hold dear. Confrontation with certain movements that, in their experience, only pull down what has been built up, prompts them into action. With some, however, one also increasingly finds forms of passive resistance: they withdraw to a sheltered place.

A central aspect is the discovery of the strength of one's own integrity. The pastors who mention this have a clear insight into their own possibilities and limitations. They know what they can ask of themselves as well as for themselves. Their own experience, frequently tested in confrontation with developments in church and society, has contributed to the development of a strong basis of their own. These pastors have also learned to articulate it concretely. They have learnt to see what ideals one does not want to aspire to (any longer), and what values are absolutely non-negotiable. It is interesting that one of these pastors points to a *"new virtue"*: the virtue of anger, which is so essential in standing up for things that really matter.

Several pastors also point out that in the process of their growing toward insight they owe a lot to some form of counselling or therapy. All these pastors looked for counselling or therapy. For some of them this took place during a period of serious personal crisis. Others were confronted with their own limitations in ministry and could not live up to other people's expectations. Therefore they tried to get some form of counselling. This counselling *"brought them back to themselves"* and made them discover that there was no longer any need for them to tax themselves to the utmost. Somebody helped them to learn how to accept their own limitations, but also to discover their own strengths and to dare to give room to the latter. Parallel to this, there is the discovery that others are capable of accepting them and believing in them.

> *My counsellor brought to the surface things within me that I had never thought possible.*

In the case of a number of pastors who do not have, or have never had, any experience with counselling, one finds a certain overstepping of their limitations in their work: an overestimation of their own abilities, but especially less insight into their own vulnerability and the ways in which it is possible to live with the latter. With a few others, one sees that they are about to succumb to feelings of inferiority. With one or two, the impression arises that these pastors are protecting themselves against criticism from other people. The pastors who do have experience with counselling or therapy appear to be capable of recognising these risks at an earlier stage.

Summary

Just over a third of the pastors appear to have a clear perception of the possibilities and limitations of their personal identity. Several of them have gained insight into their strengths and weaknesses, because they allowed themselves to be called to account by others who had direct and personal links with them, because they dared to enter into confrontation with developments in church and society, or because they were strongly confronted with their own selves in some kind of counselling. In this process the acceptance of their own limitations has grown, as has faith in their own strength. An important aspect is the significance of personal integrity, which arises particularly when pastors speak about resistance against standards and values with which they do not feel at home.

Among a small majority there is less insight into their own limitations and possibilities. This is quite apparent in the case of those pastors who run the risk of continually going beyond the limitations of their own abilities, of being overwhelmed with feelings of impotence or of being totally absorbed by their work. A passive attitude may also arise, as a result of which they hardly enter into the confrontation with their own limitations and possibilities, if they do so at all. In some, one finds a certain resignation hiding the sharp edges of some critical experience, or disguising it in general terms.

Female and male aspects

Just over half of the pastors interviewed indicate how, over the years, they have discovered and recognised their own identity as women or men. One priest, for example, says that, as a man in pastoral work, he has come to discover over the years that he has typically male features.

> *I like to be active, male. I notice that I have to be careful not to take charge of things too quickly.*

A female pastor describes how for her as a woman certain female images in the Bible act as a strong invitation precisely to recognise her womanhood quite firmly.

> *Words like 'womb of mercy', 'blessed is the fruit of thy womb', 'carrying in your womb until something has ripened' have an affirmative effect. They stimulate me to be truly a woman. The image of the midwife, for example, has a deepening effect on my pastoral work.*

For one of the male pastors the encounter and the personal relationship with a woman constitutes the confrontation with his 'macho' side. Likewise, contact with the male side of the church leadership makes female pastors acutely aware of the fact that they are not men. Parallel to this, however, there is the experience that certain groups in the church like to have contact and to work with women.

> *I discover that several parishioners choose me precisely because I am a woman. This has something to do with atmosphere, openness, spontaneous encounter.*

Some women have become increasingly aware, precisely in their resistance against a *"male church"*, how dear their womanhood and their female aspects are to them. This growing awareness is typical of women, but we also find it to a certain degree in men. Some men point out that the dominant position of men has to be broken. One pastoral worker says that in his missionary work the general policy is still determined by men. It is high time for men to start making room for women. He himself, he admits, still has a lot to learn in this respect. Another pastor says that it has become increasingly difficult for him to accept the strongly dominating, male language in the church. He feels at home in a metaphorical language that is far more comprehensive and in which male and female images are intermingled. What one notices about these pastors is that, in their awareness of female and male aspects, they experience a tension between the standards and values of the church and their own experience. In the confrontation with this tension pastors become aware of the significance of their gender. This also appears in the way they talk about their "whole being". Men discover that they have female aspects and women find out that they also have male facets.

One pastoral worker summarises it as follows: *"Male and female essentially belong together, in myself, but also in metaphorical language about God."* The foregoing description indicates, furthermore, that religious experience is also coloured by attributing gender-specific qualities to experience.

A married ex-priest describes how he did not find out until later in life, after resigning from the priesthood, and through his relationship with the woman he loves, that he is not one hundred per-cent male, but has as many female sides, like tenderness.

> *This development has made me more acutely aware of my affective possibilities and my own affective desire. I hope to be increasingly the person that I am. I am also someone who carries aspects of great sensitivity, caring and attention in myself. And I am still growing in this. I am a growing person and I realise that I am increasingly growing toward the essence of my own self.*

One of the women says that, as a woman, she is learning to deal with feminist currents, also in herself, in an increasingly balanced way. She does not wish to become dependent on an ideology in which there has to be as much resistance against men as possible. She prefers to exist *"totally"*, with her whole being, because the male aspect is not foreign to her nature. One pastoral worker shows in his homosexual orientation how one can never speak in absolute terms when it comes to his male and female sides.

> *I think that with me the balance inclines toward the homosexual side. The homo-sexual side is just a little stronger, but the other side is also in me. And I am now giving shape to it in a relationship with a friend, which makes me feel com-fortable. I cannot pin myself down by means of terminology. And this also applies to my male and female sides. I regard the receiving side as very important. I want to become aware at every occasion that I have a bond with somebody. That is what I call the female side in me. The male side is equally important, though. With respect to people around me who push away or minimise certain aspects in themselves, I am constantly engaged in making them feel: simply let it be there. Do not be so afraid of it. Both sides, male and female, are in me.*

We may conclude that nearly all the pastors who have gained an awareness of their entire human existence live in a personal rela-tionship. From this we may infer that sensitivity to male and female aspects often goes together with pastors' perceptions of their rela-tionships with others. We could, therefore, also have dealt with this part in the following section, which discusses the inter-personal aspect.

One pastor is an exception to this: he lives and works alone, but he says about himself that he has been strongly influenced by women in his environment. They have strengthened what was already going on within himself. What he has especially learned from women is the meaning of inclusive language.

A large number of pastors belonging to this group have had some kind of counselling. With respect to their female and male sides there are no explicit references to this. The general tenor of these interviews, however, gives the impression that counselling has played an important part in this process of growing awareness.

> *On the basis of my experience in psycho-synthesis, in which I was given counselling for a long time, I have often experienced the dual polarity in people around me, but also in myself. Psycho-synthesis is strongly connected with an image of human nature in which two aspects always go together: awareness and will, the male and the female side.*

Summary

It will be clear from the foregoing that, precisely in the confrontation with a dominant male culture, pastors have become aware of other, more female values. Pastors grow in the understanding of their entire human existence, and become aware of the fact that this may also have consequences for their giving concrete content to spirituality.

The group that have learned how to deal with this consciously largely overlap with those who are more aware than others of the influence of the biographical context and the experience of limitations and possibilities. The group discussed here is a little larger, though. Nearly half of the persons interviewed show a growing insight into the significance of male and female aspects.

Other pastors are less explicit in speaking about this. Some of them experience it, without expressing it in words. With a number of them this goes together with a less clear perception of their own identity.

3. *The interpersonal aspect*

Nearly a third of those interviewed have a permanent relationship. Most of the remaining pastors have opted for celibacy. For a few pastors the bond with a community or working group is of vital importance. I shall now discuss in greater detail the significance of the personal bond or relationship in the self-experience of pastors. By bond or relationship I do not only mean the personal situation in life in which somebody permanently lives together with one or several persons. I also understand by this the vital contact a pastor might have with one or several persons with whom s/he shares many things in his/her personal life and work. It is a question of a person, or persons, by whom one is known. This may be a life partner, a male or female friend, a good colleague, or a group to which one belongs.

Some interviews describe how a personal relationship can *"restore"* a pastor *"to his true self"*. A case in point is the following. A pastoral worker relates how he has learnt through bitter experience how to distance himself from the ideals of his father which he had felt he had to live up to for so long. He gets caught up in the high hopes people have about him to such a degree that he becomes dependent on everybody who comes to mean anything to him. His first relationship broke down at this point: it was *"everything or nothing"*. His life was dominated by a great fear of being let down.

Many years later, after having divorced his first wife, he came to realise how indispensable that fear had been for him. For the fear had made him shout down his real self, and caused him to over-strain himself. He had to devote himself to other people all the time. In fact, he had felt small and dependent. At the same time it was impossible for him to be small. He was unable to share things with nice people who, for their part, were quite willing to share things with him.

The discovery of all this was a turning point in his life. He found himself in a deep crisis and underwent therapy. During this therapy he gained confidence in himself and learned how to accept responsibility in more satisfactory ways. In discussion with his therapist he rediscovered the story of his life. He discerned the roots from whence he had come. This gave him new strength and he became aware of the fact that he had constantly been looking for his mother who had died years ago. He had been looking for a sense of security. A subsequent relationship provided more space: he was challenged not to be merely dependent, but, on the contrary, to become himself more and more.

I discovered that we were people together, and could look together for ways to deepen our existence.

He has gained rich experience: his life-partner *"restores him to his true self"* as a man with great possibilities, but also with limitations. He feels like a strong man, as well as a vulnerable man.

Many of the pastors who live together with a life partner indicate that one can share a lot and feel accepted in doing so. The relationship is a stimulus for becoming more and more oneself. A slightly smaller number describe their relationship as a limited living space in which one comes up against one another's hard boundaries. There appear to be considerably fewer possibilities of sharing than one had hoped for. This creates restlessness, with the not infrequent result that one starts looking for a sense of security exclusively in one's work. A strong competition then arises between work and private life.

> *There is competition between work and family. I want to do my work to the best of my abilities and I do not get any compliments. So I make the greatest possible effort to do a good job. On the other hand, my wife is criticising me about it: you are never at home, and please, pay some attention to us for once. That makes it difficult to have moments of rest and reflection.*

These interviews show that pastors in such life situations are sometimes more lonely than those who live alone. At the same time, one finds with some of them that the very effort to share things with the life partner challenges them to build up their own identity as strongly as possible. For one pastor, the fact that they cannot talk to each other sufficiently in the relationship becomes a challenge to spend a lot of time reading alone, thus taking the warnings of others seriously. Another pastor indicates that his wife's totally different views and experiences—also in the religious domain—increasingly stimulated him to find his own way and remain critically faithful to the way he experienced things and felt about them. His wife's total lack of feeling for symbolism and ritual makes him more and more aware of the actual richness of liturgy for himself. The situation also challenges him to make every effort toward developing a language that can be understood by his wife, even when it concerns experiences that are not hers.

The pastors who live in a family frequently indicate that they are kept close to themselves precisely through their children. Spending one's life with children, giving care and attention to them day in and day out, but also the special moments when children are a source of intense joy, all this creates a positive space. The children evoke something in them as a result of which they are allowed, and enabled, to be more themselves. Children knock pastors off their pedestal insofar as the latter still exists. For children the important thing is whether one is really there or not: *"The children demand real helpfulness from me, they cannot do without it."*

Living in a family and sharing life with growing children sometimes, in unexpected ways, put those things that seem so important in ministry and in the church in perspective. Neither church nor faith is the centre of everything. The family at home does not consider a number of those things that the pastor considers important and valuable equally valuable. For example: a twelve-year-old daughter thinks the church is boring, and she rather likes to spend time on biblical stories in her own way. The church has no place for her. So *"the question is whether we are doing things the right way in our ministry"*.

Putting things into perspective here means hearing the critical voices from one's own family. One of the pastors who are married explains how the children in the family indicate exactly when he is really himself, and when not: *"As soon as you are overstraining yourself or absolutely have to do things, the children say: Daddy is at it again."*

Among the others, who do not live with a life partner or with other people, there are only a few who indicate that they are really alone. One of them chooses to lead a kind of *"hermit's life"*. She tries to find her living space in a strictly planned schedule, and at the same time feels included as a member of the village community. She also regards herself as their fellow-villager. Quite simply, without any distance. She just feels she belongs to them.

With a few priests who live outside a personal relationship the impression arises that in their personal life they lack someone who at vital moments addresses them personally or affirms them. In everything that they say in the interviews they reveal their loneliness. It seems as if they have little insight into their own experience. They frequently screen their personal life with a little humour or by talking in general terms.

Others who live alone have good friends or have entered into a bond with some group. One of the priests relates in the interview how, right from childhood, he has learned to allow other people to enter his personal life. He has become sensitive to what people have to say to him personally. It has made him realise, among other things, that he is no more and no less than any other human being.

When I first came out of the monastery, and ran into someone and said: 'How are you, sir?' he replied: 'Ah, young man . . .' So that was that.

He made a habit of regularly inviting people from his environment to cook and have a meal together. It is good to have the experience of having to cope with things together with other people and of being able to learn from one another. In his ministry he badly needs the bond with colleagues. He looks for a kind of *"partnership"*. It is the only way for him not to succumb to the large amount of work to be done, and not to be too vulnerable in the face of developments in the church that he finds destructive.

This bond with colleagues means, among other things, that every now and then he is obliged to give an account of what he is doing. He is questioned critically. As a result of this he is frequently brought down to earth. This pastor knows his own possibilities and limitations; he is aware of both his vulnerable moments and his stronger side.

In the case of this pastor, as with a few other priests, it becomes clear that celibacy is in fact not an authentic living space for him. Some pastors declare outright that they would like to be married. They suffer from a situation of enforced celibacy. It is all the more reason for these priests to enter into relationships in which they are personally addressed and affirmed. For some, one way in which this can be done is through the Association of pastoral workers, where they learn concretely what personal solidarity implies: continuing to listen to, and to address, one another.

One priest who has personally experienced the crisis in the church says that he has held out because of the strong bond with a small group of colleagues. They, too, never stopped questioning him critically concerning his role and position in the church. It was in this group that he came to know his real friends. It is simply out of the question for him not to keep his appointments with them. He knows that through them he has come to know more and more about himself and has come to accept himself. It is through them that he is able to say, *"Here I stand"*.

Some pastors find that unsatisfactory or superficial forms of fraternal co-operation force them to find a place elsewhere where they feel more personally affirmed and challenged. This is given shape, for example, in a study group in which a lot of personal experiences are also shared. With one of the female pastors the bond with a circle of friends has become so strong that she finds a home with them.

She compares this with what other colleagues can experience in their families. Her celibate way of life can be meaningful, because in her circle of friends there is sufficient room for the affective dimension.

With respect to physical and sexual experience in relationships with others one or two things become clear. The importance of the body and of sexuality is most clearly articulated by those pastors who live in personal relationships and those who have learned in their contact with others to allow the language of the body to speak. The majority of those who do not dare to say much, or anything at all, explicitly about the experience of their body (a third of those interviewed) live alone and have their own home by themselves, or have a relationship in which the significance of physical being can hardly be raised, or in which actual sexual experience is impossible, or nearly so. Some of them, it is true, declare that they feel a strong need for bodily expression of their experiences with others, and that they experience the absence of this as a loss. Some of them have made some sort of peace with this, which helps them to remain sane.

> *I am celibate and that is what I want to be. At moments, however, when it is not so easy, I look for my own ways out. And I think of it—also in meditation and prayer—along something like the following lines: God, you will just have to put up with the fact that I deal with it in this way.*

In the foregoing, we have already seen that for a number of pastors the experience of sexuality includes an experience of vulnerability, but also of opportunities for communication, sometimes of a kind that is impossible with words. For several of them this also has a religious significance: religiosity and corporeality belong together for these pastors, as they do in sexuality.

Summary

Whether pastors are married or not does not seem to make such a fundamental difference as far as their perception of themselves is concerned. What is important is whether there is a real bond with one or more persons who are allowed to enter into their personal life. There are several possibilities in this regard: a lifelong relationship, a bond with friends and colleagues, or a bond with one or more persons who are able to "bring" a pastor "to his true self". When a pastor is "brought to his true self", it is possible for that pastor to arrive at active self-acceptance. It may become a challenge to pay more attention to one's own development. There is a real possibility then that the pastor's own core will be allowed to exist in softness and toughness. This is most strongly declared by that group of pastors who show the greatest awareness in dealing with their biography and with the intra-personal aspects of identity. Among this group, however, there are also a few who do not have an optimal experience of their relationships or bonds. They are strongly aware of the restrictions this places upon them. They are challenged to try to find their own way in this. Others live less consciously with the significance of the interpersonal aspect. Among them are both pastors with personal relationships and those who live as celibates.

4. *Summary of chapter 2*

We have discussed three aspects of the structure of personal identity in succession: the physical aspect, the intra-personal aspect and the interpersonal aspect. With respect to these different aspects the description showed that there are three principal factors that may have an influence on the development of the self-awareness of pastors.

Some correspondence has emerged, for example, between pastors' having developed significant self-knowledge, and the ability to articulate it on the one hand, and on the other, three different factors:

1. Pastors having a personal bond with one or more other persons (marriage, living together with friends, personal contact with one or more other persons, co-operation with colleagues, etc.). These generally appear to speak in a more explicit and more subtly articulate way about their personal identity than do pastors (including some who have permanent relationships) who live rather isolated lives. A few pastors who feel clearly restricted in their personal relationship, but are acutely aware of this, try to find opportunities of their own for developing their identity.

2. The degree to which pastors indicate that, at certain moments (personally and in their work), they have put up resistance against their environment, and at the same time, that they have grown in self-knowledge and are able to speak about it.

3. The experience of some kind of counselling or therapy. This frequently goes together with the experience that it confronted the

pastors concerned with their identity, so that they gained more self-knowledge.

These three factors do not have to occur together. It is quite certain, however, that in those cases where all three factors played a role in the life and work of a pastor, a keener self-awareness is found.

CHAPTER THREE

CULTURAL CONTEXT

A third aspect of context is the relation to culture. In this chapter we want to pay attention, especially, to developments in the religious aspects of the culture in which the pastors interviewed grew up. We understand secularisation in the religious sense as the process through which the prevailing religious culture fell apart into several cultures, giving rise to the growth of a greater flexibility. A lot of people who grew up with a traditional faith threatened to lose their roots completely and were challenged to look for new resources, new frameworks for living and working. They also had to go in search of new ways of expressing their spirituality.

For many of the 30 pastors the process of secularisation has been an experience of fundamental significance. This applies, particularly, to the older ones among them, who have experienced the revolutions of the sixties personally. The younger ones, on the other hand, grew up in a situation marked by the effects of the process of secularisation as it had taken place in the sixties.

In the religious development of pastors, answering the question about the meaning of secularisation is important, because it shows how pastors have been challenged to find their own way in the development of their spirituality, both individually and collectively, both in their personal life and in their ministry. We are especially interested in the question whether pastors have insight into their own development. Does this development become a (new) source for their spirituality?

A dilemma

André Zegveld describes the almost insoluble dilemma in which pastors have come to find themselves nowadays. The dilemma concerns the relation to the process of secularisation, which he describes in religious terms: "On the one hand, he (the pastor) represents the lost world of piety. No matter how one wishes to assess or judge secularisation, the aspect of holiness, God, has largely disappeared from people's world of experience. On the other hand, the pastor,

as a person, himself lives in that secularised world, while this
secularisation has also penetrated into his person. Moreover, the
community expects him to be able to act as the living example of possibilities of piety in a secularised age, thus giving shape to a form of
believing based on experience." (*Zegveld* 1996, 152).

Zegveld further observes that what really matters in this field of
tension is the person of the pastor and his or her actions, because
it is no longer the ministry that carries the pastor, but rather the
other way around: ministry depends on the person. Briefly, Zegveld
indicates the following triple predicament: "Firstly, as a representa-
tive of things holy, the pastor works in a secularised world in which
he is what remains (if he is not a relic) of a lost dimension. Secondly:
people expect him to show something, in his own person, of what
the influence of God and things holy can be on a human life. Thirdly,
it is imperative for him to have a well-ordered relation to things
holy himself" (Ibid. 153).

How do the pastors who have been interviewed themselves respond
to this predicament? It is important to see how they themselves
describe the process of secularisation. What do they understand by
secularisation, and what do they consider important in it? That is
what our description will start with. Then we shall raise the point
of how secularisation—according to the pastors—does or does not
compel them to make choices: do they explore the matter further,
do they reject it, do they look for a creative discussion? This marks
the beginning of a following section: the description of positive and
negative reactions to secularisation. This in turn is followed by a discussion of the question whether or not secularisation has become a
new challenge for the development of spirituality.

1. *How is secularisation looked upon?*

Seven different definitions of secularisation can be abstracted from
all the interviews taken together. They show some coherence, but
also have clearly distinctive aspects. Each description reflects in its
own way how secularisation and its effects are experienced:

  – Things worldly and profane become the starting-point for believing. The appreciation of things sacred, apart from things profane,
has disappeared. In other words: things sacred are not available separately. Things sacred and things profane are joined together. This

means that the world has to be taken seriously at all times. For some the *"world"* is manifested in *"earthly reality"*, for others in *"ordinary everyday reality"*, or in *"profane reality"*.

– Rationalisation and pragmatisation gain authority.

Secularisation implies that the spell of obviousness is broken. This means that truth is not simply accepted on exterior authority and that convictions with respect to values and standards grow on the basis of rational arguments. Pragmatisation, here, means that thought is determined by clearly demonstrable facts and verifiable reasoning processes. This means that the spontaneous acceptance of pre-determined truths has come to an end.

– Religious denomination disintegrates.

Secularisation is the process in which the role of the church as the dominant factor in life is put into perspective by social and cultural developments. This means saying good-bye to traditions of the church and Roman Catholic history insofar as they try to determine public life and the structure of personal life. There is a greater reserve toward pre-determined positions of the church in social and political life.

– Things divine become things human.

As a result of secularisation the distance between God and man is narrowed: the point at issue now is the value of humanity. The great God is coming closer and closer, is becoming more human. It is no longer possible to speak of God or things divine apart from things human.

– There is a process of growing individualisation.

Secularisation is experienced as the falling apart of great units, the fragmentation of grand systems and ideologies. Life takes place in small units. People must fall back more and more on their own responsibility. Uniformity no longer exists, but we have to base ourselves on a pluriformity of opinions and assessments.

– There is an increase in emptiness and space.

The loss of fixed frameworks of thought and life gives rise to emptiness and spaciousness. Henceforth life is determined by gaps in the system that lend greater significance to emptiness and nothingness.

– Faith and religion disappear as obvious dimensions.

This view plays a role with several of those holding the above-mentioned views. Secularisation means the rise of a non-religious society.

Secularisation proves an ambiguous concept

The manner in which the term is interpreted by the various pastors, as appears from the interviews, is often connected with the context in which they work as pastors. Pastors who work in institutions of health care are especially sensitive to the pragmatisation of culture, whereas others who have experience in parish ministry or in some form of social ministry have become sensitive to processes of individualisation.

A second factor, which is important for the interpretation of the term secularisation, is the personal development pastors have gone through. In this respect their theological education is especially important. For many, particularly for the older group, theology brought about a crisis with respect to their faith in a holy God who transcends this world.

A third factor is the fact that several pastors underwent many changes in their personal lives with respect to the way they felt about authority and obligatory forms of piety. They like to speak of humanisation, personal space and freedom in this regard.

A fourth factor is getting acquainted with contemporary literature and art in which the interest in emptiness and silence was given greater significance. Pastors who talk about this also felt sympathy for various protest movements that exposed the meaninglessness of power and violence.

Finally, the shift in the social appreciation of the pastor's position is an important factor in the interpretation of the term secularisation. Here, too, it is especially the older ones who are speaking. As pastors, they see, each in his or her own way, that the influence of the church and faith on people's social and personal lives has strongly diminished. The pastor has increasingly become a marginal figure.

A number of younger pastors, about a quarter of the total, do not speak in comparable ways of any shocking development in personal life in connection with secularisation. Rather they point out that they grew up in the midst of this developing culture in a smooth, almost natural way. This also gives rise to a different appreciation of the matter, as we shall see in the following section. They grew up with the effects of secularisation.

2. *Secularisation compels one to make choices*

Van der Ven has predicted that the church in the Netherlands will keep going further downhill, as long as a critical-constructive dialogue between the church and present-day culture fails to materialise (*Van der Ven* 1997, 22). The same can be maintained with respect to spirituality and ministry. As long as pastors will not enter into a critical-constructive dialogue with culture, and particularly with the process of secularisation as they experience it, the significance of their ministry, but also of their spirituality, will diminish. Pastors of this generation are confronted with secularisation as a part of culture. It is impossible for them to get around it.

Secularisation is not a process that leaves one unchallenged. In several ways the interviews show how pastors, both personally and in their ministry, are forced to give some answer to the process of secularisation. For the majority of the pastors interviewed secularisation is the framework within which one makes one's own choice. For some that is a fundamental choice, others speak about it as something, which does not take place as a shock, but rather spontaneously.

Among the thirty pastors three groups can be distinguished: Pastors strongly affected by the process of secularisation, who had to make fundamental choices (just under half of them); pastors who do not feel confronted with fundamental choices, and experience secularisation as a smooth process in which choices are made spontaneously and easily (just over a quarter of them); pastors who do not mention any choices (a quarter of them). We shall now discuss each of these three groups in greater detail.

Fundamental choices

With respect to the first group of pastors, who indicate that secularisation has been fundamental for them, three areas can be indicated in which the confrontation takes place, forcing the pastors to make choices:

   – Secularisation means saying good-bye to a safe, protected world. This calls for a process of letting go and making a new start. It requires saying good-bye to the parental environment. One of them, for example, explains:

> *Saying good-bye to a protected world, finding oneself in a society marked by all kinds of clashes of interests: this was very hard for me. I felt lonely. Only then*

do you realise that you had grown up and lived in such a protected environment. I felt challenged: I had to look for a new start. I am surprised at the way in which I managed to get everything done: taking action at difficult moments, continually making transitions, letting things go and starting again. It became a time when I had no grip on anything. It meant learning how to swim, because you do not simply survive the deep end automatically.

– Secularisation is a confrontation with your own weakness and strength. It forces you, with all the possibilities you have, to choose for your own responsibility.

Secularisation confronted me in a tough way with my own strength and weakness. It challenged me—through the loss of all kinds of safe frameworks, such as a church, which took care of me—to choose for my own personal way. I am amazed to see that I have dared to take that step. I am also surprised to see that a lot of others, like older people in our society, have been able to go and stand on their own two feet and that, as a result of that, they have become such rich and tolerant people. They have fought their way through the change of culture and they have become increasingly themselves.

– Secularisation is the damage done to an established form of belief in God; it challenges you to find your own way of believing.

I have certainly lost something, namely a certain obviousness in my faith. Faith was put to the test, and the question presented itself to me: is there still any sense and meaning in it? Is faith still a power, and how does it help me to find a place in this society? I chose to find my own way in it myself. Eventually I gained in the process.

Spontaneous choices

A number of pastors describe the process of secularisation as an almost natural event in which they themselves remain untouched. The choices resulting from it are indeed less fundamental than with the previous group. The following statement is typical: *"Secularisation for me is a spontaneous process of becoming free."* Somebody else says: *"It is in fact not something shocking. It just happens the way it happens."*

Smooth development probably has something to do with the fact that the group of pastors we are dealing with here is younger than the previous group. This group has not experienced the vehemence of the revolutionary developments in church and society in the sixties at first hand. Their study of theology began in the seventies, when the toughest confrontation with the change in culture was over.

No mention of choices

With a number of pastors interviewed we find practically nothing to show that some kind of choice has been made. These pastors do not talk about it. Neither positively, nor negatively do they indicate anything of the influence of the process of secularisation on their personal life or on their functioning as a pastor. It seems that they did not take any notice of this process.

3. *Appreciation of secularisation*

It has already become more or less clear in the foregoing that the appreciation of the process of secularisation can vary. It must be pointed out that the differences in appreciation do not entirely correspond with the previous division of differences in choices. A positive appreciation of one of the aspects of the process of secularisation may go together with a negative appreciation of a different aspect.

Positive appreciation

Of the pastors who give a frank opinion about the influence of the process of secularisation on their personal life and spirituality, several express positive appreciation of this process. This is articulated in terms like *"becoming free"*, *"being liberated from fixed and coercive frameworks"*, *"more space"*, and *"being able to breathe"*. Those pastors who experienced the process of secularisation as a process of change as a result of which they had to make choices, are the ones who usually make such statements. This applies to one third of the pastors interviewed. The following quotation is typical of this group.

> *I feel myself a modern human being, a human being of this generation. I have my feet firmly on the ground and I feel quite comfortable in this era. I went through some developments in my life and dared to take steps myself as a result of which I was able to free myself from a childish mentality, which was typical of the old institutions. I did not want to live my life as a dependent person kept under tutelage any longer. Once I had taken these kinds of steps, I became more and more a free person.*

It is a relief for these pastors to discover that reality offers more space than suggested by the established frameworks in the past. One of them relates how her entire development was marked by the search for a way of her own, because she did not feel at home any-where any longer. God was especially a protection and refuge in her youth, but reality was suddenly changed through the death of a good friend. That was a tough moment and at the same time this opened up the way toward the discovery of a different, open space.

> *Then I saw that that whole rosy world which had always protected me was a fiction. Reading the book 'Honest to God' by Robinson was a relief to me. It made me discover a completely different reality that was more free, so that I could choose my own way.*

Somebody else indicates that he was surprised to discover that the process of becoming free and of growing toward a responsibility of his own was not only his own development, but that all this had a place within a much broader social development. The revolutions in the study of theology, and the democratisation of a church that was being renewed in the sixties, appeared to take place in a broader climate of social and political revolutions. That *"created breathing space"*.

The younger group, namely that of pastors who experience sec-ularisation as a relaxed and smooth process, point out that secu-larised reality had already been their world since childhood—something almost taken for granted. These pastors indicate that they do not feel that they have lost something through the process of seculari-sation. They were, as it were, brought up on the idea that life is there to be lived in freedom. They gradually discover, when they think about it, that the secularised world has been their world for a long time. Nor is the church their only framework of meaning anymore. Many alternative frameworks of meaning have come into being. And these, too, are all relative. It is good to live and to act in this climate where things are put into perspective.

> *I have always felt myself a free human being. Traditional customs and usages, let alone old ideas, were hardly ever established patterns in my life. I have indeed— practically automatically—become increasingly free in my presentation in ministry and in conducting the liturgy.*

The positive appreciation of the process of secularisation is related to all the aspects mentioned in the descriptions at the beginning of this chapter. That which earlier on may have seemed a negative process has now become a new space for living and working. At the same time, however, for several persons, there is another side to this, which cannot be appreciated equally positively.

Negative appreciation: alienation

In just under a half of the interviews I found a negative appreciation of the process of secularisation. A number of these—as has already been shown in the foregoing—also indicate positive aspects. It is remarkable that the same people describe those very aspects that are appreciated positively in the process of secularisation, also in negative terms. This applies to all the views, with the exception of that of the humanisation of things divine. This aspect is appreciated only positively.

In the statements of pastors about the negative sides of secularisation the term *"alienation"* draws one's attention.

– The revaluation of things profane gives rise to alienation in the case of those people who still live very much in a sacral world when the pastors get to know them.

– Rationalisation and pragmatisation give rise to personal alienation in the case of a few pastors, as a result of which they are very concerned about the climate in which they have to work as pastors.

– The fragmentation of religious contexts creates tensions in ministry and gives rise to great conflicts that alienate pastors and various other persons from one another.

– Individualisation is a source of social alienation and isolation.

– Openness and emptiness are difficult to share with those who are, instead, accustomed to filling up everything.

A few aspects in greater detail

Secularisation occurs at the expense of vulnerable people
An industrial pastor who puts his ministry in a clearly social context and who comes across a lot of poverty and social injustice says: *"What worries me is the fact that the bonds between people at the bottom are crumbling, and that a lot of people are left to themselves."*

For one of the pastors individualisation and the individual's growing autonomy are, on the one hand, a fortunate development he can enjoy. However, he says, *"at the same time I see an achievement in the civil domain that is at the expense of vulnerable people. It is simply assumed that people are equal. The point is occasionally to show reality as it is, like, for example, the gulf between poor and rich; simply out of loyalty to those people."*

Growth of division and secularisation
A parish pastor finds it especially hard to accept that so much division has arisen among people, also within the church. He also has problems with the growing alienation from the church. It is hard to accept that more and more people only try to find contact with the church and with ministry at very special moments in their lives. Two pastors declare that they have great difficulties with the way the younger generation give content to faith, insofar as they do so at all. In this respect these pastors use terms like *"frightening changes"*.

> *It is painful to have to see how the new generation does not in the least understand the pastor's love for the church and the sacraments.*

Loss of innocence
Another parish pastor describes his problems with certain developments like the loss of a sound naivety. Secularisation has made people more free, but the result may be that people will increasingly resort to using their power, also within the church.

> *I no longer believe in the idea that all the people within the church eventually go the way of Jesus. I think there are quite a lot of them who want to do so and who indeed do so with me. I have, however, come to see more sharply that people abuse the church for playing their own power game.*

He also points out that in certain places there are people who are capable of pushing a pastor out of a parish.

> *They have tried to get rid of me too, and I discussed this openly. There were also people, then, who showed that they needed me. For me, however, it meant the loss of my innocence.*

4. *Secularisation as a new challenge*

The idea of allowing oneself to be challenged to look for new ways is especially found among those pastors who, in their interview, also indicate problems, besides showing positive appreciation for the process of secularisation. In a period of alienation from the traditional sources of spirituality pastors are challenged once more to test those sources and possibly to look for new contemporary sources of spirituality and for appropriate forms of expression. In part 2 we hope to be able to describe this. Here, we shall discuss a few aspects that may be regarded as important conditions that, according to the pastors, enable them to give specific answers to secularisation.

Looking for a new language

Pastors are compelled to work at a new language. The pastor who works in a nursing home experiences this especially in his contact with a choir in which people with different religious and non-religious backgrounds participate. That is where he feels most at home. At the same time he looks upon it as a chance to work at a new kind of communication, precisely because it has become more difficult for people to understand one another.

> *Sometimes we have to talk a lot in order to come to an understanding. It sometimes also frightens me a little. And I am concerned about it: the vagueness with which we have to formulate the things we think important, because we have gradually lost the language with which to articulate them. This is parallel to what we experience here in the nursing home, namely in the discussion about identity, in which it becomes so difficult to understand one another. Sometimes I think with terror in my heart: how are things going to be in the future? How are we to acquire a language as a connecting element in our culture that is so fragmented? . . . Now and then it weighs heavily on me that I can no longer make my choir feel why, for example, I think certain songs so beautiful. The language is then distasteful to people, but quite essential for me. It is very difficult for me to live with this, because it is a question of personal stories.*

Another pastor is looking for a language in which the humanity of vulnerable people becomes manifest. There *"every story, of whoever comes here, is important as a place of revelation of the mystery."* It is very important to look for new symbols and rituals as a result of which a language becomes possible which otherwise would have been impossible to find. Old rituals are given a new content. Sometimes they are the simplest rites, such as lighting a candle during a pastoral interview, laying on of hands in confirmation of what was achieved in the contact, spending some time together at the grave of a father or mother so as to enter into the struggle with the past.

Dealing with rationalisation: working at a new identity

A striking element is the struggle of at least one out of five pastors to deal with the strong tendency toward rationalisation. It is a challenge to work at a new recognisable identity about which it is possible to exchange views with others. In a number of pastors one sees a struggle with the surrounding medical world which has become strongly pragmatised.

> *In the pragmatisation of health care, here in the nursing home, I meet with terrible distrust. Our manner of living together and sharing the same home is increas-*

ingly being threatened by a certain chilly way of having contact with one another. The care has to be so pragmatic and there is little room for personal attention and care. I think those are frightening things.

This does not mean a total rejection of developments in health care, however. It is important to try to find new forms of personal attention within this pragmatisation process. This pastor is looking for a more comprehensive care—broader than merely the pragmatised, cold, physical care now emerging.

How can we, in our living together with one another, let our hearts speak. Now and then I have to call out in a desert, in an atmosphere of reorganisation and management culture.

When he fell ill himself, he thought it had something to do with stress, with the fact that he was going under in a way. He offered resistance and put up a fight in order to find a proper place within the domain of institutional care. His illness became a challenge to think about his position in health care. He was challenged to reflect on the process of pragmatisation. He began to discover that pragmatisation within the organisation does not only have negative effects. Ministry, too, could gain a lot from pragmatisation:

Showing in a matter-of-fact way the things we stand by and learning how to sell our product well.

With another pastor who works in psychiatry I sense the same atmosphere and tension. He has the advantage, however, that the pastoral care in the institution in which he works has a recognised position. At the same time it is a process of continually working with daggers drawn: how does one give content to one's pastoral identity in a medical world? For this pastor it means looking for openings in order to enter into a discussion with the other disciplines. In this way the differences in identity may become a subject for discussion. He also looks for possibilities of taking initiatives explicitly as a pastor, as a result of which the inmates can discover that they can get help from him in their recovery process, as well as support in their suffering. That is where questions can be discussed that do not receive real attention anywhere else.

For many pastors rationalisation is a challenge to look for a place where one can be, and remain, authentic: a place where one can give expression and shape to religiosity, and this together with others. The point is to learn how to acknowledge one's own choices openly, sincerely and honestly. What matters in the discussion is the skill of intellectual honesty: the discussion is held on the basis of verifiable arguments. It is in this discussion that a pastor becomes trustworthy and may be addressed critically. This aspect will be discussed in greater detail in the following chapter that will deal with the relation to the institution of the church.

Struggle against growing cynicism: attention for vulnerable people

In the case of an industrial pastor who is confronted with the alienation and marginalisation of deprived people, which he regards as one of the consequences of secularisation, we find the challenge to enter into the fight against growing cynicism. In this challenge he looks especially for the bond with those who have dropped out of the labour market. What is important for him in this is the value of everyone's story, no matter to whom the story refers. The language of the oppressed is a source of new faith. As a pastor, he wants to be, and remain, close to them. It is a matter of loyalty to people, and doing justice to people so that they can breathe. He is encouraged and supported in this by the fact that people, no matter how poor they are, sometimes care about and stand up for each other. At the same time the growing discrimination against the poor never ceases to arouse his anger:

> *When I see people's loyalty and when I see at the same time how these people are treated, then I feel like taking my shotgun and shooting all of them right there, just above the nape of the neck.*

Attention for humanity

Wherever secularisation is experienced as the humanisation of things divine, ministry is regarded as attention for humanity, in which the unique value of each human being is given a lot of space. A pastor in health care says about himself that he has grown very much in openness and responsiveness to each human being entering the clinic: *"Each human being entering here carries with him a unique story."* He feels increasingly challenged to discover the presence of the Unspeakable God in this concrete, vulnerable human being.

Looking for small contexts

One parish pastor finds it difficult to deal with the way in which people in his environment approach God so rationally. He is quite fascinated by the way in which groups in Latin America are able to communicate with one another. A directness and spontaneity which he also finds with Surinamese people with whom he has a lot of contact. This challenges him to look for moments in his ministry at which he can connect people with each other. He does this in small groups in which an atmosphere can arise that invites people to have spontaneous and hearty contact. Here a new kind of "obviousness" may arise.

The same can be said about his love for the church, which it is sometimes difficult for him to share with his immediate environment and with his colleagues. This love challenges him to look for new, and especially smaller, contexts in a neighbourhood where people have become strangers to one another, but also have the capacity in themselves for new forms of religious communication. At the same time, this pastor is looking for places for himself where he can relate to others in a hearty and warm manner.

Keeping things open and enduring emptiness

Putting all kinds of concepts and ideas into perspective in the process of secularisation sometimes grows into a temptation to fill the void all too rapidly with new concepts. According to some pastors, the real skill is to endure the void in the present cultural period, instead of filling it with new terms. It is better, for the present, to make do with an open space than with a space filled by concepts that have not yet been tested and verified in life. Moreover, it is an essential datum in the Jewish tradition that God cannot be put into words.

5. *Summary of chapter 3*

We started from a survey of views of secularisation. We were able to distinguish seven different views. All seven are accentuations of the way in which pastors experience and feel about the process of secularisation. Then we described how secularisation became, or did not become, a challenge for making new choices. Secularisation is appreciated both positively and negatively. Sometimes positive and negative appreciations deal with the same aspects of secularisation. In the negative appreciation, the word *"alienation"* in particular was striking. Finally, it was described how for a number of pastors secularisation can become a challenge to look for creative answers of one's own: development of a new language, formulating one's own identity, attention for human beings as vulnerable, attention for humanity, working at small frameworks and keeping emptiness open. We discovered that the answer to the question of how secularisation can become a source of spiritual development is connected with this aspect of critically finding a position.

Essential in every search on the part of pastors for finding an answer to secularisation is the attempt to find a new identity and to articulate it. This concerns both personal life and ministry.

A number of older, and some younger, pastors show that they are able to account for the position they have taken, while fully and critically aware of it. This is especially true of those pastors who have insight into the relation of tension between positive and negative aspects of secularisation. This insight clarifies their choices and helps them to put their own choices into perspective. This group largely overlaps with those whom we have characterised earlier as the group who are more fully aware than the others in dealing with their own development in life and their identity.

Others do not really give the impression in the interview that secularisation has become a source of spirituality and ministry. Generally speaking, these pastors are happy with the freedom and the space that have entered their life and work. On the other hand, they show less development in finding creative answers to secularisation and in accounting for the position they have adopted.

At the same time we have to conclude that younger pastors in particular experience the need for being fully aware in dealing with cultural developments to a far lesser extent. They grew up with them, without being confronted with vital questions in the process.

In this way, a preliminary answer has been given to André Zegveld's dilemma: culture can become a new source of religious development, to the extent that pastors take up the challenge to give a critical answer to secularisation. For younger pastors the dilemma differs from that of older pastors. Rather it is their own culture on the basis of which they are confronted with a church that in many respects is hostile to that culture.

CHAPTER FOUR

CONTEXT OF THE CHURCH

Here I shall describe how pastors feel at home in the church. Church is understood, here, as the institution of the church, the church organisation. By this we do not mean the church leadership only. It also comprises the relation between pastors and colleagues, their relation to the local church organisation and to fellow-believers. All these institutions and persons influence the position of pastors and determine whether they feel comfortable in the church.

Pastors have both positive and negative experiences with the church as institution. Negative experiences seem to predominate strongly. The following survey can be given.

– A small group speaks of a positive experience.

– A great majority indicates a negative experience. They mean by this that the institution of the church does not offer affirmation, and that they frequently meet with disapproval. A number of them, one out of four, feel hurt and wounded by the church.

– A large number of them are working at some new position in the church.

– A little more than half of them are looking for new possibilities of realising fellowship. Several pastors find here a place for expressing their own spirituality.

This survey also indicates the structure of this section.

1. Positive experience: the church is my home

A small group of pastors spontaneously give a positive answer to the question: do you feel at home in the church? For some of them it is *"the place of faith"*, others like being called *"people of the church"*, for *"I feel I belong here, in spite of all the occasional difficulties."* This group consists of three priests, one deacon and one pastoral worker.

For one of the priests the church has become a *"home"*, because he himself is greatly indebted to various people within the institution of the church for helping him to overcome a crisis. *"That strange house in which I live, that is where I feel at home. It is a pleasant place for me, because I would have felt lost otherwise. I have my roots in the church, for that matter, and that is why I am staying in it."* One might speak, here, of a kind of family relationship with the church. Another priest relates how it was precisely the strong support of his colleagues that made him dare the step toward ordination. It was they who made him a priest. The love of the church, the love of the sacrament, the love of working at redemption and liberation together with people, this is what he has to thank his colleagues for. Another interviewee, a female pastoral worker, has experienced a lot of support from the leadership in her diocese. As a result of good relations with them, she knows she is greatly appreciated and that she can always turn to them.

For one of these four pastors the negative criticism and the standoffish attitude of a lot of people with respect to the church is a great problem.

> *How terribly difficult it is to convey even a little bit of my love of the church. I thought I would succeed in making people enthusiastic and interested.*

2. *Negative experience*

More than two-thirds of the pastors interviewed indicate that they have negative experiences with the institution of the church. This negative experience is articulated in two ways: they feel disapproved of, rather than affirmed by, the institution, while a number of them feel hurt and wounded by developments and measures in the church that also affect the behaviour of church members and colleagues in ministry.

Disapproval instead of affirmation

The majority of the pastors who express this are pastoral workers, but there are also several priests, as well as a few married ex-priests, among them. Among the pastoral workers there are both men and women.

Several reasons for the negative experiences

– For many pastors their position as a male or female pastoral worker is uncertain. Pastors feel that they are the objects of *"suspicion"*; they do not feel that they *"are wanted without reserve"*; sometimes they feel that they are *"denied as persons within the institution"*. Differences as to the intensity of this experience are connected with the fact that the various dioceses all carry out their own individual policies. The experience is articulated most negatively by male and female pastoral workers who are active, albeit *"illegally"*, within the boundaries of the diocese of Roermond.

– The position of women in the church is controversial and hardly recognised in some places. This applies not only to women's experiences with the central leadership of the church. Some female pastoral workers indicate how difficult it is for them as women in pastoral work to be fully accepted at their place of work. One of the women indicates that there has never been a real place for her in the church. She has always remained *"homeless"*.

– The priests who testify to negative experiences refer to the fact that they had felt outsiders in a certain diocese and therefore had to leave for another diocese. Some of them experienced the policy in the diocese of Roermond, which was the place where they worked, as destroying their own credibility as priests.

– The married ex-priests indicate that, after their marriage, and after having been discharged from office, they felt like *"pariahs"* and *"exiles"*. It became *"a lonely period"*.

The negative experiences are, therefore, mainly connected with the position of pastors in a church that does not sufficiently recognise their position or affirm what they want to stand for as pastors.

Hurt and wounded

For a number of pastors the negative experiences with the institution of the church were the cause of permanent damage. When they speak of their feelings about the church, there is pain because of wounds that have not healed completely and for some of them *"can never heal"*. For some pastors it means that they have completely lost confidence in the church, while others are continually reminded of their disappointments and are, therefore, very vulnerable to new disappointments. With some, the feeling that people within the institution question their integrity and honesty affects them most deeply. This has to do with moments of conflict when these pastors expressed their opinion honestly. Another wound opening up repeatedly is found with women who have great problems with the fact that ordination is exclusively a male privilege. This wound is felt painfully, as soon as a man in their own environment, for example a colleague in the neighbourhood, is ordained a priest. That was the reason why, for one of these women, the ordination of women in the Anglican Church was such a painful experience.

3. *Finding one's way in a field of tension*

With many pastors a certain tension can be sensed: on the one hand there are the negative experiences, and on the other, working with people in the church in ministry—something which has become so dear to them that they cannot or will not give it up. Within this field of tension one looks for a way out.

Facing conflict

Half of the pastors indicate that, in one way or another, they did not avoid the conflicts that arose with representatives of the institution of the church. For one of them it meant that he had the courage to address a colleague personally, while for somebody else it meant trying to forge bonds with sympathisers and allies.

Many of them began to play an active role within the Association of pastoral workers. For some of them the Association was the only place for open and honest consultation. As active members of this Association, these pastors felt that they continually found themselves in a position that was not accepted by the church leadership. Organising themselves, jointly, created room *"for giving a new content to obedience: standing by the things one sincerely believes in. The bishop condemned this. Condemnation, however, became a challenge: standing together for a credible ministry"*, said one priest in the diocese of Roermond.

Working at credibility and integrity

For these pastors it is only possible to endure tensions and conflicts when, as they themselves point out, they work at credible ways of living and working as pastors. From that they derive the strength to become autonomous in the sense of no longer remaining morally dependent on the institution.

> *I will no longer allow the church to take my faith from me. I will not allow the stories that are dear to me, the perspective that I believe in, to be taken from me. They cannot take away the good things any more.*

It remains a permanent tension, however: the fear remains that one gives up a bit of one's own authenticity every time, or that one begins to put up with things for the sake of one's own survival. For a lot of pastors this is a great problem. It is quite a task not to deny oneself while staying on one's feet. One of the pastors says that this was the reason why he had to choose a work situation in which he was no longer formally bound to the authority of the bishop. He also says that, by character and by nature, he has never been someone to put up a fight.

> *I wanted to come to terms with the conflict of loyalty in that area of tension in the church. I never looked for conflict with the bishop. It was really a letdown. Out of sheer necessity, prompted by my own feelings, I had to put up that fight. Essential matters in ministry were at stake, such as the intrinsic bond between celebrating and living, sacrament and ministry. When I cannot administer the sacraments of baptism and marriage, how then can I be a pastor? I have never given up the bond with the church as a tradition of faith, though. I have, on the other hand, regretted the fact that I was forced to look for a place to work outside the official framework of the church.*

One of the priests indicates that, precisely as a priest, he keeps trying to deal with the position of male and female fellow pastoral workers in a credible way. He has the opportunity of regularly standing in at places where there is no minister. He refuses, however, simply to stand in, when it is at the expense of the position of a colleague who has not been ordained.

Creativity within the framework of the church

One finds a particular emphasis among those pastors who are looking for a way out by choosing an alternative as a result of which their own credibility is preserved for the time being. A female pastor who had administered the sacrament of baptism for years was told that she no longer had the authority to administer baptism. Nor was she allowed to administer extreme unction any longer. She says: *"I have problems with this and it fills me with pain that I am not allowed to baptise or administer extreme unction. I feel a permanent protest. I have also declared this openly, over and over again. Now, however, I am increasingly opting for a different way. I am looking for my own possibilities. For example, I make my own formula and rite for the unction. I simply do what the woman in the gospel did with a view to Jesus' funeral."*

In order to preserve their own credibility, some pastors opt for a reflection group, which enables them to remain active with the things *"that are really important for faith and ministry"*. It is also a place, however, where they have celebrations regularly, in a creative way of their own.

Trying to look with new eyes, working at a tolerant attitude

Some pastors have the capacity and the strength gradually to develop a tolerant attitude toward the church leadership, colleagues and groups in the church that deal differently with the tradition of the faith. One of them formulates it as follows: *"It is a huge task never to stop searching for the human side, precisely within our church. I am prepared to look for it, even if it requires a great effort."*

As long as people are honest, it is possible for him to continue to associate with them. Somebody else says that his attitude is connected with the plain fact that he finds himself in the church. It is partly his church. That is, in his opinion, what it will also be for others. We have to realise that a priest is speaking here. A tolerant attitude is sometimes more readily achievable in relation to the church leadership than with direct colleagues. Co-operation with colleagues is sometimes very difficult, or impossible. A female pastor has come to discover as a woman that men are also subjugated in certain ways. This makes her more tolerant, but at the same time she continues to witness that women are oppressed more seriously.

Working at a pragmatic relation with the church

In the case of a number of pastors one is struck by the fact that they have increasingly turned their relation with the institution of the church into a pragmatic relation. They have learned how to distance themselves from a kind of *"family tie"*. They feel about their position as might any *"employee"* toward an *"employer"*, and think of their working relation as an employment contract. This creates room and breathing space for just doing the job properly, and, if necessary, to discuss it in a decent way with the parties involved.

4. *Summary of chapter 4*

As a fourth aspect of the context we have described the relation of pastors to the church as an institution.

What strikes one is the large group who has had negative experiences. On the other hand, a relatively small group has had positive experiences on the basis of support received from certain people within the institution of the church.

A large group of pastors are trying to establish themselves in a new position with respect to the church. They try to find a way out of this area of tension by refusing to avoid conflict, by working at their own credibility and integrity, by looking for new frameworks and by working at a tolerant or more pragmatic attitude.

A very large number of pastors indicate explicitly during the interview that they are dealing with this set of problems consciously and actively. The large number is connected with the fact that virtually all pastors have had experiences with the institution of the church that have made deep inroads into their personal life. These experiences compelled them consciously to take a position, and to reflect on the position they have thus taken.

SUMMARY OF PART 1

In this first part we inquired into the context of spirituality. It comprised four aspects that were regarded as basic elements in the spiritual development of pastors: biography, personal identity, the relation to culture and the relation to the institution of the church.

In chapter 1, the study of the biography, two aspects were examined: the relation to parents and the influence of fundamentally important moments in the further development in life. The relation to the parents followed the course of either harmony or conflict. The conflicts concern the appreciation of things corporeal, as well as morality and religious forms of expression. In addition, the socio-economic position of the parental environment also has an influence.

With respect to the further development in life we examined how certain persons and places, training and education, social and political movements, cultural developments and developments in the church, influenced the development of pastors.

In chapter 2 the development of personal identity was described according to three aspects: the physical aspect, the intra-personal aspect and the interpersonal aspect. With respect to the physical aspect we concluded that there is an important tendency toward appreciation of it. Pastors grow toward a positive appreciation, become more sensitive to unity and integrity and the symbolic meaning of things corporeal. As far as the intrapersonal aspect is concerned, we described two facets: the perception on the part of pastors of possibilities and limitations, and the way they deal with the female and male sides of their personality.

The growth in perception of the first two aspects, namely things corporeal and the intrapersonal aspect, is subject to three factors that are of importance. The relationship with others who may have an important influence, resistance against moral standards, values and expectations on the part of the environment one comes from, the surrounding culture and the institutions of society and of the church, and finally, as a third factor, counselling and therapy. As a third aspect, we described the bond with others that is also of vital significance.

In chapter 3 the relation between pastors and their culture was described. Here, attention was given to the way in which pastors dealt with the effects of the process of secularisation. We based ourselves on an inventory we had drawn up of views of secularisation, and described positive and negative appreciations and the challenges issuing, or not issuing, from this process. A number of interviews indicate that cultural developments compel pastors to take up a position of their own. This is clearest in the case of those pastors who are active within social institutions, or practise a form of social ministry.

In chapter 4 we described the context of the church. Here, apart from some positive experiences, we encountered mainly negative experiences with the institution of the church. We described how pastors look for ways to determine their position with respect to the institution of the church in such a way that they can find sufficient space for themselves to live and work in the church. In doing so, they become less vulnerable. The number of pastors looking for a conscious answer to problems with respect to the institution of the church is greater than the number that emerged in the previous three chapters as the group with a clear awareness of the significance and influence of the aspects of the context. The groups partly overlap, however. The greater interest in the influence of the context of the church may have something to do with the fact that most pastors had experiences with the institution of the church that have made deep inroads into their personal life.

A central conclusion may be formulated as follows: the way in which pastors deal with biography, personal identity, and the context of culture and the church can make a considerable contribution to the development of a life of their own, and their positioning themselves within this context. In a number of situations in which pastors are confronted with new choices it becomes evident that pastors were able to make new choices of their own. The confrontation with the context challenged these pastors to look for new sources of life and work. We find this active attitude most pronouncedly with just over a third of the pastors interviewed. The others are less explicit about this. Among the latter are younger pastors who feel less need for saying something about this. They deal with developments more spontaneously, because they have grown up amidst these developments from their childhood onwards. There are also a number of other pastors who entered into the confrontation with the context to a far lesser degree.

PART TWO

RELATION TO GOD, JESUS AND THE SPIRIT

INTRODUCTION

In his book "The Brothers Karamazov", Dostoievsky describes a discussion in which various questions are raised about the "servants of religion". The questions concern the relation between what the officials of the churches say and do on the one hand, and what they really believe on the other. Are they both "functionaries of faith" and "functionaries without faith"?

Is there a visible connection between what pastors believe and what they preach? How can we describe pastors' faith in God? And what is the content of their spirituality, that is to say: how do they express their faith in God? In order to find answers to these questions, two dimensions of spirituality are described in this part, as they are articulated in the thirty interviews.

The first is the symbolic dimension of the relation of humanity to God, and of God to humanity. This means religious convictions, or the ways in which pastors say something in words or images about their relation to God and about the question of who God is for them. A similar inquiry is made with respect to the relation to Jesus and the Spirit. That is the content of Part 2.

The second dimension is the experiential side of spirituality. This means the aspect of experience and behaviour, that is to say: the way in which pastors express their spirituality. What is the meaning of prayer, reflection and commitment? And what are the factors that influence these forms of expression? What, for example, is the significance of discipline, study, participation in cultural demonstrations, spending time in nature, and physical work? This will be treated in Part 3.

The distinction between the two dimensions is, of course, a theoretical one. Pastors also express their spirituality in the symbolic dimension. We shall stick to the distinction, however, because in the former dimension the emphasis is more on concepts, ideas and representations of God, Jesus and the Spirit, whereas in the latter there is an emphasis on the active attitude of pastors in the way that they show, in their life and action, how they experience their relation with God, Jesus and the Spirit.

In this part—Part 2—the way pastors speak about their relation to God, Jesus and the Spirit, and the metaphors they use to describe the relation of God, Jesus and the Spirit to people, are considered.

It is, in my view, of particular importance in this study to draw attention to the Trinitarian God. According to Moltmann, an exclusively theistic or monotheistic approach runs the risk of giving the relation to God a purely political or ethical content. Faith in God, Jesus and the Spirit is a guarantee, or perhaps even a conditio sine qua non, for a liberating orientation in theology and spirituality. The point at issue is more than an ethical and/or political approach, in which God can be reduced to an ideological starting point, concept or idea. Believing is linked to a personal bond, to a relation with God who enters into a relationship with people.

According to Moltmann, the fact that God enters into a history with people is essential for the Christian tradition. The latter reaches its absolute high- and low-points in Jesus' Cross in which God gives himself away to people and imparts the Spirit to everyone who wishes to live in the love of God and of people: "God is not only elevated far above earthly reality, but also near, here and now; God is not only God, but also man; God is not only rule, authority and law, but the history of suffering, liberating love. Conversely, the death of the Son is not the death of God, but the beginning of the history of God, in which through the death of the Son and through the suffering of the Father the vivifying Spirit of love is manifested" (Moltmann 1972, p. 239. Cf. Schoonenberg 1991).

I wish to speak about the Trinitarian God from the perspective of experience. In our research we do not want to bring up the relation to God, Jesus and the Spirit in the second category of reflection, but in the first, namely in that of lived experience. Schillebeeckx indicates that the christological titles, for example, are of a relatively recent date. The basis of these titles is the religious experience of the Christians in their association with Jesus of Nazareth and, later on, in their living and believing as the community of Jesus Christ (Schillebeeckx 1974). Following the theologies of Moltmann, Schillebeeckx and Schoonenberg, as well as many others, I start from the history of God with people through Jesus and the Spirit.

CHAPTER FIVE

FAITH, HOPE AND LOVE

The relation to God can be described with reference to two aspects. We can consider this relation as a movement towards God, which is, especially, expressed in terms of faith, hope and love. However, we can also describe this relation according to the way in which we humans experience God's movement towards ourselves, and put it into words. This relation is described by means of metaphors—images used by pastors in order to articulate the way they experience and feel about God.

I shall first give a description of the way in which the pastors interviewed use the terms faith, hope and love as expressive of their relation to God. Which of these three is most important to them (chapter 5)? Then I shall describe the way in which metaphors are used to express the association with God (chapter 6).

In the Christian tradition the relation to God has always had the following structural aspects: truth, trust, hope and love. The first two, the aspects of truth and of trust, serve to give content to faith. Which of these aspects are emphasised in the interviews? Do the pastors speak about their relation to God as a belief in truths or as a faithful surrender to God? Or do they prefer using the words hope and love to indicate their relation to God? This is an important question because the way in which the relation to God is indicated strongly influences the way in which personal content is given to spirituality. The three virtues, or relational terms, of faith, hope and love will be discussed separately. It will be followed by a survey of the mutual interconnections between these three.

1. *Faith in God*

In a third of the interviews the term faith in God does not occur. Of the two-thirds who do use this term only three give a special and unique meaning to the phrase 'believing in God'. For them, believing is the term *per excellence* to indicate the relation to God. The others combine believing in God either with hope in God, or with love towards God. What content is given to the relation to God viewed from the perspective of faith? In my description I base myself, not only on the three pastors, but also on the broader group that uses the term faith in one way or another.

Wherever faith (either in a unique sense, or in combination with hope and/or love) indicates the core of the relation to God, faith in God is used in three different meanings: faith in God as ground of existence, faith in God as a companion, faith in God as destination. The terms *"ground of existence"*, *"companion"*, and *"destination"* are not used as such in the interviews. They are terms that I think can be employed to interpret various words used by the pastors to indicate their relation to God.

Faith in God as ground of existence

Faith in God is usually understood as an expression of trust in God as the basis and ground of existence. A pastor confesses: *"The fact that I am entitled to be there, that is the content of my faith. Believing is of central significance to me. I believe quite strongly that God allows me and wants me to be there."* It is, in fact, the content of the Greek word "pistis" in the gospels, which comes very close to what is meant by *"trust"*. Thomistic theology speaks in this respect of fides fiducialis. It is not surprising that the latest Willibrord (Dutch) translation of the New Testament translates the word "pistis" by "trust" in places where, until recently, it has been translated "belief". For pastors who use this term, believing expresses a trusting surrender to God who gives life and sustains life again and again. Only a small number of pastors understand this trusting surrender as an expression of a personal relationship with God of the kind that people can also have with one another.

> *I sometimes say to the one who is dear to me: I believe in you, I give myself up to you, because you make life possible for me every time. In this way I believe in Someone who is love, and to whom I give myself up.*

A slightly greater number prefer to speak about faith in God in the sense of a view or conviction. One gives oneself up to the idea, the conviction, that God is the basis of life:

> *Faith is a view which supports me in everything I do and live; it is my trust in a conviction that God eventually constitutes the foundation of everything we do on the path of justice.*

Others strongly associate faith in God with faith in people as a foundation of existence. For them, believing in God is always immediately bound up with believing in people. This also indicates an element of struggle because believing as surrender is often a long and searching process.

Those pastors who are clearly aware of the influence of the context in which they live and work, are most explicit in recognising this struggle. For them, it is the struggle to learn to understand anew the faith they have received from childhood onwards. One of them, for example, says: *"Dare I give myself up to the God who is forgiveness, or whom I have always believed to be a God of forgiveness?"*

For a number of pastors, the quest for a new content of faith in God for our time is connected to the struggle *with* God, against a background of inhuman violence and meaningless suffering. How can God be the *"source of life"*? And how is it possible that *"people destroy for each other the sources of life"*? This question is left to stand; it need not be answered immediately. Searching for an answer is in itself already an important process of faith.

Faith in God as companion

Some pastors understand faith in God as an expression of trust in Someone who, or a power which, accompanies and supports them on the way they have to go. One of them refers to the way in which Abraham embarked on his journey with God. For him, faith in God is the same as travelling on a road. Another pastor says that faith in God means strength to become increasingly oneself—through a process—and to grow in faithfulness to the road one is travelling. In this way believing is especially a verb denoting activity. Here too, however, the struggle with respect to the question of who this God may be is permanently going on. Some pastors add that people in their environment are sometimes capable of making faith in God as a companion available.

Faith in God as destination

A small group of pastors understand faith in God as a faithful surrender to the God who is a completion or destination. Here, faith in God is an expression of the conviction that it is up to God to bring the life of each human being to completion and consummation. The point at issue is ultimate acceptance, also when we humans are incapable of it. It is faith in *"God's Kingdom come"*. The few pastors who speak about this also state that faith in God as completion has everything to do with the work to be done on the road one has to travel.

Summary

Faith in God has the characteristics of a faithful surrender to God. Some pastors experience this as a personal relationship with God. For others it is a kind of trust in the view or conviction that God will be there. The faith that God will keep faith with people is the basis of existence. Thus faith in God has three meanings: it indicates the relation to God as ground of existence, companion and destination. The emphasis falls on the relation to God as ground of existence.

In the interviews faith does not mean believing in truths, convictions or fixed ideas. In other words, it is by no means something in the nature of a fides obedientialis, as described in Thomistic theology, in which formulated articles of faith are the objects of faith. It is rather a kind of faith in the living tradition: as people hand down and live the story of God, tradition becomes a living content of faith. We might, therefore, also say that articles of faith become alive and gain contemporary relevance as expressions of people's religious experience, both in the past, and here and now.

2. *Hope in God*

In the interviews, *"hope in God"* is mentioned more frequently than *"faith in God"*. Apart from six interviews in which the phrase "hope in God" does not occur, half of the pastors say that hope in God is *the* expression of their relation to God. For just under a third, hope in God goes together with faith and love.

As in the case of faith in God, the hope in God is given three different meanings: hope in God as ground of existence, hope in God as companion, and hope in God as destination. Here too, we are dealing with differences of emphasis that come quite close to one another, but are nevertheless distinct.

Hope in God as ground of existence

For a number of pastors, hope as a term for the relation to God is based on the faith that God's love or loyalty sustains us humans.

"God is the love that holds me. I profoundly hope that I will be sustained." That is indeed what the pastor who is speaking here would like to show to people most of all. It is precisely where people are vulnerable that he would like to be a living sign of this hope in God. Somebody else speaks of a kind of basic trust.

> *It does not mean just hoping. It sometimes means hesitating, though, and yet making an effort. An attitude of confidence and, to a certain extent, faith that the dark sides will not have the last word. It is that which gives me the strength to fight for the rights of people and to raise a strong protest when injustice prevails. For that is unacceptable.*

The pastor who uses the expression "hope in God" links his relation to God especially with a yearning for *"being sustained by God"*. That is precisely what he is continually looking for in the tradition, in prayers and in hymns. As a pastor in psychiatry he badly needs it.

> *Hope, that is what is most strongly alive for me here. Hope is founded on something, namely on the stories that we keep rereading, giving them contemporary relevance and translating them, the stories of the promise that the Eternal One is travelling with us. I may hope for that, for this God was there at one time, and at another time, too, and he was recognised, called upon, praised and accused. At the same time the longing is also present here and now, and I express hope by lighting a candle during a conversation with a depressed person. It is the deep longing that the dead-end situation of people here can be broken. How often do I not say inwardly: I hope that there will still be hope for you and, at any rate, that you have been accepted, that you may learn to accept yourself, and that you may know that you are still being sustained. . . . Hoping for: I think that is an expression for people staying in motion, moving on, so that they do not remain fixated on their problems. Sometimes I hope, I pray, that, for people here, the light of day may break through.*

Here, the strength of hope is connected with a constant struggle to keep the light of hope burning. This struggle is accepted, for that is what reality is like. In this quotation the hope in God as ground of existence is strongly linked to the hope in God as companion and destination. We also see this in other pastors.

Hope in God as companion

The meaning of hope in God as ground of existence is close to that of hope in God as companion: God will sustain us on the road we are travelling, and in this way God is our companion. In a number of interviews hope in God has the explicit meaning of staying on the move and not giving up, because one trusts that God as companion will continue to accompany us. For some pastors, this way of giving content to hope means strength to persevere amidst present-day developments in the church. It is precisely here that God as companion becomes visible and tangible. This is experienced as a strength with which fellow-believers persevere in solidarity with the pastor.

A missionary worker often has the feeling that social developments, such as individualisation and the decline of solidarity, have a negative influence on hope as an expression of the relation to God. The real skill, however, is not to allow oneself to lose one's resilience because of things that do not go the way one would like them to. The point is not to allow the hope that things will be different some day to be shattered. Hope in God has to do with the little things that do succeed. An example is a school that starts to use Max Havelaar coffee (coffee grown by small farmers' co-operations in the Third World, so that buying it is an expression of one's solidarity with them). Such a small sign indicates how God's strength keeps us alive on the way.

Hoping for God means daring to surrender to God in the confidence that He will take you by the hand. It is trust in God who guides us and travels with us. One of the pastors illustrates this by means of the image of someone who, unnoticed, carries people across a stretch of sand. The footprints are visible, but people do not know who carried them and when it happened. The answer is that, at those moments when people were unable to accomplish anything by themselves, it was God who carried them.

For each individual among this group of pastors it is clear that their hope of being able to press on is connected with their faith in people. There is a stream of confidence. It is people that show us how God is moving with us.

Hope in God as destination

For a number of other pastors, hope means strength with which one can change things and which helps one to be able to cope with difficult situations. Hope provides prospects for the future; it is where one finds strength. It is as if God is standing on the horizon, beckoning people to come and meet him. From this grows the confidence that there is after all some point in what we are doing. Things will turn out well in the end. Hope for the future gives strength and energy to work for the liberation of people. This realisation provides these pastors with a perspective in everything that they do. This applies, in particular, to those among them who are active in some form of social ministry. For one of them, hope in God as future gives strength to his fight against a growing cynicism, which is paralysing people.

> *In this way it becomes important now and then to tell each other how you manage to persevere. This is closely related to the love of people at the bottom, the poor, and the factory workers. And you have to be able to live with the fact that you do not see any results.*

People repeatedly give one another signs of hope, offering one another a perspective in doing so. The confidence and the faith that people give to you are a basis for keeping hope alive. And this hope is completely at odds with the reality of all kinds of tough economic interests. One of them summarises it pithily: with *"God as perspective, there is a future for people who take God as a starting-point"*.

In some interviews hope in God is linked with longing: *"longing and hope: that is what is most strongly alive for me here."* Hope in God springs from longing and at the same time hope nourishes the longing for a perspective in life. Hope strengthens my longing that, not only today, but tomorrow as well, my life is sustained by God's loyalty. For example, one pastor who has been looking for a home all his life says that his confidence in God makes him long for ultimate security with God: *"That I may live there, be at home."* It is strongly reminiscent of a statement by Augustine: *"Our hearts will not rest 'till they rest in thee"*.

In some interviews hope in God is linked to an expectant attitude. This provides courage to press on; hope also strengthens the expectation that all will be well in the end. Hope in God as destination, like hope in God as ground of existence, approximates the meaning of hope in God as companion: God sustains us towards the future, holds us and keeps us going.

Correlation between hope in God and faith in God

Hope in God in all three meanings—ground of existence, companion and destination—comes close to faith as confident surrender to God, in the sense of the Second Testament word "pistis". Hoping is cognate with trust and surrender. It is remarkable that precisely in the large number of interviews where hope in God is used as a key word for the relation to God, it is often combined with trust.

In one of the interviews the words hope, faith and trust are indeed mentioned in one breath.

> *The word for my relation to God is, first of all, hope. That is the first that occurs to me. When I keep thinking about it, I come up with the word faith as well, but it is the hope that things will turn out right with the world and that things will turn out right with people. It is faith in the sense of trust.*

Faith and hope converge in trust. Trust is both an act of faith and an act of hope. A survey of the interviews suggests that pastors prefer the words hope and trust to the term faith, because faith is still associated with rational belief in truths, dogmas, and propositions. The point at issue for them is rather confident surrender to God.

3. *Love towards God*

The word love as an expression for the relation to God predominates in a third of the interviews. In a number of interviews the term does not occur. In over a third of the interviews the term goes together with the other terms: faith and hope.

There are differences in the ways pastors use the word love as a relational term. Three of them speak about a personal love relationship with God, while others who do mention love as a relational term do not consider and experience the love relationship as a personal relation to God.

Love towards God as ground of existence

With almost a third of the pastors who speak about love as an expression of the relation to God there is no hint of a personal love relationship. Love towards God is above all a form of confident surrender to God as ground of existence.

A female pastor tells of a crisis that she once went through. While going through this crisis, she had a very unusual experience. Even so, there is for her no such thing as a love relationship towards God in the sense of a relationship that is experienced at the personal level. Rather it is the experience of being rooted in the stream of God's presence, while God is not regarded as a person. She quotes the poet Vasalis who says something about the divine mystery in the core of every human being: "In the deepest depth of my soul where it is made of stones, there I see nothing but your countenance".

I express the relation to God by using the word love. Its origin lies in my history—when I did not want to live any longer at a certain moment. We were on vacation in the mountains. And then I thought: I am not going home any more, to my parents. That's enough now, everybody and everything. And then I climbed up a mountain, not quite to the top, but still rather high. And there I sat down to meditate. And then, I do not know how, somewhere from inside or from outside or from both directions, the feeling came: you were born out of love and you will also return to love. So I could not make an end to myself then. That has been essential for me. Since then I have felt secure. That feeling has never disappeared. Yes, love is the most important thing for me.

Others speak about love but hasten to add explicitly that it should not be understood as a love relationship. Rather it is a basis of trust, a kind of ground of existence.

With a few pastors love as a relational word comes quite close to hope and trust: *"Love gives hope a chance."*

Love towards God as companion: the Loved One

Some pastors do not hesitate to speak about their relation towards God as a love relationship. One of them, for example, says:

I simply prefer terms like love and being in love. Sometimes, after a long discussion, the question is suddenly put to me: what is your idea of God? And then, without making any fuss about it, I can simply say that God loves me, and that I love God. I can say that God holds me. I recognise so much in words, hymns, and Psalms. It is God who challenges me to open up in love. I feel this coming back every time in my work, and in my preaching and praying.

Others speak lovingly about God in terms like *"my dearest"* or *"endless love"* against the background of Psalm 139 in which God's praises are sung, among other things, as the one who is our constant companion. It is in God that these pastors have found a home, a place where they are totally known and accepted. One of them went through a deep crisis during his years of study in which he experienced great emptiness and loneliness. Through the loving, personal attention of a teacher, however, he made an important discovery.

I was accepted in spite of everything. So I can say: the love relationship with God developed precisely during the time when I was completely lost, during which I became increasingly aware of the fact that God knows every inch of me as Psalm 139 says.

For another pastor there is a connection between the use of the term love and his ministry to engaged and married couples. It is all about the religious meaning of a relationship. People discover that the mystery of God's presence plays a part in a human relationship. The love relationship goes together with the hope that it is possible to make room for the coming of the Kingdom of God, precisely in the relationship. The personal love relation to God is of the same nature as faith and hope: a personal surrender to God as companion. The love towards God is described as a permanent bond with God who accompanies people like a loved one. God as the one who is intimate with people, like partners in a marriage.

Love towards God as destination

Love towards God is based on the faith that God will be faithful. Such were the experiences of the people of Israel, the prophets and Jesus. The Name of the Eternal One is associated with loyalty. The Eternal One is there, present. *"In this way I can associate loyalty with love. I can say that loyalty constitutes a kind of basis in my association with God."*

For some pastors, love is strongly linked with justice in the meaning given to it by Schillebeeckx (Schillebeeckx 1977). There, love becomes the driving force to work at our destination.

> *God is love and God is a God of life. What matters are the words used by Schillebeeckx: justice and love. When you want to work in the name of God, then those two words apply. That is the image I have to try and express. Justice creates future, creates life. Working at societal bonds, respectfully: a small human being trying to make his small contribution to a better world.*

Here the meaning of God as destination comes quite close to the meaning of God as companion, except God is not experienced as a personal partner. God's loyalty, by which my life is sustained, means strength for on the way. This calls upon me to work at justice, which will be my contribution to the consummation.

Summary

With respect to love towards God as ground of existence, as companion and as destination, some pastors speak about God in terms of a personal love relationship. God is the beloved companion. Others show more attention to God as ground of existence and destination.

4. *Reflection in and on spirituality*

We come across both forms of reflection in the pastors' speaking about their relation to God.

All the interviews show that pastors, without exception, have a reflective aspect in their experience of faith, hope and love. Several of them refer to concrete examples from their experience through which they indicate that their relation to God is often of one kind rather than another, and that this conclusion is supported by new experiences. In their very speaking during the interviews a reasoning process can be heard and felt. For example, a rational element can be discerned when they speak about faith as a confident surrender to God or about an intermingling of faith, hope and love, about the connection between hope in God and desire, or about love as a personal or impersonal bond of love. This is noticeable in the fact that pastors keep using different words, because they want to indicate that the experience is open to several interpretations.

Several pastors are aware of the transitions that have taken place in their relation to God. With a number of them, just over a third, we see that the reflection *in* their experience changes into reflection *on* that experience. This becomes apparent when, for example, they link up their faith, hope and love on the one hand, and the context on the other hand. Some of them show how, taking their biography as a starting-point, especially the growing awareness of the influence of their parents or other important persons, they struggle with a personal faith in God as the one to whom one could give oneself up. They also relate how, step by step, they could, or dared to, get as far as that, or how they are still struggling with that in which they would so much like to believe. Others show how theological developments in particular have taken hold of them and forced them towards reflection on the meaning of faith in God. Some of them tell of the connection between experiences of their own limitations and possibilities on the one hand, and the struggle with love towards God on the other. Several of them show something of the fundamental significance of developments in culture and in the church. That is what forced them to give new content to their relation to God—especially with respect to the question whether there is something like a personal relation to God—and to distance themselves from giving a dogmatic content to believing in God. They show that in the relation to God there is always something like joy and sorrow, of surrender and fear of surrender, of feeling at ease and the tragedy of not quite achieving what one would so very much hope to achieve.

Reflection on spirituality requires one to distance oneself for a moment from the concrete experience of faith, hope and love. It obliges one to ask oneself: what is happening, what is taking place in my faith, in my hope, in my love? Thus room is created for considering what this relationship implies and what it is worth.

In the interviews of just over a third of the pastors we find that they have learned how to distance themselves and how to allow for critical evaluation of their relation to God. For these pastors the confrontation with the context—their life history or culture, for example—is mostly a concrete occasion for reflection on faith, hope and love. We see in this process a gradation of more and less. We can observe how reflection emerges most strongly with those pastors who indicate how the confrontation with the context frequently confronts them with choices that again and again prove to be temporary. With them we sense that the use of certain terms that today may have a specific content, like faithful surrender, longing, God as destination etc., will be subject to criticism again tomorrow. The language these pastors use is constantly put into perspective and corrected.

5. Summary of chapter 5

When, in concentrating on the number of interviews, we restrict ourselves to those that mention explicitly one of the three virtues as the only or central expression of the relation to God, we arrive at the following survey:

> Faith in God: 3 x
> Hope in God: 16 x
> Love towards God: 11 x

It is clear that pastors prefer to use the expression 'hope in God'. When we have a closer look at the actual content of the word hope, this comes close to the word faith in the evangelical meaning of "pistis", which is best translated by trust. This is further confirmed by the fact that in the interviews the word trust is frequently linked to the word hope. As far as love towards God as a relational term is concerned, there is a clear distinction between a relatively small group of pastors who speak about love in their relation to God as beloved companion, and a larger group of pastors who experience love towards God as a relation to God as ground of existence and destination.

There is a connection between faith in God, hope in God and love towards God in all three aspects: God as ground of existence, companion and destination.

Ground of existence, companion and destination are names that we can use to give content to the relation to God in terms of faith, hope and love. These terms indicate a permanent movement, which is characteristic of God. In using these terms, pastors say that God has entered into a history with people, will continue to do so, and will consummate history with people. An important meaning of God lies in the connection between origin and destination: God as companion on the way between Alpha and Omega.

Finally, we were able to conclude that with all the pastors it is possible to point out a reflection in their spirituality with respect to the relation to God. With just over a third we find, apart from the reflection *in* spirituality, also reflection *on* spirituality—i.e. wherever pastors have learned to distance themselves and to evaluate their experience and the way they feel about things.

CHAPTER SIX

METAPHORS FOR GOD

Faith in God, hope in God, and love towards God all presuppose three aspects attributed to God: God is the ground of our existence, the destination of our existence, and the companion in our existence.

In the interviews a large number of metaphors are used to express these different aspects of God. In speaking about the way in which they experience God, pastors use metaphors to give concrete content to their experience of God as ground of existence, destination or companion.

In this chapter we shall examine, first of all, the areas of reality from which the metaphors are derived (1). We shall then describe the various metaphors derived from nature, from our dealings with nature, from personal, interpersonal and social life, and from the dimensions of space and time (2).

Then a number of fields of tension that become apparent in the use of metaphors will be described. Tension becomes apparent in a number of relations: the relation between redemption and liberation (3); the relation between liberation and exile (4); the relation between God and the other person (5); the relation between security and challenge (6); the relation between personal and impersonal metaphors (7), including the question of how pastors address God in liturgy (8); the relation between male and female metaphors (9); the relation between symbolic speaking about God and the attitude towards mystery (10).

Finally, we shall describe reflection in and on spirituality as far as the use of metaphors is concerned (11).

1. *Derived from reality*

The metaphors used by pastors to refer to God are derived from nature, or from our dealings with nature, from personal and interpersonal life, from social life, and from space and time. The way we speak about nature and about our personal life etc. is also the way in which we speak about God.

God is spoken about as source and stream, as space and depth. God's dealings with people are expressed in metaphors like creating and preserving, sustaining and healing. God's relation towards people is indicated by the notions of offering security, giving comfort, reconciling and redeeming. God is the merciful one, the other person that we meet; God calls and liberates. God is consummation and God supports us on the way to the future. Most metaphors are derived from personal and interpersonal life. In this context the metaphor of God as liberator is used most frequently. In some cases this metaphor also acquires a social meaning.

2. Different realities

Metaphors derived from nature

The images derived from nature and from our dealings with nature chiefly point to God as ground of existence. In more than a third of the interviews several of these metaphors are used. God is like a source of life, light and love, like a stream of living water, like a source of wisdom and strength. A few pastors refer to texts in the first Book of Kings where it is told of the prophet Elijah how, on his journey through the desert, he was invited to eat and drink so as to be able to continue his journey through the desert (1 Kings 19). Others like to refer to the wisdom literature in which God is described as source of wisdom, so as to indicate the strength of the hope that life is sustained by insight into what is of importance (for example Proverbs 14).

For one of them the aspects of ground of existence and destination come together in the metaphor of a *"source"*. This pastor says that the connection with the source guides and accompanies her on her life-path. It provides a permanent sense of security. In moments of crisis this experience holds and sustains her.

> *The source: the feeling that you originated from love and will return to love. That is essential for me. Since the moment when I felt this intensely during a fundamental crisis I have always felt secure, whatever happens. That feeling has never disappeared since.*

While with most metaphors derived from nature, or from our dealings with nature, the primary meaning is that of God as ground of existence, they sometimes also point to the experience of God as companion. For example, the metaphor of a *"stream"* is an image of God who sustains us. This metaphor gives to God an *"originative"* meaning, while at the same time God is seen as a movement into which we are taken up, and in which we remain. It expresses an enduring connection, as indicated by Eckhart: *"I feel enclosed in the endless stream of the sea, the ocean of God's love"* (Maas 1975, 58).

Metaphors derived from space

This also applies to the metaphors derived from space. God surrounds us as space and we receive sense or meaning because of the fact that we are enclosed within this space. God gives depth to our existence and it is from God that we derive our meaning. This is how we are on our way. We might also say that because God is experienced as ground of existence, we trust in God as the one who accompanies us as a sustaining force.

Metaphors derived from personal and interpersonal life

The metaphors derived from personal and interpersonal life mostly point to God as companion. God is near to us as someone who is travelling with us and offers us security, comforts us at difficult moments, reconciles us with ourselves, and is moved when we are hurt. God is the other person who shares our journey or whom we run up against. God invites us, and calls upon us to go further.

Metaphor derived from interpersonal and social life

The notion of God as liberator often appears. Apart from the metaphors derived from personal life, and among the metaphors derived from interpersonal life, this is the metaphor which occurs most frequently (in two-thirds of the interviews). In all four meanings given to this metaphor God is portrayed as both ground of existence and companion: God liberates from evil, God liberates from chaos and division, God liberates from established frameworks, and God liberates from injustice. There is a connection with the stories of the exodus, which mark a new beginning for the people and at the same time show God to be a loyal companion who enters upon a journey with his people.

Metaphors derived from the dimension of time

The idea of God as destination is usually expressed by a metaphor derived from the dimension of time: God will consummate. In God lies our final destination. *"I am on my way to consummation. I am in the process of becoming. And when I reach my measure, it will have happened. Then I shall then I may see God face to face."* In this metaphor the hope is expressed that we, humans, will eventually find security with God and that we shall be accepted. It is not surprising that this metaphor is frequently used in the liturgy of the funeral service in which confidence is expressed in the loyalty of God who will accept every human being beyond and through death.

Likewise, the metaphor of the *"God of exile"*, which is derived from the dimension of time, expresses longing for the future and hope for some perspective. Here, however, the emphasis is on the experience of God as companion. God accompanies us, and never ceases to sustain us, to enable us to persevere at times when any hopeful perspective fails to appear.

Summary

Surveying all the metaphors, we can conclude that the pastors use only a few metaphors to characterise God as destination and future. There is a preference for metaphors that describe God as companion. In a number of images this is connected with the experience of God as ground of existence. The emphasis is on the notion of going on a journey: trust in God as creating and recreating force sustains pastors and keeps them going. Besides, it is especially the metaphors derived from nature, and from our dealings with nature, that characterise God as ground of existence. The fact that many metaphors portray God especially as a companion coheres with the fact that most images are derived from personal and interpersonal life. The only image derived from both interpersonal life and social life, namely God as *"liberator"*, is mainly used in the interpersonal meaning. In most cases it indicates a personal movement of God towards people.

The social meaning is found especially among pastors who give a social content to their ministry. They are the pastors who work in institutions or have been appointed as industrial pastors, diaconal and missionary workers. Furthermore, those women are especially notable who are very active in a kind of ministry aimed at the liberation of women.

3. *Redeemer and liberator*

In a small number of the interviews in which the metaphor of *"redeeming"* occurs, it has something to do with freeing from evil, injustice and sin. Some pastors mention it quite emphatically, as, for example, in an interview which contains a reference to Psalm 4. Those who set their heart on trifles and run after lies is called upon to give in to God who elevates people by healing them and redeeming them from evil. In this way *"God is also redeeming for me. I am like the paralysed man who is cured and forgiven"* (Mark 2). Another pastor feels herself to be like the chaos that precedes creation. God is like the wind, the breeze. In this she experiences God's presence. Like the first *"ruach"* soaring over chaos, God is sometimes also experienced as redeemer in a similar sense. In the other interviews redemption is connected with reconciliation and healing. It means being freed, not from problems, but in such a way that one can become a free and complete human being. Creation and re-creation are closely linked to one another.

> *I think the word redemption is more difficult to use than other metaphors, because I wonder: redemption from what? I am a person of this world and I get my hands dirty. I am never called to account for that. As things are, one has to take one's share of original sin and one cannot but join in. It never interferes in the relation between God and people, though. It is never a blockade. In that sense, redemption has changed for me. I still use this metaphor, but carefully.*

Redemption is not an obvious metaphor for the pastors who speak about it. They use the word redemption cautiously. One of them says that this metaphor has some attraction for him, *"but there is something fishy about it"*. This caution has something to do with a new view of sin and evil. Reality, and especially one's own self, is not explicitly called *"sinful"*. One of the pastors, for example, is indeed prepared to use the word *"redemption"*, but then not against the background of the phrase *"vale of tears"*. It is redemption in the sense of liberation and consummation. In the majority of the interviews the word "redemption" is not used and four pastors emphasise that they have great problems with using that word. One of them articulates the development that many of the other interviewees have also gone through.

> *In my case there is a development from redemption to liberation. Liberation in connection with God highlights a more positive side. For me there is a strong link*

with the resurrection stories. I do not have an unpleasant feeling about redemption, but I notice that, as the years went by, I increasingly preferred to follow the path of liberation. Resurrection stories are stories of liberation. That is most encouraging in my ministry, especially when I see how people manage to find their own way.

In the course of their lives a third of the pastors became very interested in liberation theology. Some had personal experiences in Latin America, while others became fascinated by themes of liberation as a result of the rise of feminist theology. The latter group consists especially of women. Some pastors like to speak about liberation in connection with their ministry, which is strongly society-oriented.

4. *From exodus to exile*

With nearly half of those who spent a lot of time on liberation theology a new tendency is to be found which emerged in the course of the eighties: the God of liberation becomes the God of exile. The metaphor *"God of exile"* is used to indicate that the future is uncertain or contingent. It is impossible to predict how long the journey will take. It is a metaphor from the exilic literature. In a number of interviews one sees a transition from the image of the exodus to the image of exile. One pastor, for example, says that hope, which for him was the basis for living and working, has increasingly come to be marked by the theology of exile.

We shall have to see things through for a while. In doing so, it is less and less a matter of results and more and more a matter of doing justice disinterestedly. That is how Gustavo Guttierez speaks about it. As a theologian, he shows a strong transition from a theology of liberation to a long-term theology: it is the path of justice without many visible results. This is also to say that gratuitous justice is not hopeless. Old Jewish stories are very important for me in this respect: when you have saved a single human being, you have saved the world. Or, when you have renewed a single human being, you have renewed the whole of mankind. There seems to be no result, no appreciation and no recognition in the world. There are no visible signs of a better society. The point, however, is to do justice here and now, and there is merit in that.

It is precisely those pastors who lived at the time of enthusiastic innovations in church and society, among other things the period of the councils (the sixties), who have increasingly had to discover that the road to liberation is a long road. Travelling the road itself has become more important.

> *I have admiration for Rabin who keeps trying to get a millimetre further with the peace process around the negotiating table. This presupposes a profoundly spiritual motivation.*

The pastor who is speaking here has become more careful in her preaching. She does not just offer some rays of hope. She has learned how to handle church policy in a more creative and relaxed manner and also in the way she leads the liturgy. Until a few years ago this female pastoral worker used to administer baptism. Then her authority to do so was revoked.

> *Knowing that it will come one day but not now, surely I keep protesting against it. But I do not keep spending my energy on it. There are so many other things, and I notice that I have great stamina.*

Against the background of the image of exile, one of the pastors uses the old Twenthish and German terms 'tweeduster' and 'zwielicht': in the twilight it is not clear whether the light of the sun will break through. It may as well be the beginning of night. *"It is the border area of no longer and of not yet, not being at home yet and no longer being at home."* God here becomes the one who gives strength for seeing things through amidst the delay, which goes along with the patience of the *"one who is waiting"*. It is a matter of holding out.

The metaphor of exile expresses a yearning for security on the long journey. In fact, it is a strong appeal for seeing things through no matter how long it takes. At the same time it is a matter of recognising hard reality. There is also a growing awareness that the journey is connected with the word *"provisionality"*: we see from day to day. Believing in God is accomplished in fragments.

5. *God and the other*

In just over a third of the interviews God is spoken of as *the other*. Three aspects emerge: God is the other person, who enters into a relationship, God is the One who allows himself to be known, and God is the Wholly Other.

God as the other who enters into a relationship
God as the other enters into a dialogue and is a God of covenant. It is always a matter of a relationship, which is reciprocal. God is the one who goes with his people because a relationship has been entered into. One of the pastors who use this metaphor feels very

much at ease in Waaijman's way of speaking: *"Be-er"* is the other who says about himself: *"I shall be there".* Such is the name of God (Waaijman 1984). This, however, means reciprocity in the relationship of God and man: *"Will you also be there for me, then? . . . And: can I also be there for the other? And can another also be there for me?"*

God allows himself to be known by way of and in the other
The point here is the loving encounter, the solidarity between human beings, in which God sometimes becomes visible.

> *Thinking of Oosterhuis' book "Seeing sometimes for a moment" I believe that it is precisely in the loving encounter with the other that things divine become manifest. In my experience the essence is always the loving aspect of the encounter. This is the only way for me to speak about God.*

To describe this another pastor uses words from the story of the disciples on their way to Emmaus, who recognise the Living One in the other person who travels with them. That is the reason why this pastor has made a habit of always asking at the funeral: what has this human being of God shown? On these occasions she refers to an expression by Waaijman, who says *"The name of God has written itself in people's memory"* (Waaijman). We come across the same experience in a few others. One of them, a pastor who works in a nursing home, has gone through a strong development from an attitude of being weighed down by a demanding God to an experience of God who shows himself in people. It is a transition from *"I have to achieve something in the face of God"* to the surprising discovery that *"God shows himself in vulnerable people who become such wonderful people as a result of it."*

Others indicate that what is required is precisely a clear distinction between God and people so that people can be *"image-bearers"* of God.

> *My relation to God is not one of security. I cannot nestle in God any more than He can nestle in me. I have to use the terms purely in this sense: I am talking about God while, on the other hand, I am simultaneously talking about people. I want to keep the two sides clearly separated.*

How else, according to this woman, would it be possible for one to speak about people as image-bearers of God? From her in particular, one hears that each human being, in his or her own way, precisely as a human being, is an image-bearer of God. I do not encounter God himself in people, but they do put me on the track towards God. By way of the other person, who is my fellow human being, God calls upon me. A number of pastors feel quite at ease with Levinas' formulations about the *"countenance of the other"* as one of the tracks leading towards God. God allows himself to be known in those who call us to responsibility and solidarity. Sometimes it is an intractable experience, because the other shows, at the same time, God's being alien and different. (Levinas 1982; Engelen 1985.)

The general tendency in these interviews is that God is experienced as the one who accompanies people in the shape of the other person who finds him- or herself next to us or over against us.

God is the "Wholly Other"
This designation is used to indicate that God transcends every metaphor and can never be experienced or known completely. One of the female pastors, for example, says that she frequently moves between two extremes: the cosmic experience of God who is interwoven with the universe, and the experience that God is the Wholly Other.

> *Sometimes I am cosmic in my entire experience and sometimes God is not an Other. It is not meant in a pantheistic way, though. I do not think so myself. For me God is also the Wholly Other. The mystics in particular strongly appeal to me in this respect.*

The mystical aspect, or the feeling for mystery, will be discussed in greater detail under point 10, where the loss of all metaphors is discussed.

6. *Security and challenge*

The majority of the metaphors point to a longing for security with God. This longing is connected with pastors' experience that life is vulnerable and that they themselves are vulnerable people. It especially those who have gone through a crisis in their life, or experienced vulnerable moments in their health, who speak about God as a protecting, healing, reconciling God, who offers security.

> *I like to use images of a God who is love in which I may know myself enclosed as a vulnerable human being. I put my trust in it: we are always secure in God's first love.*

God is compared to a mother who picks up her child who has broken something, comforts it and restores it to its real self.

Yet looking forward to security with God is not an unqualified longing in these pastors. In some, a field of tension emerges as soon as they speak about God in terms of security. They feel uneasy, because the God of comfort cannot easily be related to the violence present in the world: how is it possible to be secure with God at the sight of so much inhuman violence? Or how is it possible to speak about the God of comfort when one perceives that it is so difficult to mobilise people into doing something about injustice and violence?

The pastors who show their uneasiness are, on the one hand, those who in their ministry give a lot of attention to the struggle against social and economic injustice, and on the other, those whose thoughts in fact are very often with the comforting God, while at the same time they feel a kind of "bad conscience" which tells them: should you not be more active, calling upon and challenging people, so that they are mobilised?

A number of pastors manage to handle this field of tension in a balanced way. They recognise the tension and sometimes also the conflict in themselves, but, by paying deliberate attention to it, they have developed their skill in dealing with this tension. It is not forbidden to feel the need for security, and the same applies to the experience of limitations in social engagement. Some of them show that, precisely when one is able to receive consolation, one can also develop the strength to commit oneself. In their ministry they also see this in the people with whom they associate.

7. *Personal and impersonal*

Most of the pastors indicate that they have developed a greater openness to cosmic images. These are images from nature as we have already seen in the foregoing section: source, stream, sustaining ground, and depth. For a large number of them this being open to cosmic images of God is an expression of their pastoral attitude. It is good for contemporary people for whom it is possible to find elsewhere something with which they feel more at ease than with metaphors handed down by the church—for example in the New Age-movement. In the latter case it is a comfort that so many people who can no longer find a place within the Christian tradition can find something for themselves there. A small number of pastors reveal a tension within themselves, which becomes manifest in expressions like *"on the one hand, and on the other hand"*. At one moment there is a relation to a personal God, *"Someone over against"*, and at the other moment there is an experience of the cosmic bond with everything, in which God is not given any personal names.

> *For me, it is a mixture of a bond between God and people and of God and people over against each other. Or rather: they alternate. Sometimes I feel strongly connected with the Universe, and I feel the bond of everything in and with God, and then I speak of 'stream', 'binding force'. Yet at other moments I feel, I am aware, of something of that wholly different Being, God, as something over against me that I am not up against, that my deepest self does not correspond to. The latter idea is quite challenging, often at moments of powerlessness, or when things happen that are beyond me. Then I say to myself: here I sense something over against me. That may occasionally also be something very beautiful.*

It is remarkable that God as *"something over against"* is felt and experienced at the very moment when this pastor is confronted with the finitude of life. For him it has something to do with the characteristics of secularisation: the idea of becoming aware of humanity's and the world's being finite as a result of which all the grand words about, and images of, God become relative. When words and images become relative, there is no other way to God for this pastor but by way of a personal relation to God as the one over against whom he finds himself and with whom he has to enter into the fight to find meaning and perspective.

For a pastor who works in the domain of psychiatry, the broken reality of vulnerable people evokes the desire to associate with God in a personal manner. The powerlessness because of suffering and the solidarity with people who have been hurt leads this pastor to address a direct personal prayer to God as the one whom he can address: *"God save us!"*

With these pastors, the experience of humans as vulnerable beings is not only a call to associate with these human beings, but also to address God personally. At the same time one continues to address others, like people in one's own family circle, who use only impersonal images for God.

> *The image which is most familiar to me is the image of the countenance of the other person over against me. I notice that, of late, I have been saying about God: God's countenance allows itself to be known in the countenance of vulnerable people. At the same time I am having a discussion with my wife who uses a more New-Age-like idiom, and then the phrase "God is a force" is a phrase I cannot*

> *simply accept. It keeps turning my images upside down. At the same time, how-*
> *ever, I myself also often use that image of 'sustaining force'. I have not stopped*
> *using that image. It is increasingly becoming a question, though: is that indeed the*
> *same God? I do not say no to that, but there is a shift. On the one hand, I do not*
> *restrict myself to 'something' or 'something universal'. It is closely related to incarna-*
> *tion: the recognition and experience of things divine in people's countenances, at some*
> *moments, in eyes, in attitudes. That is where I meet the other person's countenance.*

Another pastor feels there is a tension between, on the one hand, his belief that God is moving along with those who are oppressed, committing himself personally to people, and on the other, the way in which, in New Age circles, God is experienced as a kind of cosmic current running through everything, a force which pervades the whole of creation. Thus *"I experience God as a person, but also as a cosmic force."* For yet another pastor there is no such thing as an experience of a personal God. Rather it is a *"strength and source of inspiration and also a strength within myself."*

> *There is no relationship. I like to speak of the good things of God . . . and how*
> *one recognises God in the goodness of people. In the past I was not allowed to*
> *do so. It was pantheistic. The things I read about it, however, make me feel very*
> *much at ease. I do not say, however, that everything is the same as God. I have*
> *not got as far as that. I still have to think about that. I still do not know how*
> *to handle it. I only want to see the good things of God, not the bad things.*

Yet a little further on in the interview this pastor says that, in his leading of the liturgy, he addresses God personally as *"Merciful One"* and *"Challenging One"*.

The struggle between a personal and an impersonal speaking about God mostly takes place in the interviews that mention a positively critical attitude towards secularisation. On the one hand, it means paying attention to the shifting of all concepts, while on the other hand it is the struggle to find God personally in a vulnerable world. Some pastors also say that this is the only way for them: it is only with a personal God that one can enter into the fight and the struggle. It is impossible to do that with a cosmic, impersonal God.

8. *Names for God in the liturgy*

In the individual experience and speaking of God, personal images of God may not play an important role, but as soon as pastors lead in the liturgy, and especially in the prayer of the community, then

God is addressed personally. In this way a difference becomes apparent between individual spirituality and public, or functional, spirituality. On the one hand pastors call God a force which sustains them, and they speak about God as something manifest among people, while on the other hand they always address God personally in prayer.

Subsequent to the whole series of interviews the pastors were asked the question once again: how do you prefer to address God when you pray or lead in prayer? It is fascinating to see that nearly all the pastors indicate that they address God directly and personally. The following survey shows that here, too, a great diversity is to be found.

Active designations

Half of the pastors give an active name to God in prayer: *"Thou who"* or *"You who"*. Here are a number of examples.

"Thou who looks after us"
"Thou who sustains us"
"Thou who creates and re-creates us"
"Thou who makes whole"
"Thou who wants to be there for us"
"You who say you will be there for us"
"You who are our companion"
"You who move along with us"
"You who are love"
"You who know me"
"You who call for me"
"You who become manifest in people"

Here various metaphors that we have discussed in the foregoing come back. The active formulation is there, on the one hand, so as to prevent one from basing oneself on an overly familiar God who is a person, who is powerful et cetera. On the other hand these pastors want to avoid names like *"God our Lord"* or *"Father"*.

Direct designations

The remaining half of the pastors use direct designations. These direct designations also represent the diversity of the metaphors described: for example, *"source"*, *"stream of life"*, *"creator"*, *"Father"* and *"Mother"*, *"God of the people"*, *"God of people"*. Some pastors give several names at the same time. A small number of them say that they do not address God in a metaphor, but that they are always looking for words with which any positive designation of God can be undermined. They speak in terms like: *"Inexpressible One", "You still nameless one", "Unnameable One".* One of the female pastors does not lead in church celebrations. For her a personal image of God does not exist.

> *I have no personal image of God. I shall indeed never say He or She, never Father. I speak of "things divine" or I use images like wind, love, wisdom, and spirit. That is also how I pray. It is certainly over against me, but it is not a personal over against. I do not experience it as I do you sitting there opposite me. For me it is an intelligence or something like that, but I do not in the least imagine any corporeal image accompanying it. It is a presence, as a deceased person may be present. Besides, it is also something within myself.*

I shall give attention to this use of impersonal metaphors, and to the notion of breaking through all metaphors, in greater detail under point 10.

9. *Male and female metaphors*

There is a strongly prevailing tendency to refrain from any further use of exclusively male language in speaking about and addressing God.

Nearly all pastors indicate that they have learned, or are still learning, how to use inclusive language.

The following tendencies in the use of male and female metaphors may be indicated: some pastors use only male metaphors; others use both male and female metaphors; yet others use female metaphors only, for the time being; alternatively, there is a marked increase in the use of inclusive language.

Male metaphors only

A small number of pastors are at ease with the use of male language. For some of them it has something to do with the positive experience of their own father at home, while others find it strange to talk about God in female terms.

> *I experience God as a man. Texts about God as a 'she' sound strange to me. I can certainly grasp what is behind it, namely that God is not supposed to be*

> *pronouncedly male, but the one in whose image man and woman have been cre-*
> *ated. For me, however, he still remains a man, a father.*

Others share this experience. One of them, however, gives an intrinsic argument: the father always has to be consciously recognised by the child. Fatherhood is not a self-evident concept.

> *You have to believe that he is your father. The same applies to the mother. What*
> *I like about this, however, is that you are free in this respect: you do not have to*
> *recognise God as a father.*

Another argument is that Jesus speaks about *"his"* and *"our"* Father. Some pastors point out that they speak about God as Father, although they are very careful with it in liturgy so as not to hurt women. One of them says: *"I do use the words Lord and Father, but always while keeping my options open."*

Both male and female metaphors

Most pastors indicate that they have great problems with it and sometimes do not know very well what the best names are for God. A third of them use both male and female images alongside each other, however complicated that may sometimes be.

> *In the canon of the mass I deliberately say: God, Father, Mother, but also source*
> *of life, breath of life. Male and female essentially belong together, so that I think:*
> *The Lord is sure to contain all that within himself.*

Somebody else finds the continuous alternating of He/She complicated. It is simply impracticable to handle this in a proper way. At the same time he is convinced that this struggle is a good thing, for he is increasingly experiencing difficulties with the predominantly male aspect. Most pastors who have problems with it, and who increasingly learn how to distance themselves from exclusive male usage, are inspired by women in their environment and especially by female colleagues.

Only female metaphors for the time being

Against the background of the struggle of women within the church and the ministry, usage may become deliberately female with reference to God. Among female pastors the majority use female language only, because it is important for the position and experience of women.

I am one hundred percent part of contemporary society, and I let people see and hear this in my prayers and my ways of leading the liturgy. I am, for example, usually inclined to go and stand first of all on the side of women, because I myself experience very strongly what it means to be a woman in this church. I certainly see that men are subjugated in a certain way, but I side with women first of all.

For one of these pastors God can pre-eminently be designated by means of images taken from feminism: *"Virgin"* and *"Great Mother"*. Two male pastors prefer using female images, in doing which they deliberately distance themselves from male church usage. One of the other male pastors did not have a positive experience with his father at home. That is the reason why he will hardly ever call God *"Father"*.

Development towards inclusive usage

For a third of the pastors, speaking about God and addressing God only really does justice to all personal and social developments when, in designating God, both male and female aspects are transcended in a language that is open and allows room for everybody. Thus these pastors arrive at the use of open metaphors like: *"Source of life, Source of wisdom, Eternal One, Thou who art bound up with us"*.

Thus there is a predominant tendency towards non-sexist usage. This is a broad movement. Reflection on usage is remarkably widely prevalent. Pastors are obliged to think about the terms they use; they are constantly looking for words and, frequently, choices are made on the basis of that reflection. Generally speaking, there is a strong link with that which we described in chapter 2 about handling female and male aspects in personal identity.

10. *Transcending metaphors*

Two tendencies in the interviews that point to a transcending of metaphors will be discussed here.

One metaphor is followed by another, and by yet another, because each metaphor needs supplementing. We call this the 'inter-signatory' use of metaphors. Several metaphors are connected with one another.

A second tendency is to say that not a single metaphor is really satisfactory. We call this second tendency 'the coming to nothing of all metaphors'.

The inter-signatory use of metaphors

In nearly all the interviews it is said that it is impossible to refer to God by a single name or a single metaphor. The metaphor that is initially used to say something about God is very soon followed by a second and a third. Pastors immediately correct the image that is evoked.

There is more to be said about God than is possible by means of this single metaphor. In the great majority of the interviews more than three metaphors are used, while in a small number of other interviews at least two or three metaphors are used.

We can distinguish various aspects in the use of metaphors.

Shifts on the basis of one's own development

For a number of pastors the change of metaphors is related to their own development as a result of which the relation to God has changed. The relation has become less oppressive, as, for example, the following quotation illustrates very well.

> *I feel that I no longer have such a need of very concrete images. I used to have that need, though. For example, the image of God who challenges me in such a way that he makes all kinds of demands on me and over against whom I also feel guilty and small. That aspect has become much more open. I no longer think like that, or in those images. Rather, images of protection and trust predominate, that it is good that you are allowed to be there. The images also become more and more open. I hear older people say that they do not have such a need, either, to talk about God in concrete images. They keep putting their images in perspective.*

The images that have disappeared for this pastor are especially images of a moralistic God. We can also say that the images he wants to give up are images that pre-determined him as a human being. They were oppressive images, which made him small and kept him small over against a powerful God. So wherever a metaphor is likely to evoke something oppressive, it is immediately corrected by another metaphor.

Changing experience of God

A second aspect is related to the conviction that the experience of God is always a changing experience. This, too, is connected with one's own development. Every experience in life has its own metaphor of God. A feeling of relatedness marks one moment, another moment is characterised by an experience of vulnerability, and a third moment bears the stamp of forgiveness and reconciliation.

> *In this way God has a lot of faces for me, if I may say so. One moment I feel strong and glad, and I sing spontaneously: 'Lord our Lord, how powerful is your name'; this may soon change, however, for in the encounter with people I can easily feel small again all of a sudden. And then I hope for a God who holds me and accepts me. And the next day there is again an experience of being reconciled with everything and everybody.*

An exception may be indicated in the case of those pastors who point out that their life and work are determined by a single central experience, a single movement. That is, for example, the case with those pastors whose ministry bears a clear social stamp. For an industrial pastor the metaphor of the liberating and challenging God is of central significance. This metaphor is not put into perspective by other metaphors. His experience is continually characterised by the confrontation with the oppression and subjugation of people.

God transcends all images

A third aspect of the inter-signatory use is the fundamental conviction that God transcends all images and metaphors. Each statement is merely a moment, followed by another moment in which the statement fades away like a shade or tint of light.

> *In the end God is indefinable. At every moment I use different images of God. That language changes at every moment. Just as one can look at a flower which radiates colours. That flower does not have those colours. It is the radiation. When you look, the colour has already gone. Such is my relation to God. You always see God from the back. The moment you mention an aspect of God, he has disappeared again. You experience God differently each time.*

This brings us quite close to the second tendency: the coming to nothing of all metaphors.

The coming to nothing of all metaphors

In just under a third of the interviews we find a shift from speaking about God by means of concrete images and metaphors to a way of speaking in which all images are not only put into perspective by other metaphors, but are rejected as such. The above quotation already indicated this tendency. It is not surprising that the pastor who is speaking there feels at ease in the Jewish tradition in which images of God are continually being broken down. It also has something to do with God as the consummation of all life. We humans can never delimit God, for in God the whole of reality is consummated—more, higher and deeper than we shall ever be able to imagine. Another pastor closely follows this when he argues in favour of an open attitude in which there is room for God's surprising revelation.

> *God is the great nothing or the amazing void. Those are wonderful concepts for me. Then there is room. Every day I have less need of all kinds of church language that fill this space too much and too rapidly and drain it of its meaning. My concern is not to fix the matter in theories, no matter how theologically and religiously fashionable they are. I do not want to fix God and that also has repercussions for myself. I do not want to be fixed on all kinds of things myself, either. There is a great deal more to it: I think there should always be room for the unexpected, the surprising. We can get to the bottom of many things and yet . . . I can get angry when too many things are filled in and are turned tight in doing so. A lot of interests are involved. It is veiled with the cloak of piety then, or it is not really spoken.*

Here, it is not only a personal experience that is indicated; it is also stated that interests are involved.

Yet another speaks of *"God as void"* so as to keep open how God himself gives content to the way in which *"He is there for us"*. Somebody else uses the term *"supra-personal"* here, because he has come to realise increasingly that whatever images we may have of God never reach beyond the scope of our human imagination. We can only speak about it in human terms.

> *God is infinitely greater, and do not ask me why that is so.*

A lot of attention to mystery

Both tendencies, the inter-signatory use of metaphors and the coming to nothing of all metaphors, frequently go together in a number of interviews where reflection plays an important part. These pastors are fully aware and critical in handling all the terms that have to be used. Here we shall give the word to a few pastors who strongly exemplify both tendencies.

For one female pastor, mystical literature, such as that by Eckhart and John of the Cross, has become an important source. This mystical literature can nourish her against the background of her own experience of the void and the fullness: it is the *"Gelassenheit"* and the bottomless depth of God's absence. However contradictory it may sound, it is a way of fulfilment. In the void she is filled with God's infinite love, without the danger of this love ever forcing itself upon her. Mystic literature in her experience fits in with the tradition of Zen and Buddhism in which reality is reduced to the *"ulti-*

mate essence". She recognises a lot in modern sculpture and music in which *"much is indicated and expressed by means of very little"*.

Dealing with God's bottomless depth is for her, on the one hand, an experience of security. In a world in which there is no place for her to experience as a *"safe home"*, God's bottomless depth is for her the place where she is allowed to be secure. At the same time, however, this is very awkward, for this is the very reason why she has not got a home anywhere. Every time she thinks she has found herself a home, everything is turned upside down. More than all the other interviews, this interview indicates how God and things divine always transcend our human experience and thought.

A second pastor, who works in psychiatry, has gradually discovered in his life that all the images and metaphors for God are connected with the stage of life and the cultural period in which he lived. In the agrarian environment God is the creator, in the traditional piety of the family he is the mighty one who judges everything. During wartime he is the God of the oppressed. In experiences of sickness and dying in the family he is the God with whom people have an argument and in the moments of silence at the seminary he is the holy Triune God, shepherd and God of the Covenant. God gradually disappears from his throne, and becomes the God of conscience instead, the God of the people on the way, the God who becomes present in the other's countenance.

For him as the person leading in liturgy, God especially becomes the one who is recognised in the breaking of the bread. In his work as a pastor for people who are often on the way and in search of a place of their own in their lives, God becomes the one who is searched for, especially in the way people work at means of realising justice. God becomes the liberating one.

At the end of his description it becomes visible and tangible where this pastor now finds himself. In the void and the absurdity of the psychiatric clinic God becomes the *"Absent One"*. No man can guarantee God's presence in any respect. This pastor offered a text that he had published recently.

> *My fiftieth year of life over:*
> *Pastor and minister for more than a quarter of a century.*
> *Traces backward . . . leaving images behind.*
> *Living face to face.*
> *Leaving God's images behind and looking for God's traces:*
> *Cloud-of-unknowing. Wordless silence.*

Dry source. Hidden God.
Deserted void. Handed down Name.

He also indicates that, in calling out and singing together in the community liturgy, the faith tradition of centuries is the source for tracing God in a tentative, groping manner: *"Be present here, we want to see You"*.

In the most recent period of his life so far, God is indeed given names such as *"Unnameable One"*, *"Eternal One"*, or simply *"The Name"*. This pastor derives his spiritual nourishment increasingly from mystical literature, mentioning, among other things, Blaise Pascal's vision: *"Les espaces infinis m'effraient"*.

11. *Reflection in and on spirituality*

It strikes one that, in the section of the interviews where they speak about their use of metaphors, pastors are quite articulate in describing their experience. There are few hesitations, both among those pastors who positively endorse certain metaphors and among those who indicate clearly that their metaphors keep changing or are even transcended. Reflection in experience is found with all the pastors. Apart from the fact that a network of images becomes visible, one also perceives choices made by pastors on the basis of reflection at the time of their experience and feelings. The interviews also give a fairly clear picture of self-awareness when the point at issue is the question of who God is: *"Such is my image"*, or: *"Such is my evolution"*.

In just over a third reflection on their spirituality becomes visible too. The pastors belonging to this group appear to be capable of detaching themselves from direct experience. They frequently arrive at a moment of evaluation, especially at moments when they are forced to think about the influence of the context, such as, for example, the influence of the people with whom they are involved as pastors.

This reflection is found particularly clearly among those who are clearly aware of developments in their use of metaphors, especially in cases where metaphors are transcended. These pastors relate their own development, for example from an association with a moralistic God towards a God who offers far more space, to the experience that oppressive images detract from divinity rather than creating room for a faith relationship with God. By means of reflection and reasoning a relation is established between fundamental life experiences and the conviction that God will always put himself beyond any image whatsoever. It is especially the discovery that rational concepts are continually shattered, because they are deliberately and actively related to the actual developments of the context.

Reflection is also prominent in the case of those who, as a result of developments in the context, have increasingly opted for quite specific metaphors for God. This is the case with pastors working in a socio-political context, which continues to demand choices. It is also apparent in the case of a pastor who deliberately chooses the metaphor of *"Father"* so as to indicate that God always has to be recognised as such. No father automatically has a recognised position.

Just as in our description of faith, hope and love, we may conclude here that there are differences of degree among the pastors belonging to the group of those who arrive at a second reflection. One has the impression that it is those pastors who have the clearest insight into the transitions they have gone through in life and ministry who most clearly exhibit reflection on their spiritual development.

12. *Summary of chapter 6*

The metaphors derived from personal and interpersonal life appear to occur most frequently. The metaphor of *"God who liberates"*, derived from interpersonal as well as from social life, is given the highest frequency. By far the greatest significance in this respect is given to the interpersonal sphere of life.

With respect to the connection between metaphors and stories from the faith tradition, there is a tendency to move from the image of God as redeemer towards that of God as liberator. At the same time there is a certain tendency to move from liberation stories towards stories about exile. A development from the use of metaphors derived from the interpersonal and social sphere towards the use of metaphors derived from space (such as God as source or depth) and time (exile) can also be discerned. Bound up with this is the experience that the time of new initiatives, both in the field of politics and of the church, is over. The points at issue now are *"holding out for long"*, *"seeing things through"* and *"living with delay"*.

With respect to the relation between security and challenge there is a prevailing tendency towards looking for security. At the same time many pastors indicate that looking for security alone is not sufficient. Some metaphors evoke an inner conflict for some pastors: what use is consolation in a tough world? Or how do I handle the call for consolation and security in my ministry, when it is sometimes so difficult for people to allow themselves to be challenged?

The metaphors derived from either interpersonal or social life mostly point to the notion of being called. This occurs most frequently among those pastors who work in some form of ministry with a strong socio-economic orientation. This notion of being called derives from stories from the tradition that relate how God himself has looked after human beings in general and his people in particular. Those who have been liberated, or live on the basis of the stories of liberation, are called to act in a liberating manner themselves.

More than half of the interviews show that pastors become susceptible to, and tend towards, the use of impersonal metaphors: they employ images derived from nature and from dealing with nature. On the one hand, this is connected with a pastoral feeling for contemporary people who are responsive to images from the world of New Age. On the other hand, it is true of a number of pastors that they themselves are open to this kind of usage. The struggle is most evident in those pastors who deal with culture most critically.

As far as the relation between male and female metaphors is concerned, there is a clear development towards non-sexist and inclusive language. The great majority of pastors indicate that they have learned, or are still learning, how to use inclusive language in speaking of and to God. This is most clearly expressed in their manner of leading in the liturgy. Pastoral concern for a broad appeal to people is an important factor in this. It is especially the women who lead in liturgy, or who work with women in their ministry, who deliberately opt for an exclusively female usage, whereas a small group of men, and one woman, opt for an exclusively male usage.

More than half of the pastors speak about God in terms of a close bond, while at the same time indicating that, especially in moments of prayer, they experience God as "over against". This does not mean, however, that God is looked upon as a 'person' in the sense that we, humans, understand it when we speak about our dealings with one another.

Experiences of the finitude and vulnerability of life lead to the use of personal metaphors, also with those pastors who, in their own experience, tend towards the use of impersonal metaphors.

Apart from a few exceptions, as soon as pastors pray personally or lead in prayer, they address God personally. In doing so, more than half of them use an active formulation (*"Thou who"* or *"You who"*), and just under half of them address God directly by way of a metaphor (such as *"Merciful One"* or *"Source"*). A female pastor, who never leads in the liturgy and does not feel at home in it either, does not address God directly in her own rituals.

All the pastors use more than one metaphor, while a number of them indicate that all metaphors are in the end unable to say anything about God. Some of them always address God in negative terms such as the *"Inexpressible One"*, or the *"Unnameable One"*. The relation to God always demands a re-weighing of pros and cons, and the making of choices.

All the pastors exhibit reflection in their experience of God. With just over a third, this reflection on their spiritual experience emerges to various degrees.

It may be concluded that there is a connection between various aspects of speaking about God on the one hand, and the relation to the context which we considered in Part 1 on the other, and that pastors deal with this connection explicitly in their reflection on spirituality. They reflect on it consciously, thus arriving at a critical evaluation of their use of metaphors.

CHAPTER SEVEN

THE RELATION TO JESUS

In this chapter we shall study the interviews for the image pastors
have of the person of Jesus. What is their position in the theological tradition concerning *"the Son of God"*, *"Jesus the Christ"*, and *"the
man Jesus"*? Do the interviews indicate that the pastors have come
to think differently about the person of Jesus? Is it possible to detect
any shift in their experience of the significance of Jesus? This chapter will not be a long one. The interviews did not produce very
much material. This, in itself, is already a sign: pastors appear to
speak less extensively about the person of Jesus when the point at
issue is their experience of spirituality. Perhaps the reason is that it
is not all that complicated?

1. *Speaking about Jesus in the language of experience*

Pastors speak about Jesus in the language of experience. They use
words derived from what they have felt and experienced. We find
hardly anything of the language that originated during the time after
the death of Jesus, when his followers started to give all kinds of
titles to Jesus so as to express by means of them his great significance
for the Christian movement in society. Titles like *"the Christ"* and
"the Lord" are hardly found in the interviews.

> *I hardly use the term Christ in connection with Jesus. I rather talk about the per-
> son of Jesus who pre-eminently lived as God expects people to live.*

The great majority of the pastors do not feel at ease, either, in a
form of Jesus-mysticism. The central issues are God and people. Jesus
is not the centre in this, but he acts as a point of reference with
respect to God and to people:

> *Jesus is important only because he refers to somebody else. Jesus is for me not the
> last and only Son of God. He is a human being who fascinates me very much,
> but things do not stop with Jesus.*

A lot of pastors place Jesus in a wider framework. Jesus has a place
within the whole Jewish tradition. It is important to see him within

the perspective of the long tradition from whence he came. This should be a warning to Christians: we, as Christians, cannot and must not use Jesus for appropriating the Jewish tradition.

Within the Jewish tradition Jesus has a place, but not an exclusive one. According to some pastors, therefore, we had better not speak in terms of *"old"* and *"new"* covenant. We should rather speak of *"the covenant"*. This means that for these pastors the Jewish tradition has not been exhausted or brought to an end with Jesus.

2. *Concrete content of the relation with Jesus*

A large majority of the pastors speaks of Jesus as an *"example"*, *"orientation"*, *"guide"* and *"way"*. Among a small group one comes across an image which puts Jesus more clearly in the centre. There one finds a relationship based on trust. A few of them say something about a bond of affection. We shall look at the various images separately.

Jesus as embodiment of ideals

Two-thirds of the interviews show in various ways that the pastors make a distinction between the relation to God and the following of Jesus. The central point is God as ground of existence, as source of life, whereas Jesus is far more a figure who puts us on our way, a person who fascinates and challenges us to do something which follows naturally from his actions:

> *God is ground of existence and primal ground. Jesus fascinates me when it is a matter of the way in which he lived. He is an example, but he is not an object of faith and meditation. I like reading gospel stories and parables in order to get to know his way. For me he is not a centre of spirituality, though.*

For some of them Jesus is fascinating and, therefore, challenging because of the way in which he acts as a good guide and therapist of people, for others he is recognisably close, because he shows concretely which way you can go in life. That may be an important point of orientation, when as a contemporary human being you sometimes are at the end of your tether. Jesus is *"something to hold on to in times of crisis"*. For an industrial pastor it is fascinating to associate with people, for they show how Jesus lived and acted. That is something on which he can orient himself in order to find his own way. Another pastor summarises it as follows: *"I talk to God and work with Jesus as an example and as a way"*.

It is only as an example that Jesus is a source of inspiration. Jesus' being an example is given concrete content with reference to the way in which he stood up for people, the way in which he shows in his stories how humanly close God is and how one can experience God's nearness in people and can also exemplify it oneself, and the way in which, as a shepherd of people, he gives concrete content to a God who wants nobody to get lost.

To summarise, it may be said that a large number of the pastors interviewed experience Jesus as an ideal realisation of their own dreams and expectations. Jesus is an example of the hope that people can sometimes *"be as good as God"*.

Jesus as guide and companion

For a small number of pastors Jesus is not the centre of their existence, but they do experience a relationship with him as guide and companion.

> *He guides me, he walks along with me and occasionally leads me, I think. I am allowed, however, simply to come along in my own way. That is how I am on my way. It is not something from the past: if only things are all right between Jesus and me. No, that is not what I mean.*

Some pastors refer to the story of the disciples on their way to Emmaus. Jesus is the unknown companion, as in the experience of the disciples on their way to Emmaus. For somebody else who has a lot of attention for exegesis it is not the person of Jesus himself, but the stories of and about him which become so familiar that one gets a personal relationship with them.

> *I usually speak about Jesus of Nazareth, in doing which I do not make a God out of him, but want to show him as the guide who shows how you can associate with God faithfully in your life. I read the stories and the words in which he calls God Father and Creator. And it is precisely these stories that give me something to hold on to, something which serves as a handle, enabling me to get to know something of God and redemption. Thus I become more and more familiar with the texts and the stories, and I move along accompanied by them.*

Jesus as beloved

For one of the priests it is not hope or love towards God which is central, but faith. In his opinion, love, and love relationship, are the terms that apply to the relationship with Jesus. For this pastor Jesus offers, as it were, the basis for believing and living in a personal manner. And this is only possible when he works at a personal relationship with Jesus and his words.

> *I cannot say that I love God, but I do love Jesus. For me it is important to have a personal commitment to Jesus Christ as a human being, to make it somehow possible for me to see things through in my faith in God and in my belonging to the church. For me, for example, the texts from John in Eastertide are important, in which Jesus says a lot about himself. Then I have him say those words to me personally and on the basis of that relationship and on the basis of that view I try to make those words come alive. This is the only way in which the gospel becomes unique and concrete.*

Somebody else speaks warmly about the meaning of Jesus' "I-texts" in the gospel of John. He adds that he thinks it is very difficult in his ministry to convey to people a little love for Jesus himself. According to him, this is especially connected with the growing alienation from the sacraments. He regards it as a loss. He had thought that he would be able to make people enthusiastic and make them warm up to the person of Jesus and his sacraments. These two pastors, however, do explicitly add that, in the end, Jesus himself is not the central issue, but that the whole emphasis lies on Jesus as the way to the Father. It is worth noting that they are among the few who speak about God as Father.

A female pastor cautions us to be careful in giving too personal a content to the relationship with Jesus, although she does show a kind of familiarity in her own relationship with Jesus. Towards others, however, she is careful in this respect. After all it is his life as an example, rather than his person, which is important. Then there is the special case of a parish pastor who tries to see his ministry as a bond with Jesus Christ through solidarity with the poor.

> *It is difficult for me to find the right words, but I experience associating with the poor as associating with Jesus. Perhaps these are strong words, but this is how I experience it. In people's faces Jesus' countenance lies hidden. This touches my inmost self.*

Here, we sense a strong affinity with the spirituality of Vincentius à Paolo who says: "Les pauvres, ce sont le Christ!" (Van Geene 1995). By means of this expression Vincentius gives a contemporary meaning to the statement in Matthew 25: "Anything you did for one of my brothers here, however humble, you did for me" (Matt. 25,40).

Acting in solidarity becomes the place where Jesus Christ is to be found. For this pastor it is connected with the celebration of the sacraments, in particular with the Eucharist, in which the personal bond with Jesus as the Living One is celebrated. One might also say: the mystical bond with Christ in solidarity with the poor may be celebrated there. It is the encounter with the living one, the risen one.

A female pastor who, in her interest in oriental spirituality in general, and Buddhism in particular, has come to realise increasingly that she does not find what is essential there, also states this. She does find it in the figure of the risen Christ, though. The Easter perspective sustains her. This, however, is always connected with the way in which Jesus in his own life always opted for people who were hurt, and for ordinary life. That is how he highlights the shadowy side.

3. *Reflection in and on spirituality*

We may conclude that all the interviews mention reflection in spirituality. Experiences and images in the relationship with Jesus are used as basic material for pastors with which to come to the conclusion that Jesus is the way, or the example, or a beloved companion. It does not seem possible to point to any pronounced theological reflection on the significance of Jesus among the pastors. With a number of pastors we get the impression that the shift from a Christ-oriented to a Jesus-oriented approach came about automatically. Several pastors speak about it in such a self-evident manner that we may ask ourselves to what extent this way of speaking is supported by a critical reflection on the way in which Scripture and tradition are dealt with.

To be sure, theological reflection is clearly discernible among some of the pastors. They are those who, more clearly than others, account in the interview for the fact that, in their development, they have arrived at such a relationship with Jesus. This is not only the case with those pastors who regard and experience Jesus chiefly as the way and example, but also with a few who explicitly indicate what the love relation towards Jesus means for them. Here, too, we can conclude that reflection on spirituality is connected with reflection on the influence of the context in each of the four aspects, namely biography, personal identity, secularisation and church context. For some pastors there is a permanent connection with their study of the bible.

4. *Summary of chapter 7*

We may conclude that nearly all the pastors interviewed locate the significance of Jesus as an example in the concrete content he gives to the way to God. When some pastors speak of a personal bond with Jesus, it is in connection with him as a personal guide. It can also be an expression of a bond based on familiarity with the stories of and about him. As soon as the title of Christ is added to Jesus, he is not only a way to God, but the central idea is that of the risen one who pre-eminently manifests himself in solidarity with the poor here and now. In the case of two of the pastors their position does not become clear from the interview.

Looking back on the interviews, it seems a pity that I did not have the opportunity to study a number of sermons of each of the pastors who were interviewed. This might have provided more information on aspects concerning the experience of Jesus than has in fact become available. Yet a clear tendency has become apparent: Jesus is the way. He is not the centre, nor the final point.

CHAPTER EIGHT

THE RELATION TO THE SPIRIT

After all the interviews had been completed, it appeared that little
had been said about the significance of the Spirit. Not enough explicit
questions had been asked about this aspect in the interviews. In the
discussion about the metaphors used for God, the Spirit was occasionally brought up incidentally. The pastors were therefore once
more presented with the question: what is the significance of the
Spirit for you and for your spirituality? There was a surprising level
of response, which involved a lot of new, highly diverse material.

The description in this chapter will be as follows. First the difference
will be described between those interviewed for whom the Spirit
plays no, or hardly any, role, and those who attach much significance
to the Spirit. Then I shall discuss the various metaphors pastors use
to designate the Spirit. We shall use the same division as in chapter 5, where the metaphors for God were dealt with.

(In)significance of the Spirit

Five of the thirty pastors say that the Spirit has no, or hardly any,
significance in their lives and in their spirituality. In saying this, they
indicate especially that the Spirit does not play a role as a separate
person, as the *"Holy Spirit"*. For all five, however, this also means
that the Spirit as a spiritual force in people is not brought up so
explicitly. One of them indicates this in the following way, speaking
for all five.

> *The Spirit is virtually absent in my spirituality, in my ministry, prayer and preach-
> ing. S/he is not mentioned explicitly, except when I cannot avoid doing so, for
> example at Pentecost. And then it is quite difficult for me to bring up the Spirit
> credibly (that means from within). I try to live and work in the spirit of Jesus,
> the man, who is the image of God. I do not, however, regard and experience the
> Spirit as a special entity, or person, on its own.*

Some pastors say that the lack of explicit attention for the Spirit has
something to do with negative experiences relating to the leadership
in the church, who so often fix and delimit the Spirit, while there
should be space, and which sometimes even claims the Spirit as

something which is their exclusive property. In doing so, the diversity and pluriformity of spiritual powers fail to be recognised. The Spirit is not experienced as *"Spirit that blows wherever she wills"*. The Spirit has apparently been so annexed by the leadership that these pastors do not feel very much like giving attention to it or speaking about it. One of them indicates that he prefers speaking about the working of God rather than about the work of the Spirit.

> *It is God's work in me and I look for the way in which God works in people. Speaking about 'Spirit' does not add anything to this for me.*

A middle position is taken by a pastor who speaks about an inkling *"of the Spirit"*: sometimes the Spirit means sensing something, sometimes it is an absent person, sometimes a power for life.

> *I notice that I hardly pay any attention to the Spirit in my personal spirituality. I do occasionally talk about the Spirit and about spirits in my ministry, I notice that I can something use it to point out things. I often talk about fire and flames and warmth. And in that liturgical context I speak about our spirit and the Holy Spirit.*

Twenty-five of the pastors attach a clear significance to the Spirit. Several of these pastors call the Spirit the *"experienceable side of God"*: it is in and through the Spirit that God allows himself to be known and experienced tangibly. In the metaphors used by these pastors in their description of the Spirit it becomes apparent how God allows himself to be known and experienced in and through the Spirit.

Use of metaphors: who is the Spirit?

In the description of the various metaphors we shall follow the same division as in the chapter about God. The following aspects will be considered: the area of reality from which the metaphors are derived; emphasis on the Spirit as companion; security and challenge; personal and impersonal metaphors; male and female metaphors; and finally, the mystical experience of the Spirit.

1. *Origin of the metaphors*

The pastors use several different metaphors. Many metaphors occur once or twice at most. However rich some metaphors may be, there is no point in describing all of them concretely. A global survey will suffice here.

Different realities

Just like the metaphors denoting God, these metaphors are derived from all areas of earthly and human reality: nature, our dealings with nature, personal and interpersonal life, social life, space and time.

Metaphors derived from nature

Many of the metaphors derived from nature, and from our dealings with nature, are related to images that occur in the texts of the Pentecost liturgy. The Spirit is like an atmosphere of rest, like a wind blowing wherever she wills, like a gentle breeze, like the light, like breath, like a stream, a source, or warmth and fire. The working of the Spirit is compared with images like thawing what has become hardened, breaking through what has become stuck, healing what has been hurt, revealing what is hidden, renewing what has become outworn, and sustaining where life has been exhausted.

It is striking that these metaphors indicate both the strength of God and the strength of people: the Spirit reveals the countenance and the working of God by showing the ways in which people are a source of life to each other. Examples are the metaphors *"warmth and fire"*, which are often used in the interviews. These metaphors remind one of Acts 2, where the Spirit is experienced in the tongues of fire that touch the disciples and put them into motion: *"The fire that I sometimes encounter in people, the warmth of which makes me grow in strength."*

For many of them it also has a mystical side, and the metaphors point to the inner strength as a result of which people can be connected with one another: *"The holy Spirit is in our midst as a mysterious glow of warmth."*

In this way the Spirit is both a force issuing from God and an inner strength of people who *"act in the Spirit of God."*

Metaphors derived from personal and interpersonal life

The metaphors derived from personal and interpersonal life, like soul, intimacy, wisdom, consolation and enthusiasm, indicate the presence or working of the Spirit in our personal lives or point to the movement between us, humans. There are also a number of metaphors that point to the fruits of the working of the Spirit: it is through the Spirit that people become susceptible, gentle, that they open up to creative thinking and acting, find rest, act sincerely, are enthusiastic and dare to take risks. In the use of all these metaphors there is much attention to the pluriformity of the gifts of the Spirit.

Metaphors derived from social life
The metaphor "Father of the poor" is strongly connected with societal life. This metaphor is used when people speak about movements of solidarity with drifters and resident aliens, who are part of the experience of city pastors.

Metaphors derived from the dimensions of time and space
The metaphors derived from the dimension of space point to creativity and the amazing variety of spiritual gifts. The metaphors derived from the dimension of time, like perseverance, foreseeing and fulfilling, are connected with the hope and the desire to keep the movement going in a time of delay. Here, we find an echo of the confidence that we, humans, do not have to do things by ourselves, but that we may allow ourselves to be sustained by God's spiritual strength, which will bring fulfilment.

Why so many metaphors?

The large number of metaphors used to denote the Spirit may have something to do with two facts. On the one hand, a lot of pastors are concerned about a delimitation of the power of the Spirit. They sometimes experience the leadership of the church in this respect as a delimitation of the power of the Spirit: as if especially leaders are supposed to have the Spirit in themselves. On the other hand, there is great admiration for all kinds of people and movements testifying to the power of the Spirit. The Spirit as the experienceable side of God invites one to discover and acknowledge pluriformity.

2. *Attention to the Spirit as companion*

For those pastors interviewed who show a lot of attention to the Spirit, the Spirit as the experienceable side of God is an expression of the experience of the Spirit as companion and support on the way. The experience of the Spirit as companion is given the main emphasis in the interviews. This is made possible by, and has its origin in, the faith in the Spirit as *"original"*: the Spirit is the creating, re-creating, renewing, source of life. That is how God allows himself to be known and experienced. There is considerable agreement here with what we have described in the previous chapter about God. There is also a strong relation to the way in which pastors speak about Jesus as companion.

3. *Security and challenge*

Almost every metaphor points to several aspects of the many-sided power of the Spirit. Aspects that are mentioned include consolation, warm nearness and intimacy, as well as challenge, or being called. More so than the metaphors denoting God, the metaphors denoting the Spirit are used to indicate both security and being called. When the Spirit is called the *"experienceable side of God"*, this phrase is used to express God's mobilising power. We might also say: the Spirit given to people as an expression of God's warm nearness is at the same time an expression of the God who calls upon people to be a source of life for each other at the instigation of the Spirit. People can give each other warmth and security through the power of the Spirit. It is also a call for solidarity with those who do not belong to the inner circle.

4. *Spirit of liberation and perseverance*

Just as in the use of the metaphors denoting God, there is a tendency in the use of metaphors denoting the Spirit, which we indicate here, for the sake of convenience, as a transition from liberating power to strength for long-term perseverance.

In several interviews the Spirit is connected with the tradition of stories about liberation. There, however, the idea found almost everywhere is that one needs the Spirit for seeing things through, for remaining fresh and creative on the way, which may be a great deal longer than one might have expected. It is the Spirit that guards pastors against disappointment, against becoming hardened and blocked. The Spirit keeps open, engenders creativity in situations in which the range of possibilities is no longer as broad as one might have thought at first. This representation of the Spirit as strength for on the way is to be found, for example, in interviews with female pastors. They refuse to give up the struggle for a satisfactory recognition of their position within the church. Male and female pastoral workers are looking for a creative content to be given to their leadership and position as ministers.

One is struck by the way in which pastors who work in secular institutions, and those who are strongly oriented on society, experience the Spirit as a creative, indestructible power. They need that power for giving a clear identity to their ministry. It is, however, also a creative power in people who show more of God than many people think: *"the fire I sometimes encounter in people, the warmth of which makes me grow."* It is the fire people find again and again, which enables them to go further.

5. *Personal and impersonal*

Of the twenty-five pastors who accord a place of importance to the Spirit, sixteen speak about the Spirit in impersonal metaphors, while nine of them describe the Spirit as a person.

> *I think that from early childhood I have felt a bond with the Holy Spirit for which I could not find any words at the time. It manifested itself in my being fascinated by biblical stories and the spirit expressed in them. In the stories I felt that people were given strength for doing things which normally would have been beyond their powers. The Spirit has a very personal place in my life which connects me with God and with Jesus Christ, but also with all creatures in the world, with all that lives and breathes.*

The way in which these pastors write about the Spirit reminds one of a certain intimacy, although this is qualified by a certain diffidence. One reads words like: *"God in me, God close to me"*, *"inner source in me"*, *"my soul, which is touched by the soul of God"*, *"the spark of God in me, which makes me live and work from within."* One of them finds it hard to betray anything about the personal significance of the Spirit, because this *"touches the intimate relationship with the Lord"*, about which one does not so easily speak publicly. Four of the nine pastors indicate that they pray to the Spirit regularly, and that the old prayer *"Veni sancte spiritus"*, or at least some lines from it, have a concrete place here: *"breathe through me, make me gentle"*. Others pray to God for the Spirit, also using words from the Veni Sancte Spiritus.

> *In my personal life I often go back to the translation of the Veni Sancte Spiritus. For years I have been using prayers that I had composed for use at table, and many of them call upon God to make the Spirit who inspired Jesus blow in us, too. I pray for the Spirit who can comfort or inspire me, and for the Spirit who*

> *can thaw and disarm the hardening in church and society. I ask for the Spirit who is prepared to guide me at crossroads where I have to make choices.*

Here, speaking about the Spirit finds itself in a middle area: between personal and impersonal.

Spirit as spiritual power

For more than half of the pastors the Spirit is important, not as a person, but as a spiritual power, which lets itself be known in human beings, in the community, in the people and in the cosmos. This spiritual power is sometimes described as a divine spiritual power, sometimes as the spiritual power issuing from Jesus and inspiring his disciples. One of these pastors indicates characteristically that she no longer regards the Spirit as the third person of the Trinity, because the Spirit has not been done justice to by the teaching authority. She feels at ease in feminist theology where the Spirit is connected with creation.

> *In that sense she is certainly important for me. She is the Divine element that has been incarnated in the world and helps the world on its way to fulfilment. She is a dynamic principle for me. The Spirit is the contact with God (understood as the Divine element) in me. This contact is a source of Silence, of Joy in life. It makes me less dependent on my Ego, which engenders a free space in which growth and change become possible. In my pastoral activity I try to act as much as possible on the basis of this free space and to be present. It is difficult and requires daily practice in attention and concentration. In my contact with the other person I also try to create something like a free space, so that I can hear 'the Spirit' of the other person, and the other person may perhaps also be able to become aware of that.*

It has already become clear from the summary description of the metaphors that spiritual power is expressed in all kinds of ways: in creation, in people, in movements, and in creativity within the domain of working for justice.

6. *Male and female metaphors*

In two-thirds of the interviews the Spirit or spiritual power is indicated with female terms. Others do not indicate whether there is a development in the direction of female usage. They speak about the Spirit in male terms. To this group belong, among others, the pastors who do not accord a place of much importance to the Spirit.

Among the first group there are several pastors who call the Spirit, or spiritual power, pre-eminently the female side, the *"female face of God"*. One of them indicates it as follows: *"Over against the Father figure the Spirit is especially a divine person endowed with female elements"*. While this pastor experiences the Spirit as a person, others who prefer to speak about spiritual power use virtually identical terms to show how this spiritual power can be indicated by means of all kinds of female names and images from Scripture, such as *"Lady wisdom"*, the *"fiery breath animating all life because she blows wherever she wills"*. If it is possible to find an opening towards non-sexist usage for divine reality anywhere, it is through speaking about God's spiritual power. This is expressed most clearly in the interviews with the female pastors and with those who have been forced by cultural developments to think about language. They are the pastors who, also in their metaphors for God, are looking for a new language.

7. *Transcending metaphors*

More so than in the case of metaphors for God, it is in the designation of the Spirit or spiritual power that we find a succession of several metaphors. The power of the Spirit is so many-sided that we cannot confine ourselves to indication by way of a single metaphor or a single name. That is one side of the matter. On the other hand several pastors wish to indicate that the presence and power of the Spirit are quite overwhelming. That is the reason why several images are used in order to be able to say something about this. This is connected, among other things, with the multifaceted experience of God's spiritual power: comforting nearness, intimacy, bond, and, at the same time, calling upon people, challenge and movement.

Some pastors use mystical terms like *"spark in my soul"* or *"unending stream of intimacy"*. At the same time they point out that all words fall silent in the end, because the power and loving nearness of the Spirit are so overwhelming that *"we no longer understand it in any way"*. One of them says, for example, that time and again, he is so amazed at the spiritual power in people he meets that he falls completely silent. He adds that perhaps he is able to say this because he has not yet experienced very violent situations with people. On the other hand, another pastor, who does have a lot of experience in this area, says that for him the Spirit is sometimes *"the absent one"* and that he usually does not get any further than an *"inkling of the Spirit"*.

8. *Reflection in and on spirituality*

It is not very clear whether the scanty data that the interviews at first produced about the significance of the Spirit point to something like a lack of interest. When an explicit study of this was made at a later stage, there was a high level of response.

We have the impression that reflection in and on the spiritual experience of the Spirit correlates with the experience of the relation to God. This impression is connected with the conclusion that a similar, and at times even stronger, development can be pointed to in the use of metaphors, for example in the inter-signatory use and the growing interest in the mystery which transcends all metaphors. The same may be said about the development from the idea of the Spirit as personal towards the idea of the Spirit as spiritual power of God. This presupposes choices made on the basis of reflection or reasoning processes taking place in experience.

Reflection on spirituality becomes manifest among those pastors who have learned to think critically and detachedly about their experience and who are therefore capable of a critical evaluation of the way in which they speak about the Spirit and spiritual power. It becomes manifest, especially, wherever they actively engage in a confrontation with the context, for example with the ecclesial context. They opt explicitly for an experience of the Spirit as it manifests itself in people and movements. Here, too, we can conclude that just over a third of the pastors manage better than others to spend time on reflection on spirituality.

9. *Summary of chapter 8*

Several metaphors are derived from the Veni Sancte Spiritus. Nearly every metaphor indicates several aspects that come together in a many-sided spiritual power: consolation, warm nearness and intimacy, as well as the challenge to become equally close to other people in a human way.

The large number of metaphors may have something to do with the experience that the institution of the church often deals with the gifts of the Spirit in a restrictive and oppressive way. This experience may challenge pastors to deal creatively with the spiritual power in people, which shows itself in various ways and under many different forms.

The Spirit as the tangible and experienceable side of God invites one to discover and experience pluriformity in spiritual power.

It is striking that most metaphors not only indicate the experience of security with God and with people, but also call upon people to live and act on the basis of the spiritual power given to them. More so than the metaphors for God, the metaphors for the Spirit express challenge.

We may conclude that, in the metaphors for the Spirit, God is experienced and felt as the one who calls on us, and urges us, to travel the road of solidarity with other living beings. We find the strength to do so in God's warm nearness, which inspires us and fills us with his breath. There is a strong link between the metaphors of the Spirit and the metaphors of God as the liberator, the one who calls. It contains a link with the hope in God that we shall be sustained on our road, while retaining the perspective that we shall not have to accomplish things by ourselves and that God will fulfil everything.

In the interviews that describe the Spirit as a person, a link with the love towards God as an affective relationship can be discerned. With some pastors, there is also a link with the affective relation with Jesus. These interviews also mention a direct personal prayer to the Spirit, often as it is articulated in the Veni Sancte Spiritus.

In the interviews where the Spirit is understood as spiritual power, prayers to God for granting that Spirit, or spiritual power, which inspired the prophets and fills the earth with its breath, are mentioned.

The process of struggling with names and metaphors for the Spirit is perceived most clearly in those pastors who recognise the need for reflection on their spirituality. At the same time, a number of these pastors, especially those who are strongly oriented on society, show a strong preference for a small number of metaphors that point to the call issuing from the Spirit.

There are many links with the pastors' speaking of and to God.

Finally, we were able to state that through reflection a connection can be established between various aspects of speaking about the Spirit on the one hand, and the relation to the context which was described in Part 1 on the other.

In Part 2 the symbolic dimension of spirituality was studied.

In chapter 5 the symbolic side of the relation to God was described, first of all, in terms of faith, hope and love. There the striking thing was the great interest in the term hope, which, on further reflection, shows a strong resemblance to faith in the sense of confident surrender to God. In the relation to God in terms of faith, hope and love, God can be experienced as ground of existence, companion and destination. These terms express a constant movement characteristic of God. Pastors use these terms to say that God has entered upon a history with people and will continue with, and consummate, this history with them. The central significance of God, as it emerges in the description of faith, hope and love, lies in the connection between origin and destination: God as companion on the road to be travelled. With some pastors we found a personal love relation to God. The majority use less personal terms to indicate their relation to God.

Then, in chapter 6, the symbolic side was described in terms of the way in which pastors use metaphors to express how they experience God. It was pointed out from what areas of reality metaphors are derived: from nature, from our dealings with nature, from personal and interpersonal life, and from social life. Most metaphors are derived from personal and interpersonal life. From the frequent use of metaphors a number of tendencies become visible in the ways pastors speak of God. There is a lot of interest in the experience of God as companion. A transition is noticeable from the God of redemption to the God of liberation, and from the liberating God to the God of exile. There is a great need for images of security, and the pastors show a development towards impersonal metaphors, even though God is experienced as a person *"over against"* in situations of contingency. It is striking that pastors address God personally as soon as they lead in prayer. There is an important tendency to move from male to female, and especially towards inclusive, language. Interest in mystery is given shape in the frequent inter-signatory use of metaphors and in the way pastors show that all metaphors are ultimately unsatisfactory. An important fact is, that, in the interviews, the pastors speak about both a personal faith in God and their faith in a personal God. The pastors deal with God in a personal manner. Who God is, however, is a highly differentiated matter.

In chapter 7, relatively little was said about spirituality in connection with the relation to Jesus. Whenever Jesus is brought up as a subject it is done in the primary language, the language of experience. Here, Jesus is looked upon as the fulfilment of ideals, as an important figure for identification, as companion and Living One who reveals himself in the poor.

In chapter 8 the relation to the Spirit was described. The pastors emphasise the Spirit as the experienceable side of God. More than with the metaphors for God, there is an interest in the elements of call and challenge. This, however, goes together with the experience of the intimacy of God's nearness in the Spirit. A similar tendency may be discerned with respect to the increasing use of non-sexist language, the inter-signatory use of metaphors, and a susceptibility to mystery. It is striking that more than half of the pastors describe the Spirit as a spiritual power rather than as a divine person. Those who are most critical about using metaphors for speaking about God are equally critically aware in their speaking about the Spirit.

PART THREE

FORMS OF EXPRESSING SPIRITUALITY

INTRODUCTION

In the preceding section—Part 2—we considered the first dimension of spirituality: the relation to God, Jesus and the Spirit. We can also define this relation as the symbolic dimension. In Part 3 the second dimension will be described: the experiential side, or the way in which pastors, individually and/or together with others, express their spirituality.

The following questions were put to the pastors:
- Do you pray? When, how, and where?
- Do you engage in conscious reflection? Where, how, and when?
- What is the meaning of commitment? Where and when does it take place?

Questions were also asked about factors that possibly influence these modes of expression.
- What place do you accord to discipline?
- How important is study?
- Do you take part in cultural events?
- How important is it for you to spend time in nature?
- What place do you accord to physical work?

In addition, some questions were asked about the context of prayer, reflection and commitment: the communal aspect and the ritual aspect, or the experience of the church and the sacraments.

The arrangement of this section is as follows. I shall start with the description of the form and content of prayer (chapter 9), reflection (chapter 10) and commitment (chapter 11). This will be followed by a description of the significance of a number of factors in connection with prayer, reflection and commitment (chapter 12). The whole of Part 3 will be concluded by a summary.

CHAPTER NINE

THE PRAYER-LIFE OF PASTORS

In the interviews a number of important divergences emerge when the pastors are asked about the concrete, everyday meaning of prayer. A third of the pastors practice regular, individual prayer, but they also pray with others. Among two-thirds prayer is only engaged in together with others. A number of them pray at home or in a small group; Over a third of the pastors pray only during the liturgy (large or small group), when they themselves lead or take part in a liturgical prayer.

1. *Individual prayer*

A third of the pastors consider it important to have a moment of individual prayer every day. For these pastors it is a matter of finding a moment's rest and some breathing space in which to *"stay in touch with the source"* freely and without being disturbed. For most of them individual prayer is necessary to prevent them from being swamped by their work.

The importance of regular individual prayer is articulated by some as the need to feel oneself incorporated into a vital current. It is a moment when trust in God is put into words.

Others intimate that it is wonderful to give content to prayer in a personal way, without immediately engendering a connection with other people. What is important is *"a moment of rest and association with God, without other people asking critical questions about it"*. A pastor who regularly presides at the liturgy says that praying with others is not sufficient for him as a source of inspiration. There is also a regular need for moments, preferably at fixed times, to connect with God through prayer in peace and quiet.

Those who pray by themselves are also regularly present in places where prayers are said communally. A number of the pastors from this group indicate that reflection on meaning and form is important for prayer. They are among those who problematise their relation to God, Jesus and the Spirit. They look in different places for ways of giving content to their relation to God.

Moments, places and starting points of prayer

We shall now discuss a number of aspects of individual prayer: the moments of prayer, the places of prayer and the starting points for prayer.

Moments of prayer
The moments of prayer are typically the beginning of the day, midday or the end of the day. For some of the pastors prayer takes place in between their contacts with people. For others the early hours of the morning is a suitable moment for introducing the day that is to come with a personal prayer. The day is placed into the *"context of faith, and in the light of God's presence"*. It provides space, as well as peace and quiet for starting one's journey with people confidently, instead of having to carry along all one's cares as a burden. For yet others it is the end of the day that is an important moment for *"laying down"* all the experiences of that day *"before the face of God"*.

> *In the evening I often have a moment when I say:*
> *Dear Lord, here I give you everything . . . yes, everything. And then, thank God, I can say: I have spent enough energy on it today; tomorrow there will be another day.*

Midday is a good moment for one of the pastors, but it is often difficult to observe this midday prayer. Often something unforeseen occurs, such as a funeral or some other obligation. For some, both the beginning and the end of the day are important. They use both these moments for prayer. Some intimate that personal prayer is a kind of accompanying moment all through the day: after a conversation, on the way to a meeting, before or after a liturgy; it is good to pray every now and then.

Places of prayer
The places of prayer are quite diverse: in bed, while having a bath, at table before or after meals, in a little corner at home set apart for praying, in the church building, at one's desk or in an easy-chair in the room, in a natural setting or on the bicycle. All the pastors consider it important to pray in a place where there is peace and quiet or where they really feel at home. For some it may be a room where they can relax, while for others it is the room where they work: at their desk, for example.

Starting points for individual prayer

The starting points for individual prayer are also very diverse. Various possibilities are explored. A text—especially the Psalms—may become an invitation to prayer. For some pastors the breviary, in which the lauds and the vespers are specifically mentioned, allows room for individual prayer. A moment's silence can have an evocative effect: praying does not have to be done with words—a wordless prayer can be as rich as a prayer with words.

> *Every evening I retire for half an hour. I read and see to it that things become quiet, for I need that. Sometimes I pray with words, sometimes also without words, simply in silence.*

A moment of reflection, or the reading of literature or a poem, may call one to, and change over into, prayer. A prayer may spring up as a result of a pastoral moment, a meeting, or a conversation. While listening to music one may be moved to prayer.

> *I often listen to music, especially during my leisure moments. Sometimes it is purely instrumental music, sometimes new musical renderings of the Psalms. I may even listen ten times to my favourite Psalm. That connects me with a deep vital current. I am touched by the singing, very deep things spring up in myself, and I may even get tears in my eyes. Then I am in high spirits. I draw my confidence in God from that. I am carried along by it, incorporated into it, and that is how I move on to prayer.*

One pastor observes that he is not a man for the choir stalls.

Indeed, he does not listen to beautiful Psalms. Rather, for him, what is important is the *"complaint on the part of people that life is so unjust. I find it is very important to allow that to find a place within myself and to purify it. That is what praying means to me."*

He tells about the experience of a twenty-year-old who had become seriously ill and adopted a very aggressive attitude towards his illness. Nobody could put up with the way he felt about his situation. This pastor, however, took a liking in him, for this young person was actually gentle at heart. The boy could swear and rant and rave. He often visited this pastor and they increasingly found ways to talk. Now he is asking questions, *"and very difficult questions, indeed, about dying and things like that. And it is up to me to sort things out. Well, for me that is praying."*

These pastors indicate that individual prayer can be related to all aspects of life and that it takes place with or without words at moments that mark daily life.

2. *Praying with others*

A third of the pastors who practise an individual form of prayer also pray with others. A large number, two thirds, however, point out that they pray only with others. They never pray by themselves. On the one hand there is a practical reason for this: only when they commit themselves to others can they bring themselves to pray. That is the only way for them.

This is the reason given by most of the pastors. One of them, for example, prays with her colleague twice a day.

> *If I had to do it by myself, I would easily become lax about it. Now I simply have this arrangement. You do not make someone else get up early so as not to do it oneself. Especially if you want to share something with other people, you simply have to keep the appointment. That makes me keep up my praying.*

On the other hand it becomes clear that, for a number of pastors, praying as such is a communal activity. Rather than being simply a lack of individual prayer, it is their conviction that prayer has its basis in some form of community and should therefore also take place communally.

Places of communal prayer

The places where prayer with others is engaged in are the home, small groups and the communal liturgy.

At home, in the family

Some pastors point out how important it is for them to pray with their children, for example at the dinner table. It is about finding a form of prayer, which is thoroughly interwoven with everyday reality. Some form of ritual is very important in this respect: lighting a candle, or simply attention to the atmosphere of the meal.

The simplicity of the language, in which children are the decisive factor, and the attention for the seasons in nature are important.

For some pastors it is quite a task to keep this joint prayer in the family going and to develop sufficient creativity in this respect. It has something to do with the availability of time and space, and especially attention for one another.

> *Meals are very important in our family. We start with prayer. We try to have a little talk with each other. I worry about our being together, though. We have a strange family life indeed, as a lot of married pastors will certainly have. When*

> *the children are free, I am working, and when I am free, they are working. On Sunday mornings, for example, I am always absent. And that is precisely the family's leisure time. There are also moments, however, that are very precious, for example with my wife in the evening, when we have a glass of wine together, and the occasions when, together with the children, we create a festive atmosphere at home.*

Some pastors indicate that they find it increasingly difficult to give shape to their joint prayers with their partner and their children. One reason for this is the fact that the partner may not feel comfortable with the form of prayer, which the pastor concerned might prefer. Another reason is that, in the partner's experience, the word praying may carry negative associations that arouse a lot of resistsance, with the result that it becomes nearly impossible to give shape to it together.

The small group or community
Some pastors live in a religious community and find a common form of prayer there. For one of them, however, it is fairly relative. Apart from the joint prayer he needs a moment of his own to bring himself *"to really pray"*. Other pastors have found a group comprising colleagues and other people who have committed themselves to some form of common prayer. A highly individual emphasis is brought forward by the same pastor who, in the foregoing, spoke of listening to music as a form of prayer.

> *Singing together is like a vital current which gives me back, ever anew, my confidence in God. Singing Psalms most of all gives me a feeling of security. These prayers find a place through repetition. They offer words that I can easily pray with others. Singing has a deepening effect.*

A parish pastor considers it important to have regular meetings with a group in the church who seek to connect with one another in silence, in song and in prayer. There is an open invitation to anybody who wishes to join in.

> *At eight o'clock in the morning I unlock the church. Then there is a small group. Hardly anyone knows of this. I have told a few people that I say prayers in the morning, with Psalms and a few hymns—every day without fail. Sometimes I also sit there all by myself. I actually think, though: praying is something you ought to do together. I am also part of a group of colleagues who eat together every Thursday and pray together afterwards.*

The communal liturgy
Most of the pastors regularly preside at the liturgy. Many of them experience this, apart from other moments, as a central place for

their prayer. More than a third indicate that it is the only place where they pray, either because it is impossible for them to imagine any other place, or because for them liturgical prayer is prayer *per excellence*. A number of aspects also emerge here.

For some, joint liturgical prayer is only meaningful and possible when it is based on mutual care. Leading in prayer should therefore go together with ministry. For a few others it is difficult to lead in a large, pluriform parish. Their only places of prayer are small group celebrations, for example on weekdays. For some, taking part in a liturgy at which they do not have to preside is an important moment. Sometimes it is good to attend the liturgy of others, without having to play an active role oneself. Some prefer going to another church where nobody knows them and where no demands are therefore made on them.

Liturgy becomes a place for prayer, when it is possible to work at creative forms and possibilities so that everybody can express themselves through them. Looking for rituals of one's own is essential in this respect. It may just create room for joint prayer. Looking for a language through which people can be touched together is a constant task. This is typical in the case of, for example, female pastors and pastors active in health care, who are confronted with people who, as a result of a physical or mental handicap, have problems in articulating prayers.

One of the pastors who does not feel at home in any ecclesial context has had to admit that there is no place for her to participate in joint prayer, except insofar as she creates room for it at home, with her children. For somebody else the only liturgical place is the ecumenical evening prayer in which he occasionally takes part. This is *the* moment of prayer for him.

Of great importance, especially for the parish pastors, is the community aspect in the weekend liturgy. When the atmosphere in the liturgy leads to a joint experience, there is room for prayer. A number of these observations also apply to the domain of the communal and the ritual, which we shall discuss further in Part 4.

3. *Reflection in and on spirituality*

Reflection occurs, both in individual prayer and in joint prayer. The interviews show that pastors reflect on the meaning and significance of their prayer, while praying, and that they are aware of the way in which prayer is engendered, what sort of relation to God it expresses and how it develops in connection with day-to-day life in general, and ministry in particular. We hear several of them speak of their difficulties with individual prayer or, by contrast, of the joy and the rest that they draw from it. These experiences are formulated on the basis of inner processes of reasoning and reflection.

Some pastors have learned through experience how to choose those moments during the day that provide the best opportunities for personal prayer. For others, reflection during their leading in prayer in the liturgy showed them that this was the most suitable form of prayer for them.

Among a number of pastors, just over a third, the second form of reflection also occurs. They indicate that the context makes it necessary for them to review their experiences in prayer. The context of the church is one of the factors that play a role in this respect: a number of pastors have discovered through reflection that they can only really bring themselves to pray in small-group settings where people understand one another, and offer one another tangible signs of the bond that unites them. For others, like those who give a strong social content to their ministry, their confrontations with violence, or with the oppression of economically dependent groups, constitute a challenge to give a new content to their personal prayers, connecting them to such experiences.

Such instances of the second form of reflection are closely bound up with what we described earlier about shifts in the metaphors for God. Those pastors who, more than others, reflect consciously on their association with God are also the ones who exemplify this form of reflection in connection with their prayer-life.

4. *Summary of chapter 9*

When one considers the patterns of individual and joint prayer emerging from the interviews, it appears that pastors either attach a lot of importance to both individual and joint prayer, or consider joint prayer *the* pre-eminent form of praying. Some of them find it important not to be completely dependent on the possibilities of praying with others. Moreover, individual prayer is necessary for functioning properly in the community.

Most pastors pray with others, either for practical reasons, or because for some of them joint prayer is the only acceptable form of praying. More than half of them never pray by themselves. There is a strong link with their presiding at the liturgy. In their view, praying has something to do with the experience of God as "our God". From the community coming together in prayer the individual pastor receives the strength to live in an intimate relationship with God. We shall discuss the communal aspects of prayer further in chapter 13.

For many pastors their pastoral function plays an important role. Viewed from the perspective of content, too, for many of them praying is oriented on their work. Apart from that, it is important for a number of male and female pastoral workers to develop suitable forms of family prayer. At the same time some of them point out how difficult this is.

Finally, we may conclude that reflection in prayer occurs among all the pastors interviewed. Among a number of them, just over a third of those interviewed, the second form of reflection also occurs.

CHAPTER TEN

THE REFLECTIVE LIFE OF PASTORS

The same arrangement will be followed here as in the preceding chapter. The subjects of investigation are individual reflection and joint reflection. Attention will also be given to those who cannot bring themselves to reflect on things, and those who say that they feel the need for more routine reflection. A separate point is the tension between action and contemplation.

1. *Individual reflection*

A large group, half of the thirty pastors, intimate that they regularly engage in individual reflection. For a number of them it is *"wonderful to have a quiet moment for thinking, for reflecting on everything I do"*. A number of them also say that they can occasionally bring themselves to reflect. We may conclude that two out of three pastors take a moment to reflect occasionally, or regularly.

I do not use the word meditation here, but the word 'reflection': the latter term has a broader range of meaning than the word meditation. Meditation requires a certain structure and form, whereas reflection can have a more open, unstructured, form. Reflection is also a term that the pastors use far more frequently than the word meditation. In the following it will also become clear that reflection is mainly a form of self-reflection. It is a moment of thinking about, and focussing on, the things one experiences and does. The pastors who can bring themselves to a regular and structured form of reflection are those who show that they are well versed in some form of self-reflection.

The importance of such individual reflection is indicated by the need to have moments of rest and inward movement. Anybody who lives an active life needs moments for being *"close to the source"*. A female pastor who calls herself *"contemplative by nature"* has something to say on this matter with which all those pastors who regularly engage in reflection can identify. She uses the word meditation, though.

On the one hand, I am very active, with plenty of energy, and on the other hand I really need meditation. Sometimes this can mean reading something that acts as a kind of meditation and brings me to my real self. Then I think of a text by Etty Hillesum in which she says that God lies buried very deeply, and that he is covered by a whole lot of rubble. You have to remove that in order to find God again. I also think of the image of St. John of the Cross, who says that God is the source from which springs the water of life. You have to discover the source again and again, though.

Another pastor articulates the importance of individual reflection in terms of the necessity to remain open and available in an appropriate way.

Ministry is a bottomless pit. I have so many questions coming at me all the time. I actually have to decide to have moments for thought, not only professionally, but also for the sake of my spiritual well being. I have to do that myself. I am not the type of person who likes to be swamped by work. I can work in an orderly manner and also quietly postpone the things I do not have to do today. The result is that I am indeed really available when I am present.

Reflection is needed so as not to neglect one's own essential being, and for protecting and strengthening one's availability for others.

Moments, places and starting points

Here, too, we shall discuss moments, places and starting points of reflection.

Moments of individual reflection

Just like the moments for prayer, moments of individual reflection vary greatly: for some pastors the early hours of the morning, right at the beginning of the working day, is a suitable moment. There is still enough *"space"* then. For another pastor, however, a moment during the day is suitable, because he feels a desire to look for a concrete link with everything he encounters in his work. For a third pastor the beginning or the end of the evening is suitable for reviewing everything quietly. Practical considerations are relevant here: in the morning, sleep easily becomes a problem. One of the pastors prefers a number of days in the peaceful seclusion of the abbey in order to have plenty of time for reflection. In his view, reflection is an aspect of his daily encounters with people. Specific days are necessary, however, to bring oneself *"fully"* to reflection.

Places of individual reflection
The places for individual reflection also vary greatly: outdoors, in nature, in the garden, on the way, in the study behind one's desk, in a quiet spot at home, in the church building, in a place of prayer in the house, or in the silence of an abbey. It is worth noting that a number of pastors testify that they can bring themselves to reflect while riding on their bicycle or taking a walk outdoors. One of them describes how important cycling is to him.

> *I have two important moments. It is a good thing for me to cycle to my work in the morning, and back home in the evening. My route goes through the woods, far from all the noise and at a distance from people. It includes a small part through the woods where I never meet anybody, except for old trees and that splendid light that falls on the fields. My need to pass by there has grown as I myself have grown older. It includes a small part that has become very dear to me: a place where the landscape is very wide and spacious and where one cycles in between farmlands. The meditative moment is perhaps the preparation for the day that is beginning.*
>
> *It is also a moment for becoming receptive. Therefore I do not cycle fast, but take my time. It has become important for me to carry on with my work, but also to go back in the evening, to allow the things that have happened to sink in, to allow them to settle on the ground of my existence and so to let go of them. Sometimes I have to go by car, because there has been severe frost and the road is not suitable for cycling. I regard that as a disaster. When I have taken the car, I remain locked up within myself. Openness, precisely as a result of the route through nature, is closely linked in my experience with receptivity to light. All shades of light are there, both in the morning and in the evening.*

Others just walk into the garden or into the woods early in the morning or around midday. Somebody else describes how, walking about the Old City, he is brought to reflection.

> *There I can distance myself from all kinds of things. The place has something about it of the spiritual city. Walking raises me above myself. There is something sacred about it. For example, when I lay my hand on an old stone, then I imagine what that stone might be able to tell me: stories about all those people who pass this stone. Hope and despair, that which moves people . . . I feel it in myself then. How many deeply moving feelings in people have not passed this way?*

For some pastors it is important in the morning, before work begins, to read a text quietly while sitting behind their desk, and to enter into it in preparation for the day. One pastor prefers *"a moment's silence in the living room or in the bedroom"*. For others the spaciousness of the church is a suitable place, provided one can be there alone. Precisely there, silence can become an appropriate space.

Starting points for individual reflection

For more than half of the pastors who can bring themselves regularly or occasionally to reflect, a text is a good starting point. It may be a text from Scripture or a Psalm, a special text for the day, or a mystical text. A few pastors have no need of any such text. The silence (in nature or in the room where one finds oneself) invites one to think about the meaning of one's work, one's contacts with others, and the way in which one gives shape to one's personal life. Some say that *"simply doing nothing"* is already sufficient occasion for being brought to reflection. For a few the so-called *"Jesus-prayer"* is important: the repetition of a few words creates a rhythm for reflection.

> *For me, meditation has something to do with very short sentences. For example, what Thomas said on seeing the risen Christ: "My Lord and my God". It was a little phrase St. Francis used for his meditation. It is a sentence which you can pronounce in different ways: when I am looking at something in bewilderment, or at moments when I feel that I am being sustained in spite of everything. I use such a small sentence to re-establish contact with experience: what is it that actually sustains me in my personal life, in my family, in my ministry?*

For a few other pastors, practising Zen meditation is helpful. This creates space for silence and reflection. Some pastors point out that they have tried to practise Zen meditation at one time, but that they did not succeed in turning it into a permanent way of meditation. One of them says that it made him go mad, for he is *"an active person"*.

2. *Joint reflection*

Several pastors who engage in reflection individually also practise it together with others. This is in fact the group who bring themselves to reflect most frequently—that is to say, nearly one out of three pastors. For some, joint reflection is achieved in a moment together with the family, especially with the children, during meals or in an organised setting with several families. Others share a reflection group with several colleagues, in which reading texts or articulating one's own experiences are the starting point for regular, recurrent reflection. For four pastors joint reflection is the only form in which conscious reflection occurs. When it does not happen with others, *"nothing much comes of it"*. One pastor organises a moment of reflection together with her colleague, while another organises a group, or joins in when somebody else arranges something. A third can find a place in the joint reflection of the religious community. A fourth has had a strong study group for more than ten years in which, apart from studying, they also stop to reflect.

3. *Reflection as reflection on work*

For half of those who practise reflection regularly, it is especially related to working experiences, planning for work and evaluation of work. For some, reflection means *"going through things once more"*, while for someone else it is a moment *"for thinking about the question: why am I doing what I am doing and what influences me in doing it?"* For most of them reflection has something to do with the preparation of a liturgical service, a sermon, or a meeting with a working group. These are good occasions for bringing oneself to reflect. In fact, reflection here is reflection on the ministry.

4. *No reflection at all*

Four pastors point out that they absolutely lack either the peace and quiet, or the very need for such a moment of silence and reflection. In the view of one of them, people used to handle the idea of reflection in such a forced and strained manner in the past, for example at the seminary or in the monastery, that he cannot stand the word reflection anymore. Another pastor simply does not need such a moment: *"I cannot sit still in one place; I do not feel like it"*. These are the same pastors who exhibit little or no self-reflection in the interviews. It is as if their lives take place in the outward movement. Their life consists of contacts with others and there is no clear distinction between their private life and their work. The same applies, although to a lesser degree, to those who only occasionally bring themselves to reflect.

5. *Tension between contemplation and action*

For a number of pastors a constant issue is the following question: is it sufficient for me that I can bring myself to moments of reflection during my work? Or is it necessary to arrange a separate time and place? Some pastors express a great desire for being able to set apart more time.

I simply long for being together with others for one hour every day or simply to reflect and be silent. I sometimes feel that I am being lived.

Some of them point out how their life and work are determined by the tension between action and contemplation. The term *"tension"* is not used negatively here. Some pastors have learned to discover the basis of their commitment through clinical pastoral training. For one of them this has something to do with the *"close connection between action and contemplation"*. For another it is fascinating and exciting to keep up the constant alternation between action and contemplation, between political engagement and mysticism.

It is really a matter of my keeping up that alternating movement again and again. And this always takes me back to the question: is it sufficient simply to spend the day breathing or do I constantly need separate moments, which I simply have to arrange? Sometimes things are all right for a long time without such separate moments. Then, however, I suddenly feel that I am getting out of breath. Then it is time for me to pay extra attention to something.

In my view these pastors are the ones who, more than others, are capable of a critical attitude towards their life and work.

6. *Reflection in and on spirituality*

For most of the pastors reflection takes the form of self-reflection and this is mostly identical with reflection on work. So, when we speak about reflection in and on spirituality, we are talking about reflection in and on self-reflection.

Once more it is clear that all those pastors who bring themselves to reflect, exhibit reflection *in* their reflection. This becomes clear from the choices that are made concerning the time and place for reflection, as well as from what they relate about their experience, for instance that joint reflection is the only appropriate form for them or, by contrast, that it is precisely individual reflection that is an important source for their life and work. With the small number of pastors who never pause to reflect, the question arises whether we may speak of reflection in their spirituality in this respect.

The second form of reflection is especially found among those pastors who are aware of the tension between action and contemplation, and thus pay explicit attention to it. They realise that circumstances, and developments in life and work, force them to handle their time, and the arrangement of their life and work, in such a way that there will be sufficient room to breathe and, in so doing, also to breathe life into their own life and work. It is striking that this group comprises especially those pastors who are active in a pronouncedly secular environment, and who accord a place of importance to the degree of tension obtaining between action and contemplation. Their reflection *on* their reflection has taught them to realise what that reflection means for their life and work.

7. *Summary of chapter 10*

Among the pastors interviewed, those who bring themselves to reflect individually are more numerous than those who pray individually.

Just over a third are engaged in reflection in a regular and organised way. Most of them also engage in forms of joint reflection.

Reflection takes the form of self-reflection and for a number of pastors it also, even predominantly, has issues related to work as its content.

Concerning those pastors who never take a moment to reflect the question arises whether they can be said to exhibit reflection in their spirituality in this respect. Among all the others the first form of reflection is to be found, while a number of them attach great significance to the second form of reflection as well. In this group a fascinating tension emerges between action and contemplation. They belong to the group showing a strongly developed reflective attitude.

CHAPTER ELEVEN

THE COMMITMENT OF PASTORS

This chapter will describe a third mode of expressing spirituality. We shall be inquiring how pastors express their spirituality in the practical, ethical sphere. By this I mean the question of how pastors show their spirituality in their practical action and in their commitment. The following questions will be dealt with:

How do pastors define their understanding of values and norms: what is the shape of their morality?

How do they express solidarity with the less fortunate? The question here is how, in this respect, the relation between personal life and work is made visible. And how are pastors touched emotionally; how do they come to join movements of solidarity?

What, finally, can be said about the lifestyle of pastors with regard to sobriety, hospitality and the like?

1. *Views on morality*

Field of tension between old and new

One of the priests indicates how much he lives and works in a constant field of tension as far as moral norms and values are concerned. He knows that he often allows himself to be led to think and talk in moral terms. He blames especially his education and training for this. At the same time he wishes *"to learn increasingly how to handle morality in a playful manner. In fact I very much want to handle it in a flexible way."* This tendency can be observed in many of the pastors. They seek to give a broader, freer content to norms and values. At the same time a number of pastors are worried about the uncertainty felt by a lot of people as far as values and norms are concerned. One of them speaks about this tension, saying:

> *On the one hand, I am opposed to the old ideals and virtues, and on the other it would be a good thing for people in our time and culture to have a better perception of what is good and bad. I say this in connection with the growing chaos in our personal existence and in society.*

Strong emphasis on justice

In nearly all the interviews (some pastors are very inarticulate about it) a major shift is apparent in the appreciation of, and the content given to, moral virtues. Instead of a legalistic morality it is increasingly a matter of a personal choice in favour of justice, when other people's welfare is at stake. One of them speaks for most pastors in saying:

> *I am no longer disciplined in the sense of nicely obeying the rules. Actually, in my view, all kinds of laws should be broken down. In fact, all the structures that confine people should be broken down. At the same time, however, it is certainly important for me to practise being prepared to account for myself and for what I am doing. Of crucial importance in this regard are respect, esteem and wisdom in associating with people. I try to live a moderate and sober life—a simple lifestyle—but I do like to play the host. I very much like to eat with other people. I have never been anything in the nature of a strong man. I am not strong, actually. That is why I think it is important to work with others, also in joint resistance against the unjust structures in our church. I cannot accomplish anything on my own. We can only do it if we do it in a playful manner, putting things into perspective. Only with music, says the fairytale of Oinkbeest. I think that is wonderful. I myself am convinced that only together, step by step, with a lot of patience and respect, can we build up something in order to accomplish what we actually wish to accomplish. I think justice is a central virtue in the process: precisely there where people are being pulled to pieces. And justice is a leitmotiv in this.*

The relational character of the virtues, with an emphasis on integrity

Moral virtues have acquired a markedly relational character in the experience of these pastors during the course of their lives. Working at what is morally good at the individual level is no longer the central issue. It rather has something to do with the relation to the other person. In the discussion about moral virtues, pastors speak of flexibility, freedom, simplicity, sincerity, compassion, mercy, respect and esteem, sobriety, righteousness, letting justice prevail, rationality and strength. The emphasis lies on personal integrity and autonomy. The point is *"that you learn to live in an inviting way so that you oppress or restrict neither yourself nor others, but that you dare to live honestly"*. This certainly presupposes, according to the interviewees, that one practise simplicity and sincerity, and exhibit agreement between what one says and what one does.

Among this category of pastors there is a particular emphasis on the virtues of reliability, being true to oneself, honesty, a sense of vulnerability and being prepared to account for one's actions. It is remarkable in this respect that male pastors have developed a greater interest in virtues like tenderness and respect, and female pastors a greater interest in rationality and strength. An important supplement to the customary series of moral virtues is added by one of them: the virtue of anger. One is certainly struck by the fact that, within this very general picture, a number of aspects stand out in the case of those pastors who have some personal relationship and who indicate that they have entered into a confrontation with prevailing norms and values. They have also been challenged by experiences of crisis to look for some kind of counselling.

Rational accountability

A widely attested position is that morality is meaningless, and goes against life itself, when it implies a narrow-minded lifestyle. Therefore it is important to think critically and not to be guided by emotions alone. One of the women summarises her moral `self` in three words: *"justice, rationality and strength".*

> *I think, first of all, of justice, which means doing justice to every human being, especially vulnerable human beings, just as every flower is accorded its own place in a bouquet. This is closely bound up with God's justice: not breaking off the broken reed. It is followed by the word rationality, which means acting in a sensible way, thinking about God, learning how to look critically at society and at my own life. In my ministry it means trying to liberate people from their fear of God and of themselves. And, as a third word, I like the virtue of strength: in our religious community we have given a place to two statues, namely two angels, one of whom is standing proudly upright, while the other is bending down. For me these are two attitudes which essentially belong together.*

She takes her starting point in two biblical images: the healing of the crippled woman and the recurring call to give oneself up to the unconditional.

2. *Commitment to the less fortunate*

Here we shall discuss the question whether and how pastors are personally and emotionally touched by the things they encounter in their lives; the question of how they give content to their ministry, and how this personal commitment is related to their ministry.

Being emotionally touched

A large number of pastors describe how they, personally, are regularly touched deeply by the brokenness and injustice they experience in the world around them. For certain female pastors the situation of underprivileged women stands out. For pastors working in the Old City quarters it is the outcasts, foreigners and vagrants who draw their attention. For an industrial pastor it is the people who find themselves excluded from employment, or who become victims of the system. For pastors working in health care it is those who are severely handicapped, either physically or mentally.

Solidarity from within

A third of the pastors describe how it is possible to experience a strong bond with certain groups or individuals, because one has experienced in one's own life history what it means to be a vulnerable human being. For one of them it is the—premature—confrontation with death in his family, for another the experience that he did not have a place of his own to live in. For a third it is the experience of many years of contact with a mentally handicapped brother of child, and for yet others it is the experience of having found oneself in a deep crisis at one time. Finally, for one pastor, the experience of a difficult situation of poverty during childhood is an important point of recognition.

Rational basis of solidarity
Some pastors point out that they want to deal with injustice as much as possible in a practical and matter-of-fact way. They say that they always have a very good look at what is happening, and that they try to orient themselves as broadly as possible with respect to the relevant politico-economic factors. This prevents an overly *"naive or hasty commitment"*.

Commitment connected or unconnected with the work situation
For the majority of pastors, commitment to the less fortunate fully coincides with their ministry as such. They describe, in particular, how in their work they let themselves be called upon by those who are less privileged than others within the community or group for which they work as a pastor. One of them says: *"My personal solidarity and professional solidarity constantly overlap"*. A relatively small group of pastors indicate that they consider it important to associate with

underprivileged people outside their own work situation. It is a sort of test of whatever bonds there may be, but then against existence as a whole. In concrete terms it means that these pastors keep associating for years with certain people who have few or no contacts with, or no access to, other people. This kind of contact also remains after they have left a certain place of work.

A separate aspect is the extent to which the pastor's family also gets involved, whether under duress or otherwise, in some movement of solidarity. Some pastors say that their commitment is under a permanent strain as a result of the question that keeps arising: how far can I go in my identification, and am I not allowing myself to be overtaxed? For some it can become simply too much: *"This is all I can handle; the things I come across in my work are already more than enough for me"*. At the same time, this same pastor says that within his religious community he helps with sheltering refugees in the building. Another pastor says that he does not go out of his way to look for situations requiring commitment, for he is bound to come across them in his ministry. Sometimes one comes across a bad conscience: should I not have paid more attention to certain groups in my work area? Some pastors make excuses for themselves, saying: *"There are so few really poor people in my work area"*.

Commitment to social movements

A number of pastors formulate solidarity and commitment in such a way as to associate it with social, ecclesial and political movements of renewal. The following movements are mentioned: Pax Christi, the IKV (Interdenominational Peace Council), Solidaridad, and the "Vastenaktie" (Lenten fund-raising appeal for missionary activities in developing countries), ecology movements, the Association of Pastoral Workers, the "Acht Mei Beweging" (the Eighth of May Movement: a collective of catholic progressive groups and base communities), political parties and local social organisations. For example, an action group is mentioned, which is engaged in the protection of city monuments, or a Third-World shop (Oxfam shop), or an organisation for asylum seekers.

> *Work pressure in the ministry is no excuse for not being actively involved in a social renewal movement. Many colleagues are ashamed, for example, to be actively involved in the Association of Pastoral Workers and Priests—because of the great amount of work. I could also be ashamed, but I am not. For I think it is important to be involved in it.*

Sometimes it is certainly a problem that there are many meetings and much talking, but little real, committed action.

Awareness of social position

Only a small group explicitly mention an awareness of the social position they have as pastors. It is especially those pastors who orient themselves socially and politically in their ministry, and those working in institutions of health care, who show awareness in this area. Some of the pastors say: *"My thinking and acting have their foundation in this society, in which I occupy a position as a pastor"*. The pastors who are aware of their social position are mainly those who are active in non-parish contexts. However, some of them are parish-priests.

3. *Lifestyle as a basis for solidarity*

A number of pastors relate how they consciously apply themselves to a moderate and sober lifestyle, together with their family, or in their personal relationship. Others who live by themselves also point out that they apply themselves to this individually. Some pastors belonging to a religious order consider it important that this should take place in the context of the community. This lifestyle is expressed in conscious purchasing behaviour, sobriety and moderation with regard to food and drink (on certain days), a conscious effort at living in an ecologically sound manner, and paying attention to the way in which one makes use of means of transport.

Besides, with some there is a lot of interest in hospitality. One of them points out how one's personal lifestyle may become the basis for a broader, political commitment.

> *At home we practise a sober lifestyle. We are continually thinking about the contribution we can make and how we can conserve creation a little and protect all the good things contained in creation. We shall also have to make an effort towards this politically, but we shall have to find our own way of making a contribution. Very conscious purchasing behaviour and critical consumer behaviour are important. Five years ago we got rid of our car. It was not out of principle or anything like that. We simply said to one another: Let us see whether we can also do without that. We bought fold-up bicycles. And to our surprise, in spite of the fact that we both like driving a lot, we discovered that we are quite happy with it.*

Most of the pastors feel about this less strongly than this pastor indicates. However, it becomes clear that the connection between one's lifestyle and one's own political engagement is considered to be important by those who take a critical view of their solidarity. Some pastors add that it is not about an overly strict way of life, as if things have to be done by all means. They say they are quite happy with their *"playful way of handling ordinary things"*. Thus sobriety and enjoyment of life go together very well. It is on the basis of this very combination that hospitality thrives.

4. *Reflection in and on spirituality*

When the pastors discuss the way they feel about morality, they all exhibit the first form of reflection. One notices how they show a development on the basis of their own experiences, and of the way they feel about things. One also notices how the content of moral values and norms changes as a result of reflection on experience, and the way they feel about things. Choices are clearly made and pastors are on the whole able to indicate how they live and act. This can be most clearly observed in connection with the theme of integrity. The same applies to their commitment and solidarity. Several of them also show quite clearly that their development is not yet over in these two respects.

The second form of reflection is found among those pastors who indicate how socio-cultural developments, and their own biography, play a role in their appreciation of, and feelings about, values and norms. This applies especially in those cases where pastors are aware of their social position and its significance for personal life and ministry. They show that they are capable of giving an account of themselves in a rational way, in that they are consciously looking for moments in which to take some distance in order to think about their commitment and personal lifestyle. With these pastors, more than with others, it becomes apparent how they (have to) take care not to exceed the limitations of their commitment. This is connected with the development of their personal identity, as far as it concerns the skill of dealing with possibilities and limitations.

5. *Summary of chapter 11*

With regard to the experience of norms and values there is a strong tendency among the majority of pastors towards a more open and free attitude.

Concern for justice is the central idea.

A significant point is personal integrity, which is especially manifest in the interviews in which self-reflection is considered to be very important.

For most pastors who mention this, commitment to the less fortunate is closely bound up with their work as pastors. Some of them attach great importance to practising solidarity independently of their ministry.

Few pastors are aware of their social position. Awareness of their social position is most pronounced among those pastors who attach great importance to reflection on their own life and work. Generally speaking, these are the pastors who show a strong social and political orientation, or who are employed in institutions of health care.

CHAPTER TWELVE

INFLUENCING FACTORS

It appears from the interviews that a number of factors have an influence on prayer and reflection, or their absence, on the regularity and content of prayer and reflection, and on the way in which pastors are committed. The following factors are mentioned: discipline, study, taking part in cultural events, spending time in nature, and physical work. Concerning each of these factors it will be inquired to what extent they promote prayer, reflection and commitment, and influence their content.

1. *Discipline*

In the interviews discipline is understood in two ways: as time-management, and as exercising oneself in a certain lifestyle as a basis for commitment. The former understanding has something to do with the way in which one structures one's daily program; the latter meaning is connected with the way in which the pastors practise certain attitudes as a result of which commitment is enhanced.

How do pastors approach time-management? Is there any structure to their daily program, which determines its content? How do pastors look for a structure with which to separate work and private life in an appropriate manner? And how do pastors practise commitment? We shall discuss, successively, the significance pastors attach to time-management and to practice, after which the question will be considered of how discipline influences prayer, reflection and commitment.

Taking leave of forced structures

In our description of pastors' commitment, it has already emerged that it is especially the older group of pastors who testify that they are averse to the kind of coercion they used to experience in their upbringing and, subsequently, during their training. They have fought their way out of a rigid and dry discipline. Whenever the word 'discipline' is spoken in the interview, there is a knee-jerk defensive reaction. At the same time it is emphasised that there is now a great need for the freedom to find one's own way, as a result of which life and work can acquire a new, freely chosen, structure. It is not necessary that there be a new, strict plan of action; there should be room for anything.

One of them points to this as the reason why it is so difficult for him to work at a structure. Moreover, the things demanding his attention continually disturb this structure. For another pastor the best thing is to break down all the laws and regulations that tend to fixate life in one way or another. This will create room for establishing a new structure oneself. Thus the views on discipline have a markedly liberating orientation. Discipline, both as time-management and as exercise, is only meaningful insofar as it creates room for going one's own way. This kind of discipline has a major influence on the way in which pastors commit themselves. At the same time it becomes clear that practice is required, especially in order to achieve a credible lifestyle.

Planning one's daily program as structuring of time and space

One out of six pastors indicate that they are (virtually) incapable of retaining control over their daily program. Some of the pastors are always rushing from one thing to another. One parish-priest, for example, says something, which equally characterises the others' experience.

> *My life is being structured, my diary is being filled in. I am not at all good at structuring things. In our parish the things I have structured are continually being infringed upon.*

It is especially typical of parish-priests that they find it difficult to structure things. For one of them this is a reason to look for a different function in which it will be easier for him to watch his own daily program very closely. For another pastor it is important to have friends who can support him in finding a structure. A third indicates a great need for planning and structure. These are, on the whole, the same pastors as those described above.

The wish for structure arises as soon as the necessity of it makes itself felt: *"I am beginning to realise that I shall drown if I do not do anything about it"*. Tensions arise between the sphere of work and the private domain; one begins to realise that there is little room left for personal interests. Above all, there is not sufficient time for simply being at home and having attention to, and room for, the family, whether the partner or the children. Sometimes it is a happy circumstance that work and private life take place in separate places. In any case, this enables one to have a regular transition from one place to the other. However, the real point at issue for the pastors who speak about this is the following.

I need constant practice in order not to let myself be completely determined by work. It is an exercise in freedom, and creating space. And this depends on whether I am, and continue to be, capable of repeatedly breaking through certain fixed patterns. I increasingly have problems with colleagues who allow themselves to be determined too much by their work.

A framework is required in order to structure and to practise

In the foregoing it has already been stated that the separation of work and private life presents an important framework. Another framework is the rhythm of time: of the day and of the year. Some pastors indicate how the rhythms of the seasons and of the Christian year offer a suitable framework for them.

One of them, for example, tries to stay attentive to the periods of the Christian year, together with his family, in order to observe certain customs as well as moments of moderation and sobriety. For another the changing of the seasons offers a proper framework for establishing a structure, together with the children, as a result of which life itself is allowed full play. Spring requires a specific way of life; summer asks for yet another approach. Observing these customs creates space. Another framework is offered by the bond with others: appointments with colleagues and people in responsible positions, and with members of the parish committee or other pastoral associations. Working at annual plans and reports is a necessary element in this.

In about a third of the interviews one gets the impression that the daily program has a clear structure. For some pastors the division into sectors of life automatically determines it. Something that is a source of problems for some pastors is felt by others to be a suitable framework.

Structuring takes place in the combination of three aspects: being a pastor, being a husband and being the father of children. The distance between living and work-

ing already involves deliberate planning as far as accessibility is concerned. It helps to pay constant attention to the fact that I have to be with the children in time, and certainly not for too brief a time.

This pastor has the advantage that, as a pastoral worker, he does not often have to preside at the liturgy during weekends. At the same time, home is such a totally different environment for him that it enables him always to go back to work refreshed and renewed, as it were. For him it is a matter of really being there when he is somewhere, wherever that may be. This is true for him as a pastor, as a partner and as a father to his children.

For another pastor it has become very important to learn how to deal with his work methodically, because periods of hard work alternate with periods when there is less activity. He has learned how to establish a sound division: *"There are times for working, and there are times for celebrating"*.

Some pastors were brought up with strong discipline, which they have never come to dislike. They are quite happy to draw on it in giving structure to their use of time. For those who live in a religious community there is the daily rhythm of the group: the order of the day, which safeguards some space for them and guards people against entirely succumbing to work.

In some interviews it becomes clear that effective time-management has an influence on many aspects of life and work. Attention to each single moment is made possible through it.

For me discipline is required at various moments during the day: getting up in time, reading the newspaper in time, and not wasting energy on things that do not merit it.

The central point in structuring is the skill of concentrating on what is happening here and now. Those who deal with time in a disorganised way run the risk of not really having time for anything. *"I hope to be there when I get there"*.

The significance of discipline for prayer, reflection and commitment

As is clear from the foregoing, the interviews show an important connection between time-management on the one hand, and attention to prayer and reflection on the other. On closer examination it also appears that the pastors who deal with time and space in an organised way can also bring themselves regularly to pray, or to meditate and reflect. They also tend to be among those who pay particular attention to a concrete lifestyle as the basis for commitment. One of them says something the others are bound to recognise.

> *As soon as I maintain a less strict rule, I find myself losing awareness of things and acting automatically. I want to know what I am doing. Discipline is important for me. Discipline for me is a form of concentration. This is the only way for me to make contact with things divine. However, you understand that I am inclined to overdo things.*

It is also evident that discipline can never result from outside pressure. Pastors point out that they opt for it themselves and that it is they who need to pay particular attention to it.

An important aspect is the idea of safeguarding personal moments, which prevents pastors from becoming totally dependent on their work. For many pastors this is a serious problem. It appears from the foregoing that, for those who allow the content of their daily program to be determined by others, it is difficult to find time for reflection and rest. On the other hand, the description of prayer, reflection and commitment showed that for a large number of pastors prayer is only possible in communion with others. For a number of them it is given shape only in the liturgy at which they preside. The same applies, to a slightly lesser degree, to reflection. Here there are slightly more possibilities for individual forms of expression.

Time-management is equally important when the pastors associate with others in order to arrive at shared forms of prayer and reflection. There are dangers involved when both prayer and reflection completely coincide with functioning in the work situation—dangers in the sense that the question arises whether pastors retain sufficient opportunities to remain creative in this respect. A number of them indicate that it is only through considerable efforts that they themselves, as ministers, succeed in spending sufficient time with the *"source"*. Likewise, a smaller number also clearly state that it is important for their personal life to work at forms of commitment to people and to movements, and to apply themselves to a lifestyle which can serve as the basis for a credible commitment.

2. *Study*

In the inquiry into the significance pastors attach to study I was mainly interested in the question of whether and how they pay particular attention to goal-oriented study. By this I do not mean occasionally reading something or looking into a text for a moment. Study has something to do with familiarising oneself with new things from literature, reading over and over again, thinking about what is being read, making notes, and trying to establish connections between what is being read and one's own experience, thought and work.

Just over a third of those interviewed read regularly

By regularly we mean that these pastors take time for reading methodically. This can mean one moment each day or every week, or a longer period once a month. Study means that one regularly reads an article, or sometimes a whole book. For the majority of these pastors the aim of their study is their work. Among this group are a great many pastors who understand regularity as devoting a lot of time to study—and not only a lot of time, but also much diversity in what one reads and studies. These pastors show a *"broad orientation"*. Not only theological or biblical-exegetical texts fill their desks, but also modern novels, mystical texts and contributions from other disciplines.

A number of them indicate that it is precisely their work that forces them to read and study a lot—especially those pastors who work in institutions of health care (a nursing home or psychiatric institution), or those who, because of an interest in special groups and sectors in their ministry, are obliged to remain well-informed about backgrounds, developments and current reflections on them. There are, for example, a few female pastors who have made a thorough study of feminist literature, and an industrial pastor who spends a lot of time on economic and socialist literature. Another example is a pastor who regards it as his ministerial speciality to stay abreast of Jewish literature. Yet another pastor is convinced that one cannot function properly as a pastor in modern culture without being well acquainted with modern literature.

Study depends on time planning and the organisation of the context. The pastors who study a lot have learned how to plan and take the time for it. Some of them study every day at a certain time, for example at the beginning of the day, sitting behind their desks. Others find a suitable context in study meetings with other people. The members of the group mutually commit themselves to prepare their common study on a regular basis. Sometimes group meetings are held, for a shorter or longer period, in the presence of a supervisor. A lot depends on the internal coherence of such a group.

Almost two-thirds say that they study little, or not enough

Among this group of pastors there are some, just under a third, who indicate that they only occasionally read something in connection with their work. Mostly it is an article from a magazine. No mention is made of studying books. Sometimes only a few novels are read, or only very practical literature. Some say that they feel a need to spend more time on, and make more room for, study. However, they do not know how. A framework is necessary in order to bring oneself to study and to keep to it. Some can only bring themselves to read a good article or a book during the holidays. Others say that they get insufficient support from their environment, or from their colleagues.

The significance of study for prayer, reflection and commitment

There is considerable overlap between those who pay special attention to study and those who can bring themselves regularly to individual and/or joint prayer and reflection. It is mainly the pastors with a critically developed awareness who mention both aspects and who also point out that what they study has value for their prayer-life and reflection. Study invites one to reflect and, in some situations, to pray. A connection can be established, in particular, in the case of pastors who pay special attention to group reflection and liturgy. This does not necessarily mean that they spend most of their time on these two aspects, comparatively speaking. It does mean, however, that they are looking for contemporary, creative forms of leading in prayer and reflection. Likewise, those pastors who exhibit a strong social orientation pay particular attention to study. Among them there is a link with reflection, which is closely bound up with reflection on their work, and with a desire to give critical content to their commitment. Those pastors who exhibit a strong social commitment, both in their private life and in their work, say that they profit considerably from studying regularly and keeping abreast of literature that is important for their purposes.

We may conclude that those who do not study do not reflect much either. The same cannot be stated categorically about the relation between study and prayer. With some pastors one finds prayer in spite of the absence of regular study. This has to do, of course, with the fact that many pastors regularly lead others in prayer.

3. *Participation in cultural events*

By cultural events we understand: drama, music, film, expressive arts (sculpture and painting), dance and poetry.

A large number regularly participate in cultural events

Listening to music in the concert hall or at home is at the top of the list: more than half of the pastors consider this to be an important moment. Most of them prefer classical music. For one of them pop music is of central significance, for another opera or ballet music, and for yet others especially church music. After music, come sculpture and painting: just under half of them mention expressive arts (sculpture and painting) as a second aspect. A third of them mention regular visits to museums. A number of them like to see modern films. One of them spends as much time on this as possible, for *"films are the mirror of our time"*. A small group mention that they pay regular visits to the theatre.

A small number hardly participate in cultural events at all

A third of those interviewed say that for them it is a neglected area, or that interest in art and culture has remained an underdeveloped area all their lives. One of them says that he has simply never put much energy into it. For another, a married pastor, it is too expensive for the family. Some say that they feel a growing desire to make room for participation in art and culture. A female pastor says that in recent years she has begun to discover it and that she hopes that there will really be opportunities and time for it now.

Participation is linked to deliberate planning

Nearly all the pastors who regularly participate in cultural events, deliberately take time, and set aside fixed moments, for it. With some it is evident that there is always room for it. A number of pastors have the opportunity to plan occasions, together with their partner or friends, to go to the theatre, concert hall or museum regularly. It is especially difficult for parish-priests, because so many evenings are already occupied by work.

Culture and art help pastors find themselves and nourish their desire

For several pastors who regularly participate in cultural events artistic expressions are capable of bringing them to their real selves and of allowing them to find contact with their own emotions and desires. This statement made by one of them will easily be recognised by a great many others.

> *Art and culture are for me creative expressions of people of long ago, or of contemporaries, that show me where I stand and where others stand in life. They nourish me, articulate and represent aspects of my desire or of realities that are difficult for me to deal with. They sometimes give shape to my emotions and give words to it, and sometimes clarify the emotions of others next to me.*

Connection with work

It is remarkable that only a few pastors participate in cultural events on the grounds that it *"is good for my work or my function"*. Three pastors out of twenty say that they go to a concert or visit a museum because it is meaningful in connection with getting a sound knowledge of culture. The others say that they personally enjoy it, *"simply like it, for it is after all part of your life"*.

Significance for prayer, reflection and commitment

A third of the pastors point out that taking part in cultural events is an important source for their spirituality. For example, one of them says: *"Looking at art is essential for my spirituality"*. For another, art, and especially the beauty of architecture, is an image of the *"infinite beauty of God"* and that is the reason why looking at art touches him deeply. For somebody else the depth of sculpture and painting evokes emotion because of the fact that *"what lives inside people is made visible"*. In this connection, a few others speak about the wealth of simplicity in art, as a result of which the core becomes transparent. It is especially music, as some articulate it, which has concrete significance as a source and opportunity for religious reflection.

> *Music can carry me away, beyond the ordinary. Especially singing is a kind of vital current. I am touched while singing; deep layers within me come to the surface anew. Then I can even get tears in my eyes; I can become extremely happy then. It puts me in high spirits. It restores my trust in God, the deepest trust I have. I say this carefully, but even so, I feel: I am taken up in it, carried along.*

Hardly anything specific is said about the connection between participation in cultural events on the one hand, and commitment on the other. Some pastors give some slight indication of it when they speak about the significance of the culture of developing countries, the culture of the working class and the *"culture of the street"*. These are important resources for them, because these cultures invite them to concrete commitment.

4. *Spending time in nature*

Nearly all the pastors speak about the significance of nature in positive, sometimes glorifying terms. They like spending time in nature and mention the sea, the woods, the plains, the highlands, the starry skies, or a garden. The interviews give the impression that the pastors like to be in touch with nature.

Several aspects in the experience of nature

One of the qualities of nature is that it is capable of taking up and surrounding people completely. It is, says one of them, *"wonderful to feel completely taken up into it"* or *"to become part of such an immense whole"*. This pastor says that this is the reason why he likes walking outside in storm and rain so as to become completely imbued with the elements.

Several pastors point out that they like walking and cycling in nature, so as to experience peace and quiet. They prefer walking or cycling to work and back.

Contact with nature may become a fundamental experience of the grandeur as well as the vulnerability of the earth and all that lives on it. Experiencing the peace and quiet, feeling the ground under one's feet, these are moments for becoming fully human again, or for *"restoring me to my true self"*. One of them indicates that he rediscovers himself in nature as part of a far larger whole.

> *Spending time in nature brings me to myself, shows me where I stand, and often gives my life a place of its own within the larger whole. It shows me how the life of others and of myself take place as part of a larger whole, as a moment in time somewhere between the seasons, as a sign of the life cycle of being born, blossoming, flourishing and dying to become new seed for another cycle.*

Nature engenders respect and awe, and sometimes it is overwhelming. For one pastoral worker spending time in nature is a constant appeal for respect, a call for handling the beauty of everything with care. Although nature is not sacred in itself, it is a constant source of esteem and respect. For some pastors it is sometimes an overwhelming experience when they allow themselves a moment's rest to expose all their senses completely to nature.

A small group of pastors reveal a fascination with the seasonal cycle. Among them are especially the ones who like to do things in the garden. For one of them the experience of autumn is a concrete experience of her own autumn which has now arrived in her own life. A female pastor has developed a great love, together with her children, for the seasons, each of which has acquired a specific meaning. The seasons have become opportunities for special rituals.

> *In spring, around Easter for example, we do the necessary work in the garden. For me there is something highly religious about that: letting the children join me in putting seeds into the ground, and the knowledge that it will then germinate. And when the first fruits come from our kitchen garden, we treat ourselves to a dinner. Then the children are allowed to invite other children, and we invite a few friends. That is an important ritual for us.*

Nature as occasion and source for prayer, reflection and commitment

From the foregoing it has become clear that contact with nature is an important occasion and source for prayer and reflection. As we have already indicated in the description of prayer and reflection, for one out of three pastors nature is the environment in which, while walking and cycling, they can bring themselves to pray. Although nature itself is not sacred, it is capable of bringing them to themselves and enabling them to rise above themselves. In this way, nature itself becomes a source of religious experience. It not only offers beautiful religious images, but, using a phrase by Huub Oosterhuis, the earth itself is *"filled with grace"*. The power of this lies in the close bond between nature, people and God. One pastor describes the way he feels about nature as a mystical experience in which grandeur and tragedy go together:

> *I could describe one day when, fascinated by the morning dawn, I suddenly saw a buzzard with a small rabbit in its claws. That was overwhelming. I do not know whether that is mysticism, but the experience at that moment is quite fundamental: a transcending experience of creation, beauty, tragedy and violence.*

The connection with commitment is made especially by those pastors who are interested in environmental issues, both in private life and in their ministry. The experience of the vulnerable sides of nature not only fits in with the experience of one's own vulnerability, but is simultaneously an appeal for commitment to movements that are concerned with the environment. It also becomes manifest in a sober, non-consumerist lifestyle.

5. Physical work

By physical work the pastors mean various activities: household management, work in the garden, technical and creative work such as carpentry, creative sewing, and practising sports.

A number of pastors have virtually no experience with physical work. Several others occasionally spend time on housekeeping and/or in the garden. Nearly two-thirds point out that they do manual work regularly, much of which is around the house or in the garden. Technical manual work and practising sports are mentioned less frequently.

Housekeeping

Among the pastors who mention this, there are a number of women. The men live on their own or share the household work with their wives and families. For most of them household work is something which simply has to be done and at the same time is a welcome change, while certain sorts of work are more attractive than others. One of the women paints a picture in which the others, each with their own likes and dislikes, will be able to recognise themselves very easily.

> *The daily, ordinary things like cooking and washing the dishes have a positive effect on me as a change in my rhythm. It is good for me to use my powers in a different way. It allows me to relax. I enjoy the other household chores like washing, ironing, and tidying up cupboards, but these are often done in between other things. Cleaning is something I do when I have to, but it is not my favourite chore.*

Working in the garden

It is especially men who like to work in the garden. For some of them heavy manual work in particular has a positive effect. A typical statement runs: *"There are moments when I think: I wish I had a job in which I could simply work all day with my body and my hands. At those moments the scales are tipped to the wrong side. I get out of balance when I cannot work hard regularly. During some periods I do not get around to that often enough".*

For some pastors hard work in the garden *"gives you a pleasant feeling of tiredness".* Another aspect of working in the garden is that which some of them indicate by mentioning their fascination with what is happening under their very hands: life growing and flourishing in the soil.

Technical and creative manual work

This may consist of maintenance work in and around the house, or working at a hobby, such as creative carpentry, painting, or sewing. The pastors who mention this aspect speak about it with much enthusiasm, but some of them immediately add that, in fact, they do not get around to it often enough. It requires *"concentration and total engagement".*

Practising sports

This aspect is only mentioned explicitly by three pastors. Perhaps most pastors do not make a connection between practising sports and physical work. For one of them practising sports on a regular basis, jogging in the peace and quiet of nature, is a good moment for finding himself again amidst all the hasty work, and for being confronted with himself in a different way.

Insufficient time and space

The pastors who cannot bring themselves to do physical work, or get around to it only occasionally, point out that they have never learned how to do it and have never been accustomed to it, or simply do not have the time for it. It never happens because, again and again, their ministry demands all their attention. Several of them express a desire that more time and space would become available for it. *"I shall really have to make more time for it".*

Significance of physical work for prayer, reflection and commitment

No explicit connection is made. In the foregoing it became apparent, though, that bodily work is a suitable diversion from ministerial work which some of them call *"working with your head".* Besides, it is a good exercise for finding peace and quiet, for regaining oneself. Thus the pastors are *"confronted with themselves in one way or another".*

6. *Reflection in and on spirituality*

While, in the interviews, all the pastors exhibit reflection in their experience of the factors we described in the foregoing, a number of them also indicate that they sometimes distance themselves to some extent in order to have a critical look at the significance and the influence of these factors. This occurs especially when a connection is made between discipline, study and spending time in nature, on the one hand, and prayer, reflection and commitment on the other hand. Here, it also becomes clear that choices are made on the basis of critical reflection on discipline, study and spending time in nature.

7. *Summary of chapter 12*

Discipline, study and spending time in nature in particular are factors that exhibit a strong connection with prayer, reflection and commitment. This applies to a lesser degree to participation in cultural events, and even less to physical work.

SUMMARY OF PART 3

In Part 3 the experiential dimension was described: the way in which the pastors express their feelings about their relation to God, Jesus and the Spirit, in prayer (chapter 9), reflection (chapter 10) and commitment (chapter 11).

We were able to conclude that most of the pastors only pray with others. Half of the pastors do not pray by themselves. The connection with presiding at the liturgy is very strong.

As far as reflection is concerned, the difference in comparison to prayer is that pastors are more inclined to bring themselves to reflect individually. Among them, a third is regularly and methodically engaged in reflection. Most of them are also involved in communal forms of reflection. Those who hardly ever, or never, pause to reflect, exhibit the least developed form of reflection *on* their spirituality. Reflection, when it takes place, surpasses prayer in that it is directed towards work and mostly happens at moments when pastors are on duty.

Commitment has its basis in a radically changed view of, and feeling about, moral values and norms. The emphasis lies on justice and integrity. Morality has a strongly relational character. Commitment requires personal involvement. For a lot of pastors commitment is closely bound up with aspects of their ministry. Only a small group among them consider it important to develop forms of solidarity in personal life, apart from work, and to work at a lifestyle which supports commitment.

In chapter 12 we described a number of factors that may have an influence on prayer, reflection and commitment: discipline, understood as time-management and exercise, study, participation in cultural events, spending time in nature, and physical work. We were able to conclude that pastors experience discipline, study and spending time in nature as particularly important factors. Here, we also saw a connection between the level of reflection and the importance of these three factors, with discipline and study playing a particularly prominent role. For many pastors spending time in nature is an occasion for prayer and reflection.

PART FOUR

CHURCH AND SACRAMENTS

INTRODUCTION

The modes of expressing spirituality have two special aspects that clearly mark out the space and content of the pastors' experience of spirituality: the communal aspect, especially the experience of the church as community of faith, and the ritual aspect, by which is meant the significance of the sacraments in a broad sense. These two aspects complete our description of the dimensions of spirituality. Each of them also exhibits a particular development.

CHAPTER THIRTEEN

THE COMMUNAL ASPECT

Before considering how the pastors experience the church, we shall
have to look at the place where, according to the interviewees, God's
presence is experienced and where they experience spiritual power.
Taking that as a starting point, it will be possible to describe how
the pastors experience the place of God and of the Spirit. In doing
so, we shall offer a supplement to our description of the metaphors
used by the pastors in speaking of their relation to God, Jesus and
the Spirit.

1. *Locating God: where does God transpire?*

Striking differences can be discerned among the interviewees with
respect to the way in which God is 'located'.
   There are differences with respect to the experience of where God
can be encountered.
   – The place can be determined individually:
Some pastors speak of *"my God"*.
   – The place of God can be the community:
Some pastors speak of *"our God"*, the *"God of the people"*, or the *"God
of the covenant"*.
   – The place of God can be *"the whole of humanity"*:
Some pastors speak of the *"God of all people"* or the *"God of humanity"*.
   – The place of God can be the cosmos, the universe:
Some pastors speak of the *"God of everything"*.

The following survey may be given here
   – A number of pastors say that they are increasingly growing
towards the idea of God as *"You"*. Some of them also speak of *"our
God"*.
   – Some preferably speak of God as *"our God"*, an expression which,
as we shall see, is given a number of totally different meanings.
   – Yet others prefer to speak of the God who manifests himself
"in the other person", or *"in people created in God's image"*; some insist that
they cannot speak of God as *"our God"*.

– Some pastors who speak of *"our God"* find it increasingly difficult to refer to God as a *"person"*, yet some do experience God as *"over against"*.

The God of the individual

One pastor who works in a hospital mentions as one of the problems arising from secularisation the shift from *"our God"* towards a God who is experienced individually. He experienced this in the transition from the village community of his birth and childhood to the anonymity characteristic of the urbanised western part of the country where he now works. In his original environment, an agrarian village community, he still encounters an atmosphere of *"we together"*, whenever he meets his family and fellow-villagers for a feast or a funeral.

> *In the village, people say 'we' and 'our village'; we tackle things together there, and we speak of 'our God'. At the moment, here in the West, I do not feel anything when people say 'our God'. There is no community. Here in the hospital it is always a matter of individual visitors, and the district in which I live is not a community.*

The pastor who is speaking here is filled with nostalgia for a time when it was really possible to speak of *"our God"*. He feels a connection to the place where that is still possible: the village where he comes from. His longing is tangible: imagine that all this was still possible even now, in secular society, and in the fragmented world of health care in which he works as a pastor!

Several pastors say that they are aware of a transition from *"our God"* to *"my God"*. The shift towards addressing God as *"You"* rather than *"Thou"* is also related to this development. It almost goes without saying that those pastors who describe their relation to God as a personal love relationship address God quite personally, although one of them prefers speaking of the manifestation of God's love in the relation between people. An industrial pastor who likes to speak of the *"God of the poor"* also says of himself that, to his own surprise, he is increasingly capable of addressing God as *"You"*.

> *You are there for me, You who say that you will be there for people, will be there for me. Those are the only terms in which I can relate or express myself, although I do not picture a personal God to myself. The fact, however, that I call Him 'You' says something about myself: it is obviously familiar—not Thou, but You. It is about Another Being with a capital letter, and at my best moments I feel sustained by it.*

Another pastor has increasingly outgrown the habit of speaking of God in elevated terms. It appears from the interview that, standing in the tradition of liberation theology, he has gradually discovered that his social ministry only finds a fruitful soil to the extent that he pays attention to the vulnerability of others and of himself. That is the context in which he can associate personally with God, who is committed to individual vulnerable human beings.

Something similar is noticeable in the pastor who works in psychiatry. Apart from being the liberating God, God is also increasingly experienced as the healing and reconciling God who is there for people, personally. The same goes for a female pastor who likes to speak of God as *"the healer"* and *"the one who nourishes"*. One gets the impression that, as a female minister, she avails herself of every opportunity to associate with God in a personal way—and indeed in such a way that every individual is allowed to experience God personally.

> *I dislike impersonal words. I prefer words like 'You', words that indicate a relationship, especially in my personal prayer. When I preside at the liturgy, I find it more difficult, because then I stand before a community. However, when I am leading a prayer service as minister, I translate all the 'Thou's' into 'You's'. I feel at ease with texts in which God is addressed as 'You.*

The God of the community

Half of the interviewees mention *"our God"* in the sense of the *"God of the community"*. However, various explanations of its content are offered.

– Some pastors base themselves on their own feelings when they speak of a community liturgy in which the feeling of *"we together"* prevails.

– A number of them speak of the *"God of the people"* or *"the God of the poor"*.

– A few of them speak of the *"God of the Covenant"*, where God is felt to be the one who travels along with us humans as a companion.

God in the community liturgy

During the liturgy, one of the parish pastors experiences God as the God of the community.

> *I often speak of 'us'. I am also encouraged to do that in this parish: on Sundays the church is filled with people, among whom are lots of young people, children et*

cetera. This can only be 'we'. They sing, wish each other peace enthusiastically, and pray together. An enormous power emanates from it. And then I think: God not only belongs to me or to you or to us alone.

These words are from a parish pastor who draws much strength from the Sunday liturgy, where people succeed in turning it into something communal. One is struck by the fact that the pastors who speak of their feelings about God in the communal liturgy are all parish pastors. One of them says, for example, that he is occasionally nourished by the blessed relatedness characteristic of the parish-liturgy, so that he can say whole-heartedly: *"God, Thou who art willing to be there for us, Thou who art willing to inspire us"*. Some of them, however, point out that it requires quite an effort on their part to bring about something *"communal"*. It takes considerable effort to bring about communal experiences.

All this fashionable talk about 'church', and 'we together', is something you will never hear from me. I prefer speaking of 'we humans'.

This means, in concrete terms, that a lot of pastoral effort will have to be put into daily contact with people, something which this pastor takes a lot of pleasure in anyhow. Another pastor considers it his task to give many opportunities precisely to that group in the parish who does not get a chance to do something very often, especially the youth. Only when one works at this methodically can one really speak of community.

God of the people: God of the poor
A number of pastors can only speak of *"our God"* insofar it denotes siding with the poor, or making a stand for justice. A pastoral community worker, who experiences his relation to God in terms of the hope to find a perspective, says: *"I want to suggest to people that God is a God who stands up for the poor. That does indicate a certain direction."* That direction means working for justice *"free of charge"*. This pastor has made certain choices as far as society is concerned. In several of the places where he has worked, the central issue for him was to make room, and show respect, for the less fortunate in society. In fact, it involves a choice *"for standing up sincerely and honestly for one's opinion and making one's contribution to the church so that she will take sides. And that is where my intellectual honesty begins: entering into the fight on the basis of arguments."* He draws his inspiration for that from Bonhoeffer and later liberation theologians.

Two others also participate in forms of pastoral work in which social and political choices are virtually unavoidable: industrial ministry and missionary work. When the industrial pastor says that *"the personal God is a God of the people"*, he compares this with the *"tree of justice"*, which sometimes suffers a lot of damage through violence, yet remains standing because the people continue the work of justice. He speaks from his own experience and suffering. One of his brothers, who worked among the poor in the Third World, was killed. He can speak about it in terms of fruitfulness, because he has seen how people can be mobilised when someone, like his brother, dares to devote himself consistently to the poor.

For the three pastors quoted here, it is not a question of abstract justice. A fourth pastor, who is a parish pastor and has a lot of contact with vagrants and refugees in his district, vigorously articulates this. In the bond among vagrants and refugees God is given the name of *"our companion"* and *"our God"*. On the basis of his own history this pastor feels attached to these vagrants and refugees, who are in search of a place of their own. He comes from a large family, as a result of which he could never find a place for himself at home. He finds this place now in solidarity, which is *"a bond from within"*. This becomes a *"home"* for him. At the same time, this pastor finds the idea of rationalising one's association with God hard to swallow. Solidarity has a warm meaning for him. He feels connected with Latin American movements in which belief in God is far more self-evident than in *"our rational West"*.

A female pastor endorses this. She, too, feels attracted to *"the church of the poor"*, for example the Brazilian base communities where she had a work placement for some time. She has a lot of admiration for the way in which precisely the poor support each other in the hope for liberation.

> *Supporting each other by means of particular and common stories is a great strength in their lives. There is a strong belief in people's strength, the feeling of making a stand together. It is never an individual thing. Sometimes they have to take a step backward in order to give others a chance to join the movement.*

The God of the covenant

The two pastors who spend a lot of time on biblical exegesis and Jewish literature preferably speak of God as the *"God of the Covenant"*. One of them refrains from speaking of God as a person, or as the

God of the people, but can speak in terms of God's loyalty to the covenant with people. In using these terms he avoids words like *"old"* and *"new"* covenant, as if with Jesus everything connected with God became radically different and new: *"Many things led up to Jesus"*. The second pastor feels that his ministry is dominated by the idea of entering into a covenant with the people with whom he associates as a pastor.

> *That is the way it goes with God: we stand together.*

The God of humanity

One of the pastors experiences God as a person, but then as part of a large whole.

> *I do not now have the impression that God is paying attention to me personally every day. As far as that is concerned I rather feel included in a larger group, humanity in the broadest sense, which God is looking after. God is personally looking after each human being.*

The term *"our God"* is meant here in a wider sense than are expressions like the God of *"our group"*. This pastor owes much to the ecumenical experience he had already gained at the time of his theological study. He was brought up with the idea that life is a life in harmony with the whole of reality. Divisions have no place in it. Another pastor has many international contacts and, because of his work as a school catechist, was obliged to gain a more in-depth knowledge of world religions. Therefore with him there was a broadening from *"our God"* to *"the God of all people"*.

> *Therefore it is interesting for me that the present Pope meets the leaders of the world religions in prayer to the one God. That is the way in which I like to meet people from different countries and religions.*

He has contact with refugees of various religious backgrounds.

God of the cosmos

Nowhere is there any explicit reference to the *"God of the cosmos"* or the *"God of the universe"*. However, there are hints in those interviews where metaphors are used that are derived from nature, especially the one referring to God as a *"current"*.

> *I sometimes feel closely bound up with the universe, and then I feel the bond of everything in and with God, and then I speak of a 'current' or 'connecting power'.*

In that sense God is addressed by some as the *"God of all life"* or *"the breath that inspires everything."*

Summary

On the one hand there is a tendency among a number of pastors to address God as "You". On the other, there is a considerable group of pastors who speak about God in terms of "our God", an expression that can be understood in various ways: as an experience during the communal liturgy, as the God of humans or, especially, as the God of the poor or the God of the covenant. The God of the cosmos is only spoken of indirectly. From their ways of addressing God it appears where and how the pastors experience God's presence. A number of pastors ask critical questions regarding all these places assigned to God. They are aware of the fact that one cannot simply speak of *"our"* God, without making an effort towards enabling more people to join and to celebrate in the community. Among the latter group the second type of reflection can be discerned most clearly.

2. *Locating the Spirit: where is the Spirit?*

The Spirit can reveal itself in individuals or in the community, in people, and in cosmic reality. With some pastors the place of the Spirit seems to be continually shifting: now in the individual person, then in others, and then in the community, or in the cosmos.

The spiritual power in individuals

The Spirit is described by a number of pastors as a power that activates, vitalises and inspires people to set out on their journey and to take risks. It is a kind of *"lubricant"* that keeps one going, it is the *"soft breeze"* in which the mild side of God makes itself felt and through which people are also given strength to be able to cope in vulnerable situations. It is the *"sustaining power that vitalises me and keeps me going"* or the *"fire of enthusiasm, of fervour as an inner power"*. For these pastors, believing in the spiritual power as it reveals itself in people is bound up with believing in these people as made in God's image.

If you believe that grand image which the story of Creation offers us, you associate with people very carefully, for they are made in God's image. So far I have been able to believe in that, perhaps also because I have not yet experienced any really horrible things in connection with people. But what if I had? In my ministry I base myself on that and I see human beings, those who are ill, hurt, or divorced, the sociable and the troublesome, as people who carry God's spirit in them.

A special place for the Spirit's manifestation is in prophetic figures. Here the central point is the spiritual power that was active in Jesus and in many prophets before him, and which is now recognisable in people around us.

I mean the Spirit by whose inspiration Jesus acted and by whose inspiration, among others, the great prophets acted—especially the farmer's son, Amos. He is really something of an inspiration to me. I recognise that spirit in 'unassuming' people who persevere in spite of everything. I find that Spirit in Muhammad, a man who has worked in the steel industry for thirty years, a man whose back is broken, a thoroughly honest man who will not betray his comrades, although they do not behave very nicely towards him. Every night at home, and every morning on his bicycle, this man prays to Allah that he may stick it out in the factory for another few years. He lives with Allah in a very serene way without the slightest trace of fundamentalism or anything like that. He prays for those one hundred colleagues of his who are to be sacked this week.

This Spirit is also a spiritual power of resistance against injustice, a spirit that can make one angry about the injustices that occur. It is this spiritual power which makes people offer resistance again and again, also against the threatening rigidity of the institute of the church.

The spiritual power in the community

A number of interviews contain references to the spiritual power in the community. A few pastors understand *"community"* in a narrow sense: the power of the Spirit can be felt in the love of one human being towards another, in the personal relationship of affection, in a personal bond, and in the latter's erotic expression.

Several pastors who speak about spiritual power are mainly fascinated by what they experience in their community. They speak of people's *"creativity and enthusiasm"*, the *"diversity in the abilities"* of people who inspire and stimulate each other to remain active. This is what makes the community alive and fascinating. Spiritual power helps to create space and an atmosphere of compassion. Thus it becomes a binding element. Some pastors are quite envious of the power of the first Christian community as described in Acts 2. One of the pastors is strongly fascinated by the power of people living under oppression in Latin America, and she hopes to come across something similar here in the West, in her own environment, and to be able to give further support to it.

> *It is a liberating current, which produces creativity, frees people from galling bonds and gives them the strength to persevere. That is the bond which exists among people who are on their way.*

Creative power in earthly reality

A small number of pastors who speak of the spiritual power in people also say something about the creative power in the cosmos, the whole earthly reality. Earlier we have already had occasion to quote a pastor who speaks of the *"dynamic principle"* in reality, which is understood to be the creative power of the divine. Someone else speaks of *"God's breath"*, which pervades everything and brings it to life, while yet another pastor uses the image of the *"vital current into which the whole of reality, including myself, is drawn"*. It is a *"flowing movement of grace"* which creates room for all living things.

Summary

There is a lot of attention among the pastors for the spiritual power of individuals, as well as in groups and movements. In this respect, the diversity of spiritual powers is a fascinating datum, especially when it is translated into working for the cause of justice. The pastors who, more than others, have a critical attitude towards the experienceable character of the Spirit, also exhibit more strongly the second form of reflection.

3. *The church as a community of faith*

In chapter 4 we described the context of the church. There we were able to see how pastors are looking for ways of finding the space to live and work within the institute of the church. Following up on that we can now ask: where do they find places for communal expression of spirituality? In spite of, and apart from, the pain that many of them experience due to the church, many of them intimate that there are several places to be found within the community of the church where they can express their spirituality. A few of them do not share this opinion.

The broad liturgical community

The pastors indicate in a variety of ways that, as ministers, for example during the weekend celebrations, they can find a proper place for their own religious experience in the communal celebration. This depends, however, on the extent to which a bond is created during the celebration.

There has to be a direct link between the celebration and life as it is shared at other moments throughout the week. Several pastors who put a lot of time and energy into personal ministry observe that they experience a lot in liturgy precisely because of the pastoral contacts outside the liturgical context.

According to other pastors, an atmosphere of mutual solidarity has to be created during the celebration as a result of the way in which a dialogue is brought about in the liturgy. A parish pastor who does quite a lot of work with young families relates enthusiastically how he feels sustained by praying and singing together alternately. That is why another pastor only occasionally experiences a living moment in the parish-liturgy during the weekend. When one *"really succeeds in celebrating together"*, there is an experience of *"being included, sustained in one's own experience of the faith"*.

In a small group

Many pastors experience celebrations in small groups as an opportunity for expressing their own religious feelings. Parish pastors mention the celebrations during the week with a limited group; female pastors refer to the richness to be found in celebrations specifically for women; a catechist has positive experiences with celebrations within the framework of adult catechesis. The small group offers opportunities for creatively giving a content of one's own to the proceedings, apart from the fact that it offers a lot of room for peace and quiet.

Special celebrations

Parish pastors speak appreciatively about the liturgy of the funeral service and of the marriage service, where there is an opportunity to pay attention to people's concrete life situations. For the pastors themselves it often provides a wider experience than might be possible in the Sunday liturgy, because people try to be sincerely engaged in such special moments. One pastoral worker looks upon the celebration with young people as an important event, because contemporary language is spoken there. Some parish pastors take enormous pleasure in ordinary prayer services where they are not bound by formal liturgical regulations. Another pastor talks enthusiastically about the annual hour of adoration on Holy Thursday. Special celebrations in a small circle, such as extreme unction or a Communion celebration in the family circle, can sometimes be memorable.

Presiding at, and participating in, the liturgy

Some pastors point out that they consider it important not to have to preside at the liturgy themselves all the time, and to have the opportunity to take part in celebrations led by others. For one parish-priest it is important to be simply one of the faithful. He thinks it is a good thing occasionally to attend and experience a liturgy in a quite different role.

> Sometimes it is nice to attend the liturgy presided at by a colleague. In that case I am often obliged to go to another parish church. For there I will not run into people who want something from me.

Looking for a proper place when one never presides at the liturgy

For a few pastors who never or seldom preside at the liturgy it is sometimes difficult to find a suitable place of their own. For those who are married it is important to find such a place together with their family. A pastoral worker who used to associate actively with the student church knows that he has to find a place where his children can come more into their own. His heart is with the student church, but at the same time his heart is with the future of his children. Some pastors do not find such a place; they do not really feel at home anywhere. Sometimes it is just for a moment, for example during an ecumenical prayer meeting, that they find such a place.

Liturgy is relative

A few pastors have become more and more convinced that liturgy, in whatever form, is a highly relative matter. Spirituality is not irrevocably bound up with liturgy or praying together.

> I occasionally preside at the liturgy, and I do that in an honest way. Apart from that, however, I simply work from Monday morning to Friday evening. That is the time when things have to happen.

4. *Reflection in and on spirituality*

The pastors who are both critical and creative in dealing with the
church as a place for religious experience pay a lot of attention to
reflection on life and work. Clear choices are made, in which the
experience of possibilities and limitations, of joys and disappointments, is given a prominent place.

It is a striking fact that the second form of reflection is found
comparatively frequently in the experience of the relation to the
church as community. Pastors are obliged by their position within
the church to maintain distance, to think about the significance they
give to the church as a space for spirituality. They have to think
about what actually happens to them when they speak of the church
as community. This has to do with questions concerning developments in ministry and concrete church politics.

5. *Summary of chapter 13*

While a small group have positive feelings about the institute of the
church and its representatives, the majority of the pastors are challenged by their negative experiences with the institute of the church
to look for new ways of doing things. They look for credible ways
of, and places for, expressing their spirituality together with fellow-
believers, among whom are their colleagues. The central issue is to
develop an authentic way of being connected, and of celebrating.
For a number of them this is closely linked to their own role as minister, while for others there does not always have to be such a link.

It appears that a sense of community does not simply arise automatically. A lot has to be done to bring it about. For many pastors
the small circle is an important, if not the most important, place for
this. Liturgy is very important for many of them, whereas for a small
group liturgy has become something relative.

CHAPTER FOURTEEN

THE RITUAL ASPECT

Following our inquiry into the significance of the church as a place
for expressing and experiencing spirituality, this section will deal with
the question of the significance of rites. What significance do sacramental rites have for the pastors? At the same time the question will
be raised whether new, alternative rites are being developed by the
pastors with which to express their spirituality.

Differences in the experience of the sacraments

We can base ourselves on the following survey in which the differences
between the pastors' experiences are manifest.

– A large number of pastors highlight the significance of being
connected with others, no matter which rite is involved.

– Sacramental rites that are mentioned include baptism, marriage,
the Eucharist and extreme unction.

– The Eucharist is mentioned most frequently; for a third of those
interviewed the Eucharist (or the celebration of the Eucharist as experienced by pastors) constitutes an important centre.

– A quarter of the pastors interviewed give a broader significance
and content to the sacraments.

– Nearly a quarter of them is looking for new, alternative rites.
This survey also indicates the structure of this section. First, however, something has to be said, following up on the previous chapter about the communal aspect, about the church in its relation to
the sacraments.

1. *The experience of church and sacraments*

When, in the interviews, the point of discussion is the significance
of rites and, in combination with it, the place of the sacraments of
the church, a number of aspects automatically come up for discussion once again.

The influence of church-political aspects

Many of the pastors point out that the experience of sacraments is influenced negatively by what many of them call *"church-political aspects"*. A large number of female pastoral workers, that is to say, half of the total number of those interviewed, as well as a small number of priests, state, sometimes explicitly, but mostly indirectly, that the sacraments have become the object of power politics on the part of the church.

Since the institute of the church is experienced negatively, various rules, and especially restrictions, with respect to the sacramental rites are also experienced negatively by these pastors.

The question of ordination and authorisation

In the discussion about the significance of the sacraments, both male and female pastoral workers, as well as some priests, raise the question of ordination and the authorisation to preside at sacramental celebrations. A female pastoral worker expresses well what is regularly put forward by both male and female pastoral workers.

> *I am not a priest, which is something I find extremely annoying. In my present situation, in my work, I think, in fact, that I must be ordained. I simply have to be able to preside at the celebration of the Eucharist, also in this church, otherwise I would not be able to do what I am doing now: ministry. Taking into account the way I am working now, it is absurd that I am not allowed certain things.*

Large groups of different people

For many parish pastors it is not at all easy to give a positive significance to ritual during the weekend celebrations, when they are confronted with a large group of churchgoers. Half of the parish pastors would probably agree with what one of them says about this:

> *I do not find it easy to preside at the liturgy on Sundays, because I am often confronted with such a great variety of people. The larger the group, the more difficult it is for me. And the smaller the group, the more easily I can handle things. Yet I do not want to belie my character.*

2. *Strong emphasis on solidarity*

This has already been indicated in the above quotation: small groups offer greater opportunity for solidarity during the celebration of rites.

Two-thirds of the pastors find it important that all those who are assembled around a ritual experience solidarity with each other. When this is not possible, the rite, in whatever form, is empty. This is closely connected with the way in which one is able to give content to one's presiding at the liturgy, and to the link made to one's personal contacts in ministry. The celebration of a rite, such as the Eucharist, has to be a space for the operation of God's spiritual power as expressed in the intense solidarity of people with one another.

By this the pastors indicate that a rite in itself does not yet mean anything. Not until people experience solidarity among themselves, and not until space is created for the operation of God's spiritual power, does something happen. This is the meaning of the statement by several pastors about the sacraments as *"moments of crystallisation"* or *"moments of concentration"* or *"moments of condensation"* in the life cycle of people.

> *Important moments in life, or transitions in life, are celebrated in the sacraments in a more condensed way and, through the signs we erect, concentrated moments of our life are included in God's story with us humans.*

However, it is precisely in this respect that it is important that the connection between living and celebrating be made visible and tangible.

3. *The Eucharist as centre*

For a third of the pastors the Eucharist is central to their religious experience. This may be expressed both in the weekend celebration and in celebrations in smaller contexts. These pastors, each of them in their own way, confirm what is said by one of the parish-priests: *"That is when I feel close to the source"*.

For some pastors, presiding at the celebration of the Eucharist is therefore a high point. It is pre-eminently a prayer for the nearness of, and security with, God. It is a ritual experience of *"being healed and liberated"* by God. For one of them the Eucharistic piety in the

procession and the adoration on Holy Thursday, and always at the
moment after Holy Communion, are precious moments. The element of adoration is something that is essential for him.

*Space is available at such moments for allowing everything to sound forth from
my heart, a moment of profound awareness of Jesus' presence.*

One of the parish-priests describes the concrete meaning of the Eucharist, and especially his presiding at it, for his spiritual experience.

*Celebrating the Eucharist is hardly ever too much for me. I am sometimes ashamed
that there are hardly any limits for me in dealing with it. It will undoubtedly
have something to do with character features: being at the centre of things for a
moment, and having people's attention for a moment. Also: I like touching and
holding something. In my view there is something concrete about the Eucharist,
something you have in your hands, and yet do not really have in your hands.
However, in my view the Eucharist also has something to do with the generosity
of the Most High. God is generous and likes to give freely. In that space, Eucharist
is for me a moment of intimacy, which is shared, and at the same time an amazing moment at which so many different people—different as regards age, culture,
and level of education—are brought together. And I am one of them. I draw quite
directly from a source from which a lot of people draw. The fact that I often celebrate the Eucharist also kept me going in periods of depression or disappointment.
For me it is a medicine, bread for on the way, rather than an expression of 'how
far and how good I am already'. It is relief rather than high point. For me the
Eucharist also has an element of forgiveness. I live rather intensely with the feeling of being dependent on the Merciful One, who is patient. That is badly needed
because of the idealistic and high-flown ideas of what a priest should be. I carry
those ideas with me as inconvenient luggage.*

He adds that he commemorates the day of his ordination rather
than the day when he started his ministry. This means that that day
has preserved a special significance for him. A few other priests point
out, like this priest, that, in the light of the central significance of
the Eucharist, they repeatedly have an important experience relating to the fact that they are ordained ministers. One of them says
that the fact of his ordination demands more from him than would
be the case if he were not ordained: the work is done entirely from
within, more so than if one were not ordained.

A striking fact in connection with the Eucharist as central rite is
the fact that the male and female pastoral workers experience a great
deal during the celebrations of the Word and of Holy Communion,
at which they preside regularly. They experience the celebrations of
the Word and of Holy Communion as the celebration of the Eucharist.

One of them adds that, initially, he was rather sceptical about the services of the Word and of Holy Communion. At that time, he was not yet employed as the only pastor in a nursing home. As soon as he started to preside at the liturgy *"with his people"* almost every weekend, and during special celebrations during the week, his scepticism vanished completely. *"This is where I experience the Eucharist, and that is essential for me."*

4. *Sacraments are relative*

For two-thirds of the pastors the celebration of the Eucharist is not really the central moment in their spiritual experience. For some priests a word of conversation between one human being and another is sometimes a clearer sign of being connected with God. Many pastors say, not only about the Eucharist, but also about all the sacraments of the church, that they are not so important for their own spiritual experience.

> *The word sacramental does not mean very much to me and I do not think that my spirituality has a sacramental dimension, certainly not when the term 'sacramentality' is used to indicate the sacraments of the church.*

According to these pastors, this does not detract from their actual spiritual experience.

> *Certainly at quite different moments I am allowed to experience something of the gracious nearness of the Most High. However, in my opinion, this has hardly anything to do with the sacraments.*

5. *Sacraments are to be understood in a broader sense*

For nearly a third of those interviewed the sacraments should be understood in a broader sense than the usual seven sacraments of the church. Whenever people become connected with each other in faith, and when they give each other signs of this solidarity in the sphere of God's spiritual power, one may speak of a sacramental event. In this sense, there are many sacramental moments, like a good conversation, the sharing of food, sharing each other's lives, and so on. An industrial pastor says that the *"sacramental aspect"* takes place precisely in the solidarity at the workplace. And this happens on weekdays. This broader conception of sacramentality also has something to do with the growing interest these pastors show in the rich significance of symbols for life.

6. *Looking for new, alternative rites*

A number of pastors speak of the significance of new, alternative rites. Among this group are especially those pastors who work in institutions of health care. In personal contact and in communal celebrations they are faced with the task of finding a language which can establish connections, and looking for rites that can mean something in the lives of people who are physically or mentally handicapped. The *"play of the imagination"* is important. Lighting a candle can be very effective in supporting a pastoral talk; the laying on of hands can become a powerful symbol of affirmation and encouragement. Rituals are always somewhat ambiguous and open-ended. It usually involves a fleeting experience.

> *When we find a sign together which is suitable for this moment; this creates space for the experience of brokenness and vulnerability, but also for hope and longing for healing and reconciliation.*

One of the women, whom I have already quoted in previous chapters, has developed a ritual of her own with her children. It is a substitute, because she has not been able to find a home in the church. The ritual is closely bound up with the cycle of the seasons. Moreover, she says something about the power of the laying on of hands.

> *Thus we are often engaged in a physical and natural way, also with the laying on of hands. We learned this when my autistic son was so terrified and unable to talk. Now we always do it spontaneously, at all kinds of occasions, as when somebody is sad, or when there is something wrong. Our hands are very important in our mutual contacts.*

Some female pastoral workers have developed their own rituals for the farewell at the end of a life, or in cases of serious illness. They themselves experience quite a lot through such rituals.

7. *Reflection in and on spirituality*

Reflection is found in the personal experience of the sacraments and especially in the presiding at ritual celebrations. This is apparent from the way pastors speak of their struggle with the sacraments of the church, and their search for authentic rituals in which solidarity is celebrated, particularly within a concrete community. The pastors show that they think about their own experiences, thereby arriving at new choices. This is clearly expressed, for example, in their articulation of the significance of the Eucharist.

Among a number of them the first form of reflection changes over into the second, in which process the confrontation with the context in each of its four aspects (biography, identity, culture and church) plays an important role. For example, reflection on the experience of spirituality leads to several of them explicitly distancing themselves from the significance eucharistic piety used to have for them, or from the significance the authority of the church now attaches to the sacraments. In reflection *on* spirituality, various factors simultaneously play a role in this respect: theological developments, the influence of secularisation on the experience of God's nearness, and developments in the church with respect to ministry, in which especially the role of the minister is at issue. The degree to which reflection *on* spirituality occurs is roughly equal to the level of reflection in connection with the experience of the church.

8. *Summary of chapter 14*

Sacraments are important rites. For a third of those interviewed the Eucharist occupies an important place among these rites. The Eucharist is important for the majority of the priests, but also—in the form of services of the Word and Holy Communion—for a few male and female pastoral workers. In that connection the question of extending the criteria for priesthood is also a point of discussion. The significance of the Eucharist is of special importance to those pastors who experience a personal relationship with Jesus.

For two-thirds of the pastors the Eucharist and other rites are not the be all and end all. Various questions relating to ministry play a role here, and at the same time it is a question of a new development. As soon as people experience solidarity in God's spiritual power, there is room for rites. Concrete contact with people, especially in vulnerable situations, invites them to look for new, alternative, rites.

The pastors who engage in critical discussion with the church and with present-day culture are able to offer new rites through which they themselves also experience quite a lot: at the same time it serves as a ritual expression of their own spirituality. Some of them experience little or nothing in rituals. They find the expression of their spirituality in their work throughout the week.

SUMMARY OF PART 4

In Part 4 two specific aspects marking the framework of the concrete experience of spirituality were studied: the communal aspect,
or the relation to the church as community (chapter 13), and the
ritual aspect, or the relation to the sacraments (chapter 14). With
respect to both aspects we were able to discern a strong development among the pastors. The increasingly critical relation to the
church induces pastors to look for appropriate places for the communal experience of spirituality. A striking fact, in this respect, is
the significance of small, conveniently arranged contexts. Several pastors are critical of words like: *"our God"*. In relation to the ritual
aspect, or the sacraments, a similar critical development can be
observed, namely that several pastors distance themselves from the
customary sacramental moments. They look for ways to give a broader
content to the sacraments. For a comparatively small group, especially priests, the Eucharist is a central moment.

On the whole, the pastors show during the interviews that some
form of reflection is involved *in* their experience of spirituality, while
a third of them also exhibit reflection *on* their spirituality. Because
they often take a certain distance, in order to think about what is
happening in their experience and praxis, this group is critical towards
all the standard forms of expression of spirituality. For some of them
this means a critical revaluation of the traditional forms and contexts in which spirituality is expressed. For others it means taking
leave of all that, and facing the challenge to search for other possible forms of spirituality. These new forms emerge in some of the
interviews, for example in the interest in new symbols that express
a connection with the earth.

PART FIVE

SPIRITUALITY AND MINISTRY

INTRODUCTION

Having described the communal and the ritual aspects, we shall now proceed to give direct attention to ministry in connection with spirituality. The fact that we deal with the relation between spirituality and ministry in a separate section has to do with the fact that the point at issue here has received increasing attention in recent years.

In an inquiry into the spirituality of pastors it is important to study whether and how their spirituality is related to their ministry. In particular, the question may be raised whether these people who, in a way, regard spirituality as their 'area of expertise', speak of their own spirituality in connection with, or apart from, their work. Is their religious experience entirely bound up with their ministry? In other words: is the spirituality of pastors an integral part of their professional attitude? Is it possible that perceptions of what a professional attitude should involve could constitute an obstacle to spirituality?

I shall take 'professional attitude' to mean the systematic and explicit use of sound scientific knowledge, insights, and skills, as well as well-reasoned attitudes, in the exercise of pastoral leadership. In short: a professional pastor knows what he/she is doing and why he/she is doing it. This description is based on the idea that spirituality as an 'attitude' is an integral part of the picture. It will also be clear from all the foregoing that the central point for us is a 'well-reasoned attitude'. The question in this part—Part 5—is whether and how the pastors endorse such a view of professionalism.

The question of the relation between spirituality and ministry is of topical interest in the present development of the church. The question is relevant at various levels:

– The level of church politics, in which the policy with respect to ministry is at issue.

– The level of the discussion about professionalism in the ministry, in which the relation between ministry and spirituality is especially at issue.

– The level of ministerial formation, where all sorts of questions present themselves concerning the necessity and desirability of a specifically spiritual training for prospective ordained ministers.

In this section we shall therefore pay attention to the significance of spirituality in relation to a professional attitude to ministry and vice versa. Is ministry simply an occupation, like all other professional occupations? Is spirituality part of the professional occupation, and if so, how? Is it possible to be a pastor without being able to rely on a specific sort of spirituality? And of what nature is the influence of ministry on the pastor's spirituality?

In order to find answers in the interviews, three aspects will be studied that bear upon the relation between the spirituality of pastors and their ministry.

1. Target conceptions of ministry: What metaphors are used by pastors to describe what they hope to achieve through their ministry?

2. The significance of one's own spirituality for one's target conception of ministry: Does spirituality add something essential, something peculiar, to the pastor's profession? Do the pastors speak of their spirituality as a specific dimension in their professional attitude, and if so, what does this imply? Or is spirituality to be understood as an aspect apart from ministry?

3. The significance of ministry for spirituality: Is the spiritual experience of the pastors nourished and influenced by their ministry?

On the basis of these three aspects we shall be able to formulate some conclusions concerning the relation between professionalism and spirituality.

The structure is as follows: in the first place, a number of key words that are used by the pastors interviewed to indicate the aim of their ministry are described. For each of these descriptions the question will then be posed to what extent spirituality adds a peculiar emphasis to this understanding of ministry and, finally, how the ministry influences the spirituality of these pastors.

CHAPTER FIFTEEN

FIVE TARGET CONCEPTIONS OF MINISTRY

When, in the interviews, the significance and experience of the ministry are discussed, pastors use certain words recurrently. These might be understood as images indicating the meaning and aim ministry. They are not comprehensive definitions of ministry, but rather central aspects from which one can surmise what the pastors regard as important in their work. These central aspects touch the heart of their profession.

Five distinct target conceptions can be identified:
- ministry as the discovery and revelation of God's presence
- ministry as creating a space in which people are given a unique value
- ministry as fulfilling a mediating function
- ministry as liberation
- ministry as protecting and healing

All the pastors offer several of these descriptions, but some lay greater emphasis on the first description, others on the second, et cetera. In our description of the separate aspects, we shall pay attention in every case to those pastors who attach particular importance to that specific aspect.

1. *Revelation of God's presence*

In the case of five of the pastors—four priests and one pastoral worker—a development with respect to their conception of ministry can be observed, in which they are less and less concerned mainly with what people expect of them. More attention is paid to the question of how they can be signs of God's presence for people. Here one might also speak of ministry as 'presence' instead of ministry as 'intervention'. The emphasis is more on presence than on assistance in the sense of effecting solutions. At first, they thought they had to achieve a lot, to offer a lot to the people with whom they became involved as pastors. They had the feeling that a great deal depended on them: building the community of faith, leading groups, and intervening in difficult conflicts. Gradually they came to discover that ministry is not only about taking care of people. People's lives and faith do not really depend on the care and work of the pastor. Rather it is a matter of discovering and recognising that God is present in people's lives. Being present to people with all one's heart can make one into a sign of God's presence.

> *The centre of my ministry has shifted through the years: from acting for the benefit of people, taking care of people, and working at a certain kind of community, towards being a sign, by being truly present. By 'sign' I mean: trying to be a symbol of God's presence, and trying to bring people together, and to connect them to one another.*

One parish pastor describes his ministry as *"a way of being there"*, a *"way of being devoted"*. Others formulate this presence as *"walking part of the way with people"*, *"bestowing on people their own, unique value"* and seeing to it that *"you are there as yourself, and paying attention as such"*. Sometimes the encounter itself is more important than what actually happens or is achieved in the encounter. The emphasis is on the comforting element in ministry: in the presence of a pastor people can feel safe and secure, because the pastor is a sign of God's comforting proximity. However, the fact that the pastor discovers and recognises God in people, also makes him/her into a living invitation, a challenge to his/her fellow-believers to discover God's presence in their own lives.

Professionalism

According to the pastors, this kind of presence requires professional skill. Some formulate this more strongly than others. The pastor who works in a nursing home portrays a professional attitude to ministry as follows: ministry as a sign is not *"simply being there"*. It means hearing what people have to say (even when they lack a language in which to express themselves), offering to them a language which makes connections, being aware of how you speak of God, opening up a familiar space and developing a clear profile, and seeing to it that you are accepted as a colleague next to other social workers and professionals, and on an equal footing with them.

His position as a pastor in a secular social service institution can only be secured gradually. It requires constant critical reflection on developments in health care and in the management of social service institutions, and especially critical reflection on his own position as a pastor within the organisation as a whole. The point is that a pastor must be present in such a way that he becomes really *"visible as a professional, working next to other professionals"*. A pastor must have the skill to see and hear the religiosity in the people with whom s/he associates, and to assign to each of them a place within the institution, but also within the tradition of the faith of which s/he seeks to be an exponent.

In the case of the parish pastor who describes his ministry as a *"way of being there"* and a *"way of being devoted"* the professional attitude emerges in his critical reflection on his position as a pastor in an Old City district where ministry is one of many forces promoting the well-being of the residents. His professional attitude is distinguished from that required in other professions by the need to develop a certain *"open-mindedness"*, with which he seeks to be present as a pastor in the neighbourhood. He becomes a prominent person that people can turn to, although it is not primarily a matter of giving assistance or solving problems. Local residents, both those who have lived there for a long time, and others, such as foreigners and vagrants, run into him in all kinds of places. Sometimes such a place becomes the space for a *"real encounter"* through which people can feel recognised and accepted.

His presence can mean a great deal in that he can help people to experience that one does not always need to solve everything; nor is there anything that one has to do immediately at all costs: some things can always be dealt with at a later stage. This requires of the pastor that s/he is able to understand people, that s/he is well aware of developments in the neighbourhood, that s/he is familiar with the various cultural groups in the neighbourhood, as well as with the world of social assistance, community building, et cetera. In order to make God's presence visible and tangible, s/he has to be *"familiar with the neighbourhood"*, but also well-versed in the tradition of faith so as to be able to place the story of God alongside the stories of people and vice versa: to recognise God's story in the stories of the people of the neighbourhood.

The other three pastors formulate their professional attitude less sharply. This applies especially to a parish pastor who above all wants to be a *"nice and approachable human being"*. For him professional attitude has to do especially with dealing *"tactfully and generously"* with people. In this way, he says, he bestows on *"people their own, unique value"*.

Two others associate a professional attitude with an appropriate recognition of their own limitations and possibilities as pastors. Both of them emphasise the fact that they *"are there as themselves"*—no more, but no less either. One of them indicates this by stating: *"I am allowed to be present. I am allowed to be accepted, and the beautiful thing is that I can accept other people."* However, this requires critical reflection on all the things he actually does, having an eye for what other people can do, and regularly thinking with colleagues about what is, and what is not, being done in his ministry. When you understand your own position sufficiently well, *"you can live your life as an ordinary person. I am not 'bigger' or more 'exclusive' than other believers."*

However, the above statements have nothing whatsoever to do with what is characteristic of a professional ministry. The point at issue here is especially a basic attitude, which enables one to develop a professional attitude. A specific aspect of the ministry is highlighted by the way in which these pastors indicate their own significance as revealing God's presence in the neighbourhood, the district where they work. They have this significance on the basis of a study of the biblical tradition and of a theological reflection on present-day culture. The pastor's own contribution, here, is: showing clearly how and where the voice of God is made to speak in secular culture, and how it becomes manifest in people, when they discover each other as vehicles of God's presence.

The professional attitude of these five pastors is especially elaborated at the level of preaching. Both in liturgical services and in personal encounters in the neighbourhood, or at one's place of work, for instance in health care, God's presence is proclaimed: the fact that God 'transpires' is made tangible and visible.

Three of the pastors are not accustomed to speaking of their ministry in terms of a "professional attitude". A certain apprehension is apparent in their speaking of their target conception of the ministry: a pastor has to be the equal of his fellow-believers as much as possible. Any accentuation of his professional status can create too much distance.

One could ask in this connection whether a sound professionalism could not contribute to an even greater proximity in ministry. This is what one sees in the case of the pastor who works in a nursing home, whom we mentioned first. He works in all sorts of ways to improve his skills with a view to strengthening his position as a pastor within the culture of the institute. This pastor spends a lot of

time on study, personal reflection and fraternal talks. Attention to a
new language is the central point at stake here.

Questions about the significance of a professional attitude are also
connected with the significance of spirituality, and whether or not it
functions as an integral part of a professional attitude. Before describing this, however, we should, at this juncture, discuss another point
connected with it. It concerns the connection between themes in
ministry and themes in the biographies of the pastors (Koot, A.M.,
Zuidberg, G. 1995, pp. 10–17).

Correlation between ministry and biography

Several terms used in the description of ministry are reminiscent of
terms used by the pastors when they speak of important moments
in their life history. Both of the two pastors who were quoted first
have gone through some fundamental crisis, in which it became especially clear to them that the strength of their life does not depend
on achievements. They learned through experience that they do not
"have to deserve" their value and significance. An important term in
this respect is *"being accepted"* and *"being at home"*, or finding a *"home"*.
The more pastors find their own place in life, and are allowed to
know that they are accepted by others, the more they are able to
contribute towards making sure that fellow human beings in the institution, or in the neighbourhood, are allowed to be there just as they
are. The other three pastors point to the connection between their
ministry and their own history by using expressions like *"being accepted"*,
"being taken seriously", or *"I am just an ordinary bloke"*. Both of them,
each in his own way, indicate that their ministry, insofar as it is a
sign of God's presence, is based on their own experience that people, at important moments in their lives, have shown them that they
were allowed to be there for their fellow men, and for God. The
significance of spirituality is understood from that perspective.

The significance of spirituality

A support to professionalism

What strikes one about the description given by this group of pastors of their spirituality in its relation to their ministry, is that their
spirituality supports their ministry. Their pastoral presence is sustained and supported by the belief that they can be a *"sign"* or a
"symbol" of God's presence. The pastor him-/herself is a sign, in that

s/he is, or at least seeks to be, a *"person of God"*. Three of the five pastors point out that, in their personal religious development, they have grown towards a relationship with God, in which, as one of them says, they *"do not have to do so many things any longer, but are increasingly allowed to do things"*. One's development in ministry keeps pace with the development in one's personal religious life: being there as a sign of God's presence does not depend on achievements. It is a matter of giving oneself up to the faith, the hope, that God accepts people. These pastors feel accepted by God and believe that they can be signs for others of the faith that God also accepts them.

Discerning God's presence
A second aspect is connected with this, namely the faith that God allows himself to be known in fellow men and women. These pastors have no obsessive need to *"take"* God to people, for God is present in people. Ministry must be an invitation to recognise that fact. This is a task for pastors themselves, but also for the people they are involved with. So it is not only the pastor who is a sign of God's presence. The people with whom he or she associates are also signs. It is a matter of reciprocity. This holds true for all five pastors.

A flexible image of God
Generally speaking, one finds a flexible image of God among these pastors: the concepts of God are not fixed. God allows himself to be discovered in ever new and surprising ways. Viewed from the perspective of content, this image suggests a mild, accepting and merciful God, who is experienced as a companion.

Dedication and priesthood
One of these pastors describes spirituality, in its connection with ministry, as a form of *"dedication"* or *"being dedicated"*. He is a priest, like three others in this group. For three of the four priests, dedication is closely bound up with their being priests—their ordination. Ministry is a *"way of being there"*. For two of them the religious experience of their ordination adds something peculiar to their being a pastor. This is sometimes formulated in terms of *"more and less"*, in comparison with non-ordained pastors.

> *More is demanded from me because I am ordained. It happens more from within, more so than if you were not ordained. We all have our spirituality and you certainly have to spend some time on it. As ordained priests we have been given a special task to pay attention to that.*

For the pastoral worker dedication is not a way of being there, but the fruit of working steadily at his professionalism, of which spirituality as a professional attitude is an integral part. One of the four priests resembles him in this respect. He lays less emphasis on his ordination, and more on his professional attitude as a basis for his presence.

Significance of the Eucharist

In the experience of the four priests, presiding at the celebration of the Eucharist is an important resource in their ministry. Two of them state this explicitly as follows: *"That is where I feel close to the source. I experience a lot through it"*. One of them says that presiding at the celebration of the Eucharist is an *"expression of the presence of God"*, by which he indicates that he, as a minister, becomes even more explicitly a *"sign"* himself. A third pastor likes to celebrate the Eucharist together with a small group every morning, as an important *"moment of prayer"*, adding that he does not consider himself someone who *"merely performs the ritual of the mass"*. It is not so much he himself that is at the centre of attention, but the group that is celebrating together. For a fourth priest the Eucharist is especially an experience of *"the divine dimension in people"*.

Of particular interest here is the experience of the pastor who works in a nursing home, whom we have already mentioned before. He is a pastoral worker. In chapter 14 we cited him as one of those who experience the services of the Word and of Holy Communion as celebrations of the Eucharist. The regular celebration of these services together with patients has thus become an important Eucharistic experience for him. For him this Eucharistic moment is an indispensable resource in his ministry.

Strong correlation between spirituality and professionalism

In the case of all of the five pastors there appears to be a strong connection between spirituality and ministry. Even so, one cannot say of all of them that there is no separation or distinction whatsoever between their ministry and their spirituality. One of the priests says that he would have an equally strong development in his spirituality, even if he were not a pastor. His spirituality does not coincide with his being a pastor. This may have to do with the fact that he is a member of a religious order. His spirituality is expressed, among other things, in his regular participation in liturgies at which he does not preside. He experiences this as a major difference between him and his colleagues who never celebrate a liturgy without presiding at it themselves. This pastor suggests that his spirituality could exist apart from his ministry, however much he maintains that his spirituality is a condition for his being a good pastor. He wonders whether his spirituality is also strongly influenced by his ministry. It is worth quoting him on this.

> *It is part of my spirituality to carry out my profession as well as possible and to keep myself well-equipped as far as my profession is concerned. It is not something apart from my profession. If spirituality has to do with praying, then it is connected with my work and with my profession. While praying, I think of the people with whom I am involved professionally. In between, during and after my work, I bring people before God in prayer. I sometimes wonder how my attitude in ministry influences my own piety, in the sense that being a pastor influences my faith.*

He adds that it may have something to do with his character—the type of person he is: he is someone who allows himself to be affected by what he experiences in his profession. He experiences presiding at the liturgy in particular as a highly personal, religious event. Presiding at the liturgy influences the development of this minister's personal spirituality. This also applies to the other four pastors. It applies equally to their pastoral contacts with people in the neighbourhood: encounters with people who are experienced as signs of God's presence call for esteem and respect, but also invite the pastor to deepen his own spirituality: it is an invitation to grow in the faith that God reveals himself in day-to-day life.

Interaction between ministry and spirituality

Among this group of pastors an interaction can be discerned between ministry and spirituality. One of them, who has hardly any special experience in connection with his ordination, says that he hopes to be present for people in such a way that they are better able to find evidence of God. He himself, however, is continually being touched by these people with whom he associates. It contributes to his growth, so that perhaps those people may in turn be given a chance to grow through him. Another pastor indicates that meeting people fascinates him as a pastor and sometimes moves him so deeply that he is brought to his true self through them. This is expressed even more strongly by a pastoral worker who experiences the patients in the nursing home, with all their handicaps, as rich people who nourish him in his own faith in a God who accepts people whole-heartedly and gratuitously. At the same time the confrontation with the secular world is a challenge for him to pay a lot of attention to his own religious development. It is, however, a matter of a spirituality which takes this secular reality seriously and which, from its own resources, tries to find an answer to the questions raised by secularisation.

In the case of the parish pastor who speaks of *"dedication"*, the influence of his ministry on his spirituality emerges from what he relates about his experience—which occasionally surprises him, and catches him unawares—that Christ allows himself to be known through strangers. He uses words which, as we have already indicated in chapter 7, are strongly reminiscent of what Vincentius à Paulo says about the presence of the poor: "Les pauvres, ce sont le Christ" (Van Geene 1995).

We have already seen in previous chapters how this pastor had himself continually been searching for a place to be *"at home"*. He recognises something of himself in the strangers and vagrants in search of a place of their own. He finds his home in the *"house of God"*, by which he means God's love in which he is allowed to feel secure. It is to be wondered whether this pastor has any room for a private life. His life is so closely bound up with his ministry that he continually runs the risk of being swamped with work. The risk of this is less in the case of the other four: one of them is protected by his religious community, a second has had a serious warning as far as his health is concerned, and has learned from it to take account of his own limitations.

The pastoral worker is challenged by his family, particularly by his children, to divide his attention, while at the same time he feels a deep desire to make more room, and allow more time, for his personal religious development. The fourth pastor has learned constantly to evaluate his ministry, and to make regular appointments with colleagues. Thus he is guarding against biting off more than he can chew.

Summary

We may conclude that, when pastors experience their ministry in terms of presence, and see signs of God's presence in it, there is a strong link between ministry and spirituality. Personal religious experience is an important precondition contributing to an effective ministry.

Pastors experience their own spirituality in some of the things they do as part of their ministry, such as presiding at celebrations of the Eucharist. This applies to priests who find an important resource for themselves in presiding at the celebration of the Eucharist, while one of them finds this also in participation in the Eucharist. It also holds true for the pastoral worker who experiences the services of the Word and Holy Communion as an important Eucharistic resource.

For one of the five pastors his spirituality could also exist without his being a pastor by profession.

The interaction between ministry and spirituality also involves the risk of an excessive interwovenness of personal life and work. We see this to a great degree in one of the five, while the other four are trying to deal with this in such a way as to safeguard themselves against the dangers.

The term 'professional attitude' is used with care with respect to this group, not only because three of the five pastors do not use the term, but also because in three of the five an awareness of professional development can not be clearly demonstrated. The pastoral worker, and the priest who speaks of dedication, display the most strongly developed professional attitude. They are also among those who attach a lot of importance to reflection.

2. *Ministry as creating space*

A key phrase used by eight of the pastors, and which does not differ very much from the preceding, is *"creating space"*. Ministry can come to function as a space in which people feel welcome. This is expressed by expressions like esteem and respect for people, accepting people as they are, and being faithful to what is unique about people. Putting it negatively: a pastor should not moralise by adopting an attitude of *"I know best, and I will tell you how it must be done"*. Ministry is not a form of assistance imposed from outside.

This aspect of ministry requires patience, learning how to see what is unique in people, being loyal in the encounter with people, and fighting for space when existing policies do not allow sufficient space. This finds concrete expression in efforts to create space for women, for young people, and for other groups that are given few opportunities within the church. For the pastors who experience this central aspect in their ministry, the concept of *"justice"* is at the centre of attention.

Ministry as creating space is described in active terms by these pastors: a pastor may be expected to be prepared to fight for a structure in which people are taken seriously.

Professionalism

Such active efforts to give shape to one's ministry require a professional attitude, which may be different for every occasion, depending on the specific group the pastor is involved with at a particular time. A number of examples follow.

One of these pastors is actively involved with, and attentive to, young people. He is convinced that they are given too little space of their own within the traditional church community. That is why he is working at a policy within which the young people themselves can become active. It may be expected of him as a pastor that he knows the world of young people, while at the same time he has to be trained in the skill of perpetually negotiating with policy-making bodies in the parish, for space is something which must be deliberately created.

One female pastor knows from her own experience how little space there is for women, particularly women who occupy a marginal position socially and economically. She regards her ministry as a way of fighting alongside these women to find and create a space in which they can assert their rights. Ministry means trying to create a space in which people's autonomy can grow. This presupposes a clear social orientation, as well as psychological and sociological knowledge. One has to have knowledge of the possibilities people have to stand up for themselves and achieve autonomy, and this must be translated into ministry.

One parish priest considers it his principal task to have attention for the church's social welfare work. He thinks it important that there should be growing attention within the parish for developments in the neighbourhood: how can we make sure that the problems of the underprivileged in the neighbourhood become part of the church's agenda? However, this does not only mean that the *"parish should do something for the poor"*. Rather it is a matter of allowing them to speak for themselves and to mean something for others as people who are able to stand up for themselves. This pastor points out that he has oriented himself thoroughly in the area of social dynamics, and that he has acquired the skills necessary for teaching people how to take their life in their own hands.

A missionary worker hopes, above all, that his ministry will become the space in which all sorts of people will learn how to take small steps themselves—steps that have to do with striving for more justice. He does not have to do it for the people with whom he is involved, or in their stead. Rather, he regards it as his task to create space for people by providing information, and creating awareness of the political and economic realities in which those people live. This pastor indicates what may be the common denominator for this kind of ministry: providing space as a form of doing justice to individuals as well as to groups.

Ministry is characterised, especially among the parish pastors, by the twofold position that pastors occupy: they are close to the group that needs space, and they are close to the centre, where policy is made. A professional attitude can be most clearly discerned in two of the eight pastors. They actually use the term 'professionalism' quite easily in discussing their ministry. Both of them are also capable of looking at their professionalism, their skills and their attitudes, at some distance. They have a businesslike attitude to their work, while realising that they are also deeply touched by the people they encounter. Two others give the impression that they have developed a professional attitude to a reasonable degree.

Four of the eight pastors exhibit less development in this area. They are the ones who also indicate that they have no, or hardly any, opportunities for bringing themselves to study and reflect. Their self-reflection is also at a lower level of development.

Correlation between ministry and biography

Among these eight pastors a connection is also discernible between central themes in their ministry, and themes in their personal life histories. Interest in young people is bound up with their own experience in the past that it was difficult to get a response from parents; for the female pastor, working for justice has a basis in her experience that a considerable struggle is required to find a place which one can call one's own; for the city pastor, his efforts at involving people in the struggle to make their parish responsive to developments in the neighbourhood is connected with his own discovery that the focus should no longer be on the church, but on the coming of the Kingdom of God. He has experienced personally what it means to live and work in a secular environment. The missionary worker points to the connection between his work and his own life history, by relating how he always had to struggle to find his own way amidst the tensions at home. It was only step by step that he succeeded in finding his on way.

A clear connection can also be discerned in the case of the other four pastors. However, in the above description we restricted ourselves to the first four, who display the most strongly developed professional attitude.

The significance of spirituality for the ministry

Overflow

When we consider the significance of spirituality for this target conception of ministry, we see that the pastors' spirituality spills over, as it were, into their ministry. In the case of those pastors who describe their ministry by means of the metaphor of a *"sign of God's presence"* we saw that their spirituality supported their professionalism; here we see spirituality *"flowing on"* and *"spilling over"* into ministry. There is a difference of emphasis from the preceding group. Spirituality in relation to ministry is described in such expressions as: *"respect for people, and for God's proximity"; "loyalty"; "the central point is the Kingdom of God, which is coming"; "we should not stand in God's way"*, et cetera. The pastors use these terms to indicate that they want to be *"employees of God"*, so that *"God can transpire"*. Respect for people goes together with respect for the Holy One.

Ministry is profoundly bound up with the pastor's own faith in being known by God. Put differently: the pastor's own religious experience of security with God flows on, and spills over, into a form of ministry in which other people are offered the space necessary for finding security.

Vulnerable spirituality also flows over

One of the parish pastors is engaged, both in his ministry and in his spirituality, in a continuous fight *"against despondency"*. He uses this term, not only to refer to the fight against a negative atmosphere among people in his parish, but also to denote his own struggle to attain the assurance that he is positively accepted by his fellows and, ultimately, by God. The tension in his dealings with God spills over into the tension involved in his ministry.

Another parish pastor struggles with the tension in her life between security and challenge. In her ministry she seeks to give every person she encounters a feeling of security, but at the same time she feels a permanent restlessness about this: people also have to get moving. Her ministry, as an effort to create space, is permanently under great stress. It springs from her faith in God: there, too, there is a tension between wishing to be secure, and the restlessness of calling and mission: *"I have to get down to work!"*

Constant interaction between spirituality and ministry

This last pastor also points out that there is a constant interaction between ministry and spirituality. However, it is also clear that this interaction involves tension. Three other pastors also feel this. The restlessness involved in trying to create space in their own lives is reflected in the restlessness of a ministry aimed at creating space for other people.

One gets the impression that those pastors who were described in the previous part as indicating that they have found few forms of expression for their spirituality, also find little rest in their ministry. They express an ardent desire to find such space and rest. This coincides with a feeling that much still needs to be done to further their professionalism as pastors. It strikes one that these pastors do not assign a definite place to reflection, let alone self-reflection, in their lives. One gets the impression that their ability to have personal space at their disposal leaves something to be desired.

Other interviews breathe a more peaceful atmosphere. A number of pastors have developed a conception of a ministry with more space of its own. It is closely bound up with the space they seek to create in their own spirituality. This is expressed, for example, in a phrase like *"I am invited to remain with myself"*, for *"I feel enclosed in the space of the Great Mother"*. Typically, this pastor does not wish to let her spirituality merge completely into *"political commitment"*. Her ministry does have a strong political orientation, but political ministry is not the only thing for her. She finds the word *"encounter"* a richer word in connection with the ministry, because she feels sustained *"by a profound relationship with things divine"* as a kind of *"undercurrent"*. *"The relationship with things divine is the all-important thing in my own life"*. At the same time, however, that is the most difficult task: where can she really find a place, a space to be at home, in a religious sense? This yearning for a place to feel at home, and for knowing oneself accepted, is reflected in her ministry where, together with others, she is trying to create a space in which people are accepted both personally and socio-politically.

A peculiar difference emerges within this group of pastors: the two pastors who have developed their professional attitude most strongly, differ with respect to the development of their spirituality. The female pastor shows a strong religious development, whereas the missionary worker shows less explicit attention to this. The missionary worker prefers to formulate the space he seeks to create in his life and work in terms of remaining in good health. In his interview he does not speak explicitly of a spirituality of his own. He speaks in secular terms. He tends to articulate religious space primarily as *"looking for the peace and quiet necessary for a healthy way of working"*. This care for his private life does not fully coincide with his concern for his work.

> *Spirituality and a professionalism are interwoven and related to one another, but not always and everywhere. For I also sometimes go for a walk in order to find peace and quiet, for the sake of my health. I want to equip myself to keep my body in good health and to be able to cope with my work. It is necessary to create the space one needs to be able to put things in their proper context and perspective.*

It seems that this pastor's professional attitude could stand in the way of the development of his spirituality: sometimes his work is so much characterised by a businesslike attitude that the question arises whether a religious attitude can still be given an integral place in it. At the same time this pastor speaks of a *"faith in small steps"*, by which he indicates that his personal faith in God does affect his work.

The influence of ministry on spirituality

There is some interaction between spirituality and ministry. In this group, however, it would seem that the influence of spirituality on ministry is stronger than vice versa. At the same time one might say that the tensions involved in ministry continually affect the tensions experienced in personal life. The reverse is also true: pastors who succeed in finding moments of peace and quiet, and creating space in their own lives, manage to do the same in their ministry.

Summary

We may conclude that the target conception of ministry, which is expressed in the metaphor of space, gives an active connotation to ministry. In the case of this conception, as with the previous conception of ministry as presence, there is a relation between themes in the pastors' biographies and themes in their ministry.

A strong connection is discernable between ministry and spirituality: *"My work is permeated with my spirituality"*. The pastors' own religious experiences have their impact through the central emphases in their ministry. At the same time it becomes clear that ministry either has a direct influence on religious experience, or at least enhances the desire to find more room for oneself to develop one's spirituality.

This conception of ministry is marked by tension: ministry can either become a source of peace and quiet, or of restlessness. One's own spirituality is also characterised by tension.

Two of the pastors endure the tension between security and challenge in a balanced way, while among three others one finds a permanent restlessness in both areas: in ministry, and in their personal life.

Being actively engaged in ministry in the attempt to create space for others depends, even under the most favourable conditions, on the pastors' own experiences of peace and quiet, and the space they have created in their own lives. When this is lacking, ministry itself becomes a permanent source of restlessness.

As far as the development of a professional attitude is concerned, we find that two of the eight pastors show a strong development in this area, while two others show a reasonable development. The other four have a weakly developed professional attitude. Three of them attach great importance to reflection.

3. *Ministry as mediation*

This target conception of ministry, found among seven of the pastors, is expressed in various terms that point to mediation.

– Mediation between different groups in the church community among whom the pastor wishes to engender dialogue. The pastor is the one who represents dialogue within the pluriformity of currents.

– Mediation between the stories of people and the story of God, or between the little stories and the great story. The pastor is the interpreter, the one who offers the words for recognition and orientation.

– Mediation between the interests of the environment as a living space, and the people who might be able to serve those interests, or between the neighbourhood and the church. Here the pastor functions as an advocate.

What is at stake here is mediation between tradition and culture, neighbourhood and church.

Professionalism

Ministry as a connecting function between various groups and currents requires knowledge of, and insight into, possibilities of communication between people, and skills in the domain of relationships. Moreover, it is important for a pastor to be well-versed in hermeneutics: the art of getting the conversation between culture and tradition going and of making connections between the Story and the stories of people. In this respect there are clear differences among pastors, for example among the two parish pastors who are the most articulate in their interviews. One of them firmly believes that he has much skill in dealing with differences. A concrete example is his competence in relating the religious experience of the present generation to the ancient rituals of the church. He has learned how to establish a positive connection between the ancient tradition and present-day culture. He has knowledge of the old, but also of the new. Another parish pastor struggles to avoid the pitfalls involved in trying to fulfil a mediating function. He says of himself that he is a *"man of harmony"*, but he finds it very difficult to accept that large groups of people have become estranged from the church and from the faith. This pastor lacks a strong sensitivity to present-day culture. Study and the development of pastoral skills are also weak aspects in his armour.

> *It is so difficult to convey a little love for Jesus, for his sacrament and for the whole of the church. I regard this as a defeat, for I thought that I would be more successful in bringing about connections and making people enthusiastic.*

The two pastors who indicate that the core of their ministry lies in the connection between life and celebration or reflection, are both well-versed in dealing with the secularised world. They see it as raising many questions with regard to the attempt to give a contemporary

content to spirituality, for what can be the meaning of faith in God
if it is not intrinsically bound up with day-to-day reality? For one
pastor this implies the permanent task to ask essential questions
about everything people want to undertake and experience. The
second pastor sees it as his task to connect everyday life in a
credible way with its ritual expression, wherever life is celebrated in
all kinds of moments. Both pay a lot of attention to study and reading. The pastor who defines the mediating function as an interpretation of the little stories and the great Story, takes a great interest
in biblical exegesis. Spending time on biblical stories enables him to
look critically at the stories of contemporary people. One also comes
across this focus among some of the pastors mentioned earlier. The
pastors who characterise themselves as advocates give the impression
that they are well informed about the interests that they want to
promote. For some of them it is urban culture and art, for others
it is a good insight into neighbourhood problems and the chances
of co-operation with other disciplines. The two pastors who spend
a lot of time on bible study and exegesis emerge as the ones who
have developed their professional attitude most strongly. They spend
a lot of time on study and reflection. They are the ones who also
engage in a constructive, critical discussion with culture. Besides, one
of them shows a strong development in the area of individual pastoral counselling. Both of them pay a lot of attention to the development of their spirituality.

In the case of four of these seven pastors the professional development may be called reasonable. One of the seven may be characterised as weak in this respect. The same picture emerges with
regard to the pastors' religious development.

Correlation between ministry and biography

This connection is also found among these seven pastors. For one
pastor his skill to be a mediating figure in a diverse community of
faith is related to the experience that there have been several moments
in his own life history that have required such mediation. For another
pastor there is a connection between his function of connecting life
and celebration on the one hand, and on the other, the fact that
from childhood onwards he has been granted that connection quite
naturally. For a third pastor the connection is apparent in the fact
that since his youth he has been fascinated by urban culture. In the

case of a fourth pastor, who gives a lot of attention to poverty in the neighbourhood, there is a connection with his childhood experiences of a visible and tangible gap between poor and rich. As a child in a poor family he was aware of a great distance from wealthier families and the church.

Significance of spirituality for ministry

One pastor speaks of his own spirituality in the same way that he speaks of his ministry. He points out that his spirituality is strongly oriented on the kind of dialogue that he recognises, *inter alia*, in the figure of Abraham. Spirituality spills over into his ministry as an *"undercurrent"*, which carries him in everything he does, in his personal life as well as in his ministry.

> *If spirituality is separated from the position which I take in this society, and from my ministry, then I shall be left hanging in the air.*

Another parish pastor is absorbed by his work, while also deriving a lot of pleasure and joy from it. His is a genial and kind-hearted ministry, but one gets the impression that a less profound spirituality is reflected in a less developed professional attitude. The spirituality of the two pastors who characterise themselves as *"advocates"*, exhibits especially the features of reliability and standing up for that which they consider important in their work. Precisely because of the fact that they want to stand up strongly for what they consider important in their lives, they are able to become advocates in their ministry. It requires, as one of them says, *"loyalty to myself and to my conviction"*. Attention to urban culture is based on respect for those people who cannot enjoy or profit from it. This pastor says that it is for him a question of a *"driving force"* within himself, and that his spirituality is an important motivational factor in his work. Both pastors indicate that their spirituality is an integral part of their work, but both also say that they keep trying to create more space for themselves and for their own religious experience. In fact they refuse to accept a wholly functional spirituality. The significance of the spirituality of the two pastors who work at the connection between living and celebrating, or life and reflection, is expressed in terms that strongly indicate God's proximity: *"the earth is filled with mercy"*, or: *"spirituality means dealing in a special, reflective way with everything that exists"*—a reference to a definition of spirituality by Otger Steggink

(Steggink 1985). There is a difference, however, between the two as far as the functional character of spirituality is concerned. In one of them a fusion between ministry and spirituality can be observed.

> *Spirituality can never be separated from my profession. It has become blended into it in one way or another. It truly belongs to it. The two are tied together, especially in the person I am, and in that which I emanate towards others. It also has to do with the question of whether I feel at ease.*

The other pastor exhibits a clearer distinction. However much his spirituality may be an essential condition for a healthy ministry, he still needs separate moments to stay healthy as a person, irrespective of his work. He gives special attention to prayer and reflection, as well as certain forms of ascesis, like sobriety, awareness in dealing with the environment, and critical consumer behaviour.

The spirituality of the pastor who considers his professional attitude in terms of mediating between the stories of people and the story of God, displays a strong biblical orientation. As a result he has learned better to understand the stories that he encounters in his work here and now. Another pastor indicates this even more explicitly.

> *It strikes me that I can remember very small occurrences, stories, and sayings. Apparently I pondered over them and interpreted them and then they began to influence my spirituality. They include biblical stories. These have influenced my life story.*

The first pastor indicates that he likes to regard himself as a *"person who mediates between God and people"* in the sense that, whenever it is necessary, he is allowed to offer words that can establish links between God's story and us. It is in his respect for people that he finds an important basis for exercising his mediating function as a pastor. Respect for people's stories is linked to respect for the Story.

Influence of ministry on spirituality

It is not immediately clear to what extent ministry has an influence on religious experience. This is not articulated in precise terms.

However, the fact that two pastors indicate that they run the risk of being swamped by their work, and that they feel a great need to create more space for their own religious experience, provides a hint: ministry has an influence on the desire for spirituality. This does not yet say anything about the actual content of spirituality. With another pastor one sees how developments in ministry, and conflicts with the institution of the church, continually oblige him deliberately to look for space for himself, so as to remain a healthy human being.

Summary

In the process of giving shape to ministry as mediation, a professional attitude has to do especially with insight into possibilities in the domain of relationships, and with hermeneutic skills as a basis for the discussion between tradition and culture.

The spirituality of pastors clearly influences their ministry. Substantial attention to religious development is reflected in the substantial content given to the ministry. A spirituality with weak content effects a ministry with weak content. This group of pastors has more to say about the integration of ministry and spirituality than about the influence of ministry on spirituality. They indicate how they try to be themselves in their ministry. *"The attitude I have towards my job is the same as that which also determines my existence."* It is the experience of being accepted as a person.

For at least four of the seven pastors a functional spirituality is not sufficient. They retain the desire to give more personal content to their spirituality.

As far as the development of a professional attitude is concerned, two of the seven pastors clearly stand out. The others show less development in this respect. The two pastors that stand out in this respect also attach a lot of importance to reflection.

4. *Ministry as liberation*

Five of the pastors understand ministry in terms of liberating people, that is to say: creating inner freedom in people; fighting against socio-economic injustice; enhancing people's ability to stand up for themselves so that they can free themselves from oppressive systems; creating space for living and believing, through a learning process; and preparing people to always see new possibilities.

Professionalism

For some pastors a professional attitude has to do with the skill of seeing through everyday reality, discovering connections as a result of which one is able to *"put things into perspective"*, and to create space. People have to be able to breathe. For an industrial pastor this means that he has to make a thorough study of the socio-economic system; he is also particularly interested in the inner selves of people who have made, and are still making, socially important choices. For a parish pastor professionalism means working at close relationships with colleagues and fellow-believers for the purpose of gaining a space of one's own inside the church. This means learning to recognise new opportunities to make people aware of their social position, and of their opportunities for development. For a fourth pastor the essence of his work as a catechist consists in teaching adults to gain insight into relations, concepts, and stories from the tradition, so as to help them acquire a more independent position as believers. Finally, for a female pastor ministry involves the competence to unite people around opportunities that they discover together, in order become freer as human beings.

Two of them show a strong development in their professional attitude: the industrial pastor and the parish pastor who is mainly engaged in creating inner freedom in people. During the interviews they point out that they have learned how to view their work detachedly, and how to retain an inner freedom in doing so. They attach a lot of importance to reflection. The other three show a less marked development in their professionalism. Reflection also plays a less important role for them.

Correlation between ministry and biography

All five pastors indicate during the interviews that they have had to work for freedom in their own lives. For some this was a process in their personal life, for others it involved a struggle within societal and ecclesial institutions. For all five the emphasis is on faithfulness to their own integrity.

Influence of spirituality on ministry and vice versa

All five pastors have gone through a development in their own life, which they define as a process of becoming religiously free. In the case of three of them this is explicitly brought out in what they tell about themselves. With the two others it can be read between the lines. For these five pastors spirituality is closely bound up with their ministry. Mention is made of a strong interaction between the two.

In his fight for freedom within the institution of the church, one of the parish priests has discovered that his spirituality is closely related to his ability to assert himself. That is his basis for engendering the ability in people to stand up for themselves. And this work itself is a source of spirituality. He notices that work and personal life mutually influence each other and are sometimes subject to mutual tensions.

> *It is a matter of looking for a balance of work and life. There is a certain tension between the two. It is possible that my work is once again affirmed in my spirituality and in the way of co-operating with others, as well as the other way around.*

One of them has some reservations about the intermingling of work and spirituality. He says that there is certainly a close bond between ministry and spirituality, but that they remain distinct matters. They can never merge completely into one another. When a person does not fully coincide with his/her work, this may be a sign that s/he has acquired a sound spirituality and attitude to life.

> *Spirituality also goes a little deeper: sometimes you have to restrain yourself in your work, so as not to succumb to it completely. For me that is what it means to deal with reality in a professional manner.*

One could also interpret this precisely as indicating that spirituality is an intrinsic part of this pastor's professional attitude: the religious aspect prevents him from being swamped by his pastoral responsibilities! One gets the impression that for him a sound division between work and personal life is what provides breathing space. That is certainly important, precisely with a view to helping others to recover their breath.

An interesting contribution comes from the industrial pastor, who says that he has been fighting for years for recognition of a diversity of spiritual styles in the religious order of which he is a member. Not everybody necessarily has to be engrossed in mystical texts all the time. For him spirituality does not depend on being preoccupied with texts.

> *In the complaint of people who are exploited socially and economically I hear what I have to do. I have to let myself be touched by that harsh reality, and thus I am purified. In this way ministry becomes for me a work involving heart and soul. It strikes at my very soul.*

A little further on in the interview he relates how some of his colleagues sometimes seem to regard the work he does as an industrial pastor as of little religious significance. His reaction to that is: *"When you cannot share bread with each other during the week, you should ask yourself whether you can really do it justifiably on a Sunday."* From the interview with this pastor one gets the impression that he has developed a strong foundation of his own as a result of which he is capable of coping with these tensions in his ministry. Also: what he says about spirituality on Sundays and during the week is closely related to the religious, mystical content he gives to what he experiences in people. It is thus not a question of tension between mysticism and action. Rather the point at issue is: where do experiences occur and how are they processed? It is clear that for this group of pastors there is a permanent interaction between spirituality and ministry, and that precisely in that respect true skill is required in order to preserve a living space of one's own.

Summary

We may conclude that among the pastors who put forward liberation as the key word in their ministry, ministry and spirituality mutually influence one another. There is no spirituality apart from their work, although one of them has important reservations on this score: *"As long as the person of the pastor is not wholly absorbed in work".* Apart from this there can be no ministry without a spirituality which is thoroughly integrated into it.

Themes in the pastors' ministry reflect themes in their personal life histories and religious experience. For some this is closely bound up with the theme of hope.

The development of a professional attitude is strongly present in two of them, while in the other three there is less developed in this area. One notices, further, the considerable efforts required to pin down this development. The first two pastors also have the ability to view their professional attitude with some detachment. They attach a lot of importance to reflection, which fulfils a function with respect to the development of both their spirituality and their ministry.

5. *Ministry as protecting and healing*

Five of the pastors can be considered under this heading. In their ministry these pastors are especially involved with vulnerable people. This context determines the way in which they give shape to their ministry. This conception of ministry borders on the first one (ministry as presence), but here the emphasis lies more on ways of dealing with people's broken existence. The brokenness and contingency of existence demand a ministerial presence marked by tenderness and compassion; such a ministry seeks to encourage people to be what they can become as human beings. It is matter of loyalty to people in their vulnerability, of associating with people on a daily basis in their ordinary day-to-day concerns, and of working so that people may experience healing.

Professionalism

Two of these pastors work in a hospital setting, one in a psychiatric ward, the other in a nursing ward. Both of them have had to pay a lot of attention to determining their identity in a secularised environment, in which so many different disciplines pride themselves on their professionalism. This has meant that they have had to think critically about their position, and about the kind of space they create so as to be recognisable to the patients. One of them has already been quoted before, in the chapter about secularisation, where he spoke about the importance of the language which has to be developed all over again in order to make oneself understood as a pastor, and in order to learn to understand what patients have to say. It means, among other things, looking for rituals that may mark out a new space for religious experience. The other pastor points out that his ministry is especially concerned with the whole human being, the patient as a whole person. For both of them professionalism also has to do with their being aware of the fact that they are men.

One of the three other pastors defines his professional attitude as *"the clarification of my position vis-à-vis the other person"*. In other words: having a perception of the nature of the relation between himself as a pastor and the person with whom he associates in that capacity. One cannot begin to mean something for people until one has a proper perception of that. For a female parish pastor professionalism means first of all *"having a proper knowledge of the boundaries, knowing what I can handle as a pastor and what is beyond me"*.

Three of these five pastors exhibit a strong professional development, while in the case of the others such a development is less clearly observable. The first three also intimate that they are capable of considering this topic with some detachment, and dealing with it uninhibitedly. They are also the ones who spend a lot of time on study and reflection.

Correlation between ministry and biography

With all five pastors the theme of *"being protected"* or *"being healed"* runs like a golden thread through their personal life histories. One pastor experienced this concretely during a period of deep crisis, in which the crucial point was whether there were people who were prepared to shield and protect her. For another pastor it was the experience of a profound conflict, in which the feeling of being rejected caused deep wounds. The warm-hearted proximity of people and the loyalty of a therapist meant for him: being protected and healed. The personal lives of these pastors are marked by the same basic experience: the gratuitousness of life.

Strong interaction between spirituality and ministry

A strong interaction is apparent in the case of four of the five pastors. In their case it is almost impossible to speak of two distinct aspects: when they speak of the influence of spirituality on ministry, they are already also saying something about the influence of ministry on spirituality.

In concrete terms, this interaction can be portrayed as follows. The spirituality of the pastors in health care takes the form of a ministry that seeks to *"protect humanity"*: every human being has her or his own story, and that is important. The point at issue is how this concrete human being can be protected against destructive chaos and fear. For the pastor who works in psychiatry there is a strong connection between standing over against the Unnameable, Ineffable God, and the experience of the destruction of life. The very encounter with destruction is a confrontation and encounter with a God of whom he very much wants to believe that he is the Protector. Thus there is a constant interaction between ministry and spirituality.

> *If I am to exercise my profession properly, and also achieve a distinct profile— i.e. be a pastor as the concrete human being that I am, while continuing to stand where I stand—then I shall urgently require spirituality. But it also works the other way around: my profession has an influence on my own emotional experience, my own relation towards the Unnameable One. It is a matter of my being susceptible, and also present in a creative way.*

A strong interaction is also evident in the case of the pastor who works in a nursing home. He describes the relation between ministry and spirituality as filled with tension: tension between professional and competent action on the one hand, and on the other, knowing that one has a vocation. He sees himself as someone who has been called to proclaim the gospel in his own peculiar way. That may sometimes appear strange in a world of professionals. Wherever there is brokenness, the pastor represents healing, but then healing in the sense of being accepted by God. According to this pastor, if you take away spirituality, you take away this tension. At the same time the ministry constantly necessitates a religious development of one's own, so as to be able to fulfil one's own specific calling. For the three other pastors the core of their spirituality is described in Isaiah's words about the Anointed One: *"He will not break a bruised reed"* (Is. 42,3). It involves a decision never to write people off—a decision which is strengthened through respect and patience. For a female pastor, speaking of God as the *"bosom of compassion"* is important. For her this has everything to do with accepting the boundaries and contingencies of her own existence. She admits that she has to be professional as a pastor, but at the same time she is aware of her own limitations and her vulnerability. This is an important insight arising from her spirituality. This will be recognisable to another pastor who depicts the interaction between ministry and spirituality as follows.

> *I am increasingly aware of how one thing does not suffice without another. My spirituality demands of me that I enhance my professional attitude. And my professional attitude is in constant need of spirituality. I have always regarded professionalism as the clarification of the nature of my existence vis-à-vis the other person: relativising myself, knowing that my own emotions play a part, as do my own interests, my wish to be more important than the other person whose presence may be threatening. All this requires knowledge of my academic discipline. If I had to point to the core of my spirituality in its interconnection with my professional attitude, I would refer to the phrase: not breaking the bruised reed. This is only possible insofar as I am thoroughly in touch with myself.*

Four of the five pastors look upon their spirituality as being strongly connected and integrated with their pastoral profession. With all four of them, however, one notices that they are continually looking for separate, appropriate moments for their religious experience. There is a permanent tension between the ministry, which claims them entirely, and their quest for separate moments of prayer or reflection.

For one of the five a strong connection between ministry and spirituality is not necessary. Her spirituality persists even when her pastoral work ceases.

> *I am carried along by my own, personal current, so to speak. It does of course run through my work. However, I think that I would move along the same current, even if I did other work. Perhaps my spirituality would be of a slightly different nature in that case. However, spirituality is necessary first of all for being a healthy and sincere human being. I think that the word 'pastoral' in connection with spirituality is an addition. In the first place, you are a human being and you need spirituality for that. If you are a pastor, this also has an influence, but it is not the ministry which determines my spirituality first of all.*

Summary

Through frequent contact with vulnerable people, ministry comes to be understood in terms of protecting and healing.

The experience of boundaries and contingencies calls for an attitude of tenderness and compassion.

Professional attitude consists especially in determining one's identity in a secularised culture, and one's position vis-à-vis vulnerable people, as well as having a sound knowledge of one's own limitations. In three of the five pastors this kind of professional attitude is developed quite strongly; reflection plays an important role in this.

We can conclude that among these five pastors there is a strong interaction between themes from their personal biographies, and the concrete content they give to their ministry.

In the case of four of them there is a strong interaction between ministry and spirituality, and all of them continue to experience tension in their desire not to identify themselves completely with their work as a pastor.

For one of the five pastors the reciprocity of ministry and spirituality is always subject to review. She feels that she could develop an equally sound spirituality quite apart from her ministry.

In our study of the relation between spirituality and ministry we started from a distinction between five different target conceptions of ministry, as they emerge from the interviews. From the concrete content given to these target conceptions of ministry it becomes clear what significance the pastors attach to professionalism. From this it is also apparent that central themes in ministry tend to reflect central themes in the personal biographies of the pastors interviewed. Important life experiences are reflected in the aspects that strongly determine one's ministry.

A similar point can be made about the relation between spirituality and ministry: there is a strong correlation between the two. This correlation manifests itself in various ways.
- The spirituality of pastors plays a supporting role.
- Spirituality spills over into ministry.
- Spirituality is developed on an equal footing with ministry.
- Spirituality functions as a support from within.
- The degree to which ministry is militant corresponds to the militancy of the spirituality of the pastors concerned.

The influence of spirituality on ministry can also manifest itself in a negative way: uncertainty and tension in one's personal faith can spill over into one's ministry, so that the latter also becomes uncertain and tense. The movement can also be reversed: a restless ministry results in a restless spirituality. However, in the interviews where mention is made of a great restlessness, it seems to originate in the person: restlessness in personal life leads to restlessness in the ministry.

In the preceding part—Part 3, chapters 9, 10 and 11—we have already seen that for nearly half of the pastors their expression of spirituality coincides with their functioning as pastors: the pastors say prayers when presiding at some event, and the subject of prayer and reflection is for the most part the pastors' work and everything connected with it. This applies even more clearly to the practical, ethical aspect: almost two-thirds of the pastors indicate that their concrete commitment largely coincides with the effort put into their work. For the others—i.e. for just over half of the pastors—their expression of spirituality does not entirely coincide with their ministry. These pastors also have attention for individual prayer and reflection. For two of the pastors their spirituality would persist in equal measure, regardless of whether they were pastors or not.

The vast majority of the pastors point out that their ministry has an influence on the content they give to their spirituality. Presiding at the liturgy, and preaching, play a major role in this. Exceptions to this are the pastors who display a strong social involvement. Among a third of the pastors it is apparent that their work has come to determine their entire personal life. This lack of distance between ministry and private life constitutes a great risk.

Generally speaking, it may be concluded that spirituality is an integral part of professionalism. Of importance in this respect is the discovery, applying to a number of those interviewed, that a professional attitude with a highly distinct profile, tends to go together with a strongly developed spirituality. The reverse also applies: a ministry characterised by a professional attitude with a less distinct profile, goes together with a form of spirituality with a less distinct profile.

With respect to the group of pastors who display a highly distinct profile in this area, it may be concluded that this group attaches a lot of importance to reflection. Here a strong resemblance can be discerned with those, mentioned in previous parts, who attach great importance to reflection. They are capable of dealing critically with their own belief in God, and with their relation to Jesus and the Spirit. They have learned how to work at potential ways of their own to express their spirituality. They can distance themselves from it and deal with it critically.

One cannot conclude on the basis of the pastors' conceptions of professionalism that it involves any kind of obstruction to the development of spirituality. One pastor has some reservations here: a markedly businesslike approach characterises his ministry; this might create the impression that, in his experience, spirituality can detract from *"giving a proper professional content to ministry"*. At the same time, however, one notices in this pastor how much his faith in God, and especially his hope in God, determines his work: it is a matter of *"believing in small steps that are worth taking"*. On the whole, it would appear, not only that professionalism does not obstruct spirituality, but also that a less developed professional attitude often goes together with a less developed spirituality.

PART SIX

EVALUATION AND ASSESSMENT

INTRODUCTION

As indicated in the general introduction, one of the central findings emerging from the research of the Catholic University of Nijmegen, namely that a lot of pastors do not experience their spirituality as a separate attitude, served as the occasion for our study of the spirituality of pastors. Many pastors speak of spirituality in close connection with their ministry. At the same time, very little emerged about the concrete content of spirituality among the pastors who intimate that they no longer feel at ease in traditional forms of ministry. Therefore, the following question arose: what does a contemporary spirituality look like? And what is the nature of the correlation between this spirituality and conceptions of pastoral ministry?

I shall not go into the theological aspects in detail. I gladly leave this to Frans Haarsma, in his afterword.

CHAPTER SIXTEEN

EVALUATION

What are the results of our inquiry into the contemporary spirituality of pastors? We arrived at seven central conclusions.
1. The spirituality of pastors is a pastoral spirituality.
2. Spirituality is developed in relation to the context.
3. There is a critical relation of tension between spirituality and the church.
4. Spirituality is this-worldly.
5. Reflection in and on spirituality is an important factor in the development of spirituality.
6. Spirituality is dynamic.
7. Spirituality is non-professional.

Our description of these seven central findings will be concluded with a few practical conclusions regarding the education and training of pastors.

1. *Pastoral spirituality*

The majority of the pastors speak of their spiritual praxis—prayer, reflection and commitment—in close connection with attitudes and choices in their pastoral activity. Few pastors are able to experience these three moments apart from their pastoral practice, or wish to do so. This correlation can be established both with respect to the content of spiritual practice, and on the basis of the places and moments at which pastors engage in such practice.

The content of spiritual practice

The descriptions in chapters 9, 10 and 11 suggest that the pastors experience their prayer, reflection and commitment as oriented mainly on the content of their pastoral practice and their role as ministers. Prayer and reflection are moments that prepare, initiate, supervise, support and round off pastoral practice. The pastors express this most clearly in the case of reflection: reflection predominantly takes the form of reflection on work. Commitment, too, is for most pastors an integral aspect of their ministry.

When we look at the aspects that concern the content of the relation to God, Jesus and the Spirit, then there, too, a strong correlation with ministry becomes apparent. The relational terms of faith, hope and love, as well as the various metaphors, are given a content that corresponds to the way the pastors experience their pastoral contacts and their presiding at the liturgy. This is again confirmed in the way the pastors speak of the communal aspect and the significance of ritual.

In Part 5 we concluded with respect to the five target conceptions of ministry that the pastors understand spirituality as a support in ministry, as an element which spills over into ministry, as an aspect merged into ministry, or as a confirming moment in the ministry. The whole area displays a strong interrelatedness between spirituality and pastoral action. Spirituality has a strong influence on pastoral action. The reverse is less evident, but for the majority of the pastors the bond between ministry and spirituality manifests itself so strongly that spirituality cannot be separated from ministry. Here it becomes clear that spirituality is not only an important condition for ministry—in the experience of the pastors it is in fact bereft of any content whatsoever apart from actual pastoral action. This conclusion applies to most of the pastors interviewed.

Time and place

For most of the pastors prayer, reflection and commitment coincide partly or completely with the times and places of pastoral practice. This is most striking with respect to prayer: most pastors only pray when they preside at, or take part in, the liturgy. It applies to a lesser extent to the moments of reflection and commitment, but there, too, the same general tendency is apparent. This is connected with the yearning of many of the pastors for shared forms of expressing spirituality. It is difficult for many of them to bring themselves to prayer, reflection and commitment, either collectively or in the family circle. One needs other people if anything is to come of it. For a lot of them this means, in concrete terms, that they find the only viable modes of expressing spirituality in the context of their ministry, in which they meet others with whom they can give shape to their spirituality.

The description of the factors that may have an influence on prayer, reflection and commitment (chapter 12) shows a similar strong interrelatedness. This is expressed most pointedly in those statements that refer to a correlation between the fact that prayer and reflection occur rarely, and the specific nature of the ministry: there is insufficient room for it, because the pastoral agenda is overloaded. Likewise, for the majority of the pastors the content of study is closely tied to pastoral interests. This first finding of our inquiry confirms one of the general tendencies that had emerged from the Nijmegen research.

There is a relatively small group among the pastors interviewed for whom the interrelatedness of spirituality and ministry plays a less important role. Some pastors say that they would give the same amount of attention to prayer, reflection and commitment, even if they were not pastors.

With a relatively small group of pastors attention to communal forms of prayer, reflection and commitment goes together with a need for moments apart from work. Some of them are able to find their own way in this. Others look for friends or colleagues outside their work situation with whom they can pray or practise reflection together. At the same time, however, we were able to conclude that for these pastors reflection is also chiefly concerned with the content of their work.

For a small group it is important that their commitment, including their lifestyle development, is first of all given shape in their personal life. For an equally small group of pastors it is possible 'simply' to enjoy study, as well as other ways of regaining energy after much exertion, without any relation to their work. This is especially striking in the case of some of the pastors who display a contemplative attitude in their interviews. This latter group do feel the need for a communal setting (reading, praying, reflecting, studying and celebrating together), but they also feel a need to be alone, and to experience moments of silence. They bring themselves to personal reflection by keeping a diary and describing their own experiences.

2. Relation with the context

In our descriptions we have consistently related the content of spirituality to its context. What does the relation to the context teach us with respect to contemporary spirituality?

Let us review once again the influence of the various aspects of the context on the development of spirituality. Our descriptions have shown that pastors deal with their context in a variety of ways. They may adopt an open and receptive attitude, or a closed, defensive one; the conflict is engaged in actively, or avoided; there is, or is not, an awareness of the complexity of the context. These different attitudes, each in its own way, influence the development of spirituality. Let us look once more at the first three aspects of the context (biography, identity and culture) in order to study their impact on the development of spirituality. In each case I shall give a few examples, on the basis of my earlier descriptions, that characterise the relation to the context. The fourth aspect, the ecclesial context, is left out of consideration for the moment. This aspect will be discussed in greater detail under our third conclusion.

The influence of the biographical context on spirituality

An open attitude with respect to one's own life history implies that one does not have to deny or hide anything about one's own development in life. In the case of several pastors such an open attitude appears to form the basis for an open development of their spirituality. There is, for example, a striking connection between the way in which pastors deal with their memories of the presence or absence of an atmosphere of security and challenge in the parental environment on the one hand, and on the other, the way in which they handle the tension between security and challenge in their use of metaphors for God. An open attitude has the advantage that it can break through all sorts of forced dispositions. A closed attitude either appears to form an obstruction, or to give a rather forced character to one's dealings with God. In any case, a closed attitude with respect to one's own roots does not become a resource for the development of a free and emancipated relation to God.

A second set of attitudes concerns the facing or avoidance of conflict. Our study shows that the pastors who responded actively to the conflict with their parents (father or mother, or both), or with others (persons or institutions), during a later phase in their lives, have grown in their relation to God, by coming to see God as someone over against whom one stands as a free and responsible human being. God becomes the one who calls, and who challenges, and to whose call one can respond freely. We also saw that those pastors who did not experience their parental environment positively as a home, and who continued to struggle with this, have never stopped searching for a new home, in which God, as the one who gives space and security, offers an important foundation. Both these aspects can be regarded as a sign that the conflict has been faced up to. In the case of those pastors who did not face up to the conflict, there seems to be little room for learning how to deal with God in a mature, open-minded way. One has the impression that for these pastors God also has a less clear identity.

We described the third set of attitudes in terms of attention to the complexity of the context. Attention to the complexity of one's own biography means that both the positive and the negative sides, the clear and the obscure aspects, the challenging and the less challenging moments in one's own life history, are accepted as real. A clear example is the way in which the pastors have dealt with the influence of their parents, whether critically or more mildly. This can provide a basis for their dealing with God *and* with human beings in an authentic way, which involves not hiding anything. This also emerged clearly with respect to the experience of moral values and ideals. The tension between good and less good, between positive and negative, is allowed to exist, without having to be argued into oblivion. The result of such attention to complexity is that one's spirituality can also acquire a more complex character.

The influence of personal identity on spirituality

The pastors who have learned to take the possibilities and limitations of their identity into account, speak of their spirituality as something typical of themselves: *"That is how I am. That is what my relation to God looks like"*.

One also notices this in their way of dealing with male and female aspects. A more closed attitude appears to offer less room for the development of a pluriform, flexible spirituality.

In the case of several pastors, certain inner conflicts in the development of their identity, in which moments of crisis have played an important role, have a significant influence on the content they give to their relation to God and their fellow human beings. They have struggled to be assured that they are accepted in their relation to God and to their fellow human beings, and only thus have they developed new strength in that relationship. By contrast, those who avoided the conflict in their own development appear, as a result of this, to have less breathing space in their dealings with God and with their fellow human beings.

For several pastors, attention to the complexity of their own person, and insight into both their possibilities and their limitations, as well as the tension between light and darker sides, provide a basis for seeing the development of their spirituality as a multifaceted process. There is much room for surprise, and especially for putting things into the proper perspective. These pastors can recognise themselves in the words taken from a Eucharistic prayer by Huub Oosterhuis, which is somewhat controversial within the church: *"Thou who knowest what goes on in people's minds in terms of hope, desire, joy, and uncertainty."* Happiness and tragedy, joy and sorrow, as well as experiences of possibilities and limitations, are typical of contemporary spirituality. With other pastors, who have difficulties in accepting the complexity of their own person, there is less room for a complex spirituality.

Influence of the cultural context on spirituality

The pastors who are able to allow the cultural context, especially the consequences of secularisation, to enter into their life and work, declare themselves open to all sorts of critical questions with respect to their association with God, Jesus and the Spirit. This acts as an important catalyst for the use of metaphors for God, dealing critically with language, and looking for new contexts in a society that is falling apart into fragments. A more closed attitude towards cultural developments allows less critical reflection on one's own faith and work. A more defensive attitude is also apparent in such cases.

In the description of the relation to the cultural context it becomes clear that the pastors who respond to modern culture as a challenge, allow their spirituality to be under permanent criticism, and look for their own answers to, among other things, the negative aspects of secularisation. This is shown, *inter alia,* in the fact that metaphors are permanently put into perspective, as well as in the growing attention to mystery. The pastors struggle with language and try to give a new content to rites and sacraments.

Attention to diverse cultural developments, in which the aspects of alienation and challenge go together, creates room for a multifaceted spirituality, which is open to questions—both those that can be answered easily, and those that cannot be answered in any simple, straightforward manner. A remarkable category in this respect is the pastors who are very attentive to mystery and, at the same time, to God's proximity.

Less attention to the complexity of culture reflects less attention to the complexity of spirituality.

An important conclusion can be formulated as follows

The material which our study provides indicates in several respects that, where pastors have grown in their spirituality, this is especially the result of experiences of crisis, situations of conflict, and moments at which they could not see a way forward. It is especially the aspects of the relation to the context that required the making of new choices. Those choices could only be made in creative and critical response to the context. At the same time the pastors carry with them a number of achievements from their personal histories which, in their experience, require a contemporary articulation.

We may conclude that those who have learned consciously and actively to confront their context, tend to show a clear development in their spirituality. This applies both to the content, and to the way in which they try to capture it in language.

At the same time we can conclude that an open-minded yet critical development of a contemporary spirituality allows one to perceive the positive and negative aspects, the challenging and alienating sides, of the context.

The strongest development can be observed in just over a third of the pastors interviewed. Some of them indicate that certain situations have compelled them to search for themselves. They were forced by crisis experiences to make new choices, to review long-standing decisions, and to reformulate their convictions. They were all but forced to enter into a confrontation with their context. These are also the very persons who point out that their perception of the context has changed, and has been clarified, as a result of developments in their spirituality. They appear to deal with the context in an open-minded yet critical manner. Among the others, just under two-thirds, the development is less far-reaching. These pastors' perception of the development of their spirituality is less acute than that of the first group. The same applies to their perception of the context.

3. *A tension-filled relation with the church*

It was stated, both in chapter 4 and in chapter 13, that a large number of pastors have a critical, tension-filled relation with the church, insofar as the latter is understood as an institution.

We concluded that only a small group spontaneously speak of the church in a positive way. These are the pastors who are greatly indebted to certain representatives of the institution of the church, who have been a major support, particularly during periods of crisis. We also concluded that many of the pastors are looking for ways to determine their position with regard to the institution of the church in such a way as to leave sufficient room for themselves, and for their ministry, to be able to live and work within the church. As a result of this they also become less vulnerable. For a number of them this has meant growth towards either a more tolerant, or a more businesslike, relation to the church.

The way in which concrete content is given to spirituality in prayer, reflection and practical action is strongly marked by this tension-filled relation to the church. Many pastors point out that they are looking to smaller contexts for possibilities of giving shape to prayer, liturgy and the celebration of sacramental rites, especially in solidarity with people. A lot of tension becomes apparent as soon as the significance and position of the ministry is spoken of. This comes to the fore most clearly in questions about who is allowed to preside at which celebrations. This has several consequences, for example for the appreciation of the Eucharist as a source of nourishment and an expression of spirituality.

In most of the interviews the church as an institution is only very loosely connected, if at all, with the significance of Jesus. Jesus is experienced as the way, and as a companion on the journey of the broad movement of people who wish to travel the road of the gospel. Jesus as an example and an ideal manifests himself particularly in the communion which becomes manifest in the liturgy, but also, and for some pastors especially, in mutual solidarity among people. Some of them add that much will also have to be done in order to arrive at real communion. Some of them also accord a mystical significance to the encounter with the poor: that is where the Risen Christ becomes visible.

The conflicts with the institution of the church, and the relativising of the societal significance of the church, are connected with a growing interest among the pastors in the spiritual strength manifested in concrete solidarity among people. Instead of an established institution, the church becomes a process, carried by the diversity and pluriformity of spiritual gifts. With respect to conceptions of morality, there is a development towards values such as authenticity, credible action and integrity.

On the whole, we may conclude that contemporary spirituality may indeed be called an ecclesial spirituality, provided that church is understood primarily as a movement and community of faith.

Another striking fact is that no great difference can be observed between ordained and non-ordained pastors with respect to the development of spirituality. Throughout the interviews, priests, as well as male and female pastoral workers, speak in a similar style and language about their experience of the relationship with things divine. The same struggle can also be discerned in the ways that they deal with their context. A relatively small group of priests form an exception, in that they attach a central significance to the Eucharist. At the same time one can observe, precisely among some male and female pastoral workers, a growing interest in Eucharistic celebrations in the form of the services of the Word and Holy Communion. Surveying the whole group of pastors, however, it is clear that the attitude with respect to the sacraments, especially the Eucharist, is strongly determined by the debate on ministry.

Finally, we may conclude that a broad tendency is observable, which can be described, in my own words, as *"dedication"*. Dedication is a broader concept than *"ordination"*. For just over a third of the pastors interviewed, whether ordained or non-ordained, it is increasingly a matter of dedication to secular reality.

Relating the second conclusion (about the relation to the context) to this third conclusion (the relation to the ecclesial context), we may infer that the development of contemporary forms of spirituality among the pastors depends on their relation to the context rather than on the fact of their having been ordained or not. In connection with this it is possible to observe a further differentiation between women and men, and between pastors who have, and those who do not have, a life partner. The social contexts in which the pastors work also appear to have much influence. For the time being, we can conclude that pastors who work in secular institutions or in some form of social ministry, are more challenged to work at a contemporary form of spirituality. This development is also discernible among a few parish pastors. This is closely connected with the way in which they entered into interaction with the ecclesial context. Apart from this, it is characteristic for a number of female pastors that they feel challenged as women in ministry to try and give a new content to spirituality and ministry.

4. Attention to earthly things and to mystery

Contemporary spirituality, as an expression of the relation to God, Jesus and the Spirit, contains a number of inseparable elements. There is a constant tension between the experience of the proximity of mystery on the one hand, and on the other, the overwhelming realisation that mystery is beyond any human experience, and even shatters it. Speaking of God goes together with being silent about God. All metaphors are relative, and the intersignatory use, as well as the loss, of all metaphors stands out clearly.

An important element is the interest in humanity. A spirituality, which is not about respect for things human, is empty and lacks direction. On the one hand, God is spoken of in strongly human terms. On the other hand, one notices that the pastors struggle with the hidden God, especially where they run up against impenetrable boundaries.

One is struck by the fact that the pastors address God mainly in personal terms as soon as they lead the liturgical prayers, while a lot of them otherwise speak of God in less personal, cosmic metaphors. Here we come across two aspects that seem to contradict one another: on the one hand, God increasingly becomes a *"You"*, while on the other, there is a growing interest in the use of impersonal metaphors.

An important development in contemporary spirituality is the fact that in the relation to Jesus, any interest in christological titles has disappeared almost completely. Jesus is an example, a companion, and an embodiment of ideals. The Lord, the Risen One and the Son of God are only mentioned by a few. For them, these titles refer to the mystical presence of the Risen One among the poor, and the hope that our life may grow towards greater simplicity, thus reflecting the transparent presence of God in Jesus.

With respect to the Spirit, it is notable that pastors no longer speak of the Holy Spirit as one of the persons of the Trinity, but rather as the spiritual strength manifested in the pluriformity of creation.

5. *Reflection in and on spirituality*

In the general introduction I distinguished between two forms of reflection: reflection *in*, and reflection *on*, spirituality. The first form of reflection is accomplished in and during prayer, in contemplation, and in practical action. During prayer, contemplation, and reflective action, the pastors are engaged in reasoning processes; they arrive at choices, evaluate these choices, and discover who they are and what they are like. The second form is the first made more explicit, and is accomplished more at a distance from actual praxis. Reflection on spirituality involves critical thinking on the part of the pastors about that which occurs in their experience and in their actions. Thus they arrive at a critical evaluation of what their spirituality actually amounts to. This second form of reflection is, as it were, reflection consciously engaged in; it takes place as a result of certain developments that influence prayer, reflection or action from within or without. One could also say: it is precisely an active relation to the context that invites one to engage in the second form of reflection. In the above description of our second conclusion a brief indication of this has already been given. However, it could be useful to review the results emerging from a number of the sections of our study once more. At the end of some of the sections dealing with the symbolic and experiential dimension, in Part 2 and Part 3, we asked ourselves how pastors reflect in and on their spirituality.

The general tendency seems to be that the pastors show some form of reflection *in* their spiritual experience. In speaking of how they experience their relation to God, the pastors are aware of the fact that, whether in experience or in action, they are continually observing, feeling, seeing and hearing, and that they carry a pattern of images within themselves that influences them in their prayer, reflection and action. In prayer, reflection and commitment, various reasoning processes are involved by which the pastors arrive at conclusions concerning whether or not to continue along the road they have chosen in prayer or reflection. One can sense from, among other things, their way of speaking about their own feelings and experiences whether they feel happy, vulnerable, searching, self-assured or insecure, and how they make choices and form an opinion about them. Reflection in the first sense is found in all the pastors. On the basis of this form of reflection it becomes apparent how pastors view themselves as spiritual beings: *"That is how I am"*, or *"That is how things usually go for me"*.

The second form, reflection *on* spirituality, appears to be less self-evidently present. This form of reflection can be clearly observed in the case of those pastors who explicitly take the time, and create the space, to think about developments that call for a critical scrutiny of their life and work, as well as new choices to be made while travelling on a road the direction of which cannot be predicted in advance. Reflection on spirituality takes place whenever pastors explicitly pose the question of the significance of their life history, and its influence on their association with God and the content they give to their ministry; or when they inquire how they can give a clear response to the far-reaching influence of secularisation on church and ministry. The second form of reflection is most clearly discernible among those pastors who have had to give certain discordant moments a clear place in their lives. This applies, for example, to those who feel challenged to take a look at their own possibilities and limitations once again. This means that they explicitly look for opportunities to distance themselves from actual events momentarily, and to reflect critically on what is happening in their spirituality. Thus they come to an assessment of the road they have travelled. In the process they are increasingly enabled to perceive new prospects and possibilities, but also the tragedy of failure, the pain of ideals that have not been realised, and the shortcomings in the goals they have set for themselves. At the same time one can sense the joy and gratitude of those pastors who speak of new opportunities in life, and of the discovery of new vistas in their ministry.

In the light of all the foregoing, we may perhaps speak of a sort of continuum in the area of reflection: on this continuum the pastors move from the first towards the second form of reflection. Just over a third of the pastors reach the farthest end of this continuum. On the whole, they can be recognised by their habit of continually correcting the language that they use, and by their wish to give an adequate content to the terms used in their description of their spirituality. Prominent in this respect are the pastors who work in secular institutions, female pastors, pastors whose ministry displays a conscious social and political orientation, and a few parish-pastors who have experienced conflict with the institution of the church, and have made their own choices.

We may conclude that the pastors who exhibit both forms of reflection, also display a more integral spirituality than do the others. Their spirituality appears less fragmented. There are clear connections between their perception of the context, and their perception of their own spiritual development. They are more aware of a certain complexity involving several different aspects simultaneously. A concrete example is that the experience of a bond with God can go together with a struggle relating to God's absence. Another example is the fact that both the liberating and the alienating aspects of secularisation are incorporated as two inseparable moments in a single movement. The two different aspects belong together in the development of the whole person. During the interviews these pastors dare to say that they know themselves well, and that they have insight into the position they adopt within their context, while also being aware of which moments in their life and work have, and which have not, been integrated or worked through.

6. *Dynamic spirituality*

From the foregoing it becomes clear, first of all, that any description of contemporary spirituality must be an open description. By this I mean that spirituality is not a fixed datum or self-contained whole. Our inquiry shows that spirituality is permanently in motion because of the unavoidable and continuous confrontation with the context. This confrontation always varies: reflection on one's biography constantly reveals new, surprising elements; personal identity is never complete, but always in the making; and the cultural context is a shifting pattern of several cultures and cultural dimensions with respect to which the pastors sometimes find themselves in the centre, and at other times at the extreme margins. The relation to the structure of the church also constantly requires new decisions, and the adoption of new positions; one has to search for places where, together with others, one can express one's relation to God, Jesus and the Spirit. A description of spirituality must therefore always include reference to certain tensions and tension-filled relationships.

An important factor is, for example, the skill to deal with possibilities and limitations, both in personal life and in one's functioning as a pastor. A factor, which stands out, is the struggle with language. There is a constant tension between established concepts and formulations on the one hand, and the necessity to find new words that do justice to religious experiences in contemporary culture on the other.

At the same time, it becomes clear that contemporary spirituality has an active relation to the long tradition of faith and spirituality. In this tradition the feelings and experiences of many earlier generations have been laid down in certain formulations. The pastors enter into a dialogue with this tradition again and again. Tradition is an indispensable datum, but it requires considerable creativity to confirm established words and then translate them.

Finally, there is a strong emphasis on sincerity, integrity and authentic behaviour. It is not a question of whether one fulfils one's duties, but whether one lives one's life in an honest way—whether one is reliable and allows oneself to be called to account.

7. *Spirituality is not (yet) professional*

Four aspects of professionalism

In the general introduction we took our point of departure in a distinction between four aspects that are characteristic of a professional attitude: scientific knowledge, insight into the structures and goals of knowledge, skills and attitudes. For the sake of clarity, I shall reiterate here what I wrote about this in the introduction. The professionalism of pastors has to do with whether they possess sound scientific knowledge of their field (e.g. the biblical and Christian traditions, systematic and practical theology, and the socio-cultural context within which they work), as well as insight (into the structures and goals of that knowledge), and skills (e.g. the ability to conduct counselling sessions and to preside at the liturgy, or the capacities required for community building).

A fourth aspect of professionalism has to do with whether a pastor displays the attitudes of sincerity, evangelical orientation, collegiality and spirituality. According to this view, then, spirituality as one of the four attitudes is an aspect of professionalism. One could also say that spirituality, like knowledge, insight and skills, is an aspect that pastors have to develop, and in which they have to train themselves in order to be professional. However, this spiritual attitude is just *one* of the aspects, it is not the only condition required for ministry.

Spirituality is part of the 'craft'

What insights has our study yielded with respect to the significance of spirituality for professionalism? We have concluded that the pastors understand and interpret spirituality as pastoral spirituality. Spirituality is part of their 'craft'. For most of the pastors prayer, reflection and commitment coincide with their ministry. This strongly suggests the conclusion that one may speak of an integrated spirituality, which is part of a professional attitude. This would mean that the pastors who were interviewed experience their spirituality as an aspect alongside the other aspects of professionalism. One would then expect these pastors to be convinced that the same condition applies to spirituality, which also applies to knowledge, insight and skills.

Enhanced or functional spirituality

On the basis of our study, however, only two possibilities seem to emerge: a professional attitude is either an enhanced spirituality, or a functional spirituality.

In the first case, a professional attitude is understood as a kind of extension, strengthening or enhancement of the pastor's own spirituality. Professionalism is then viewed as an acquired attitude. Spirituality remains the starting point of a professional attitude and determines the content of that attitude. Spirituality is thus not understood as *one* of the aspects, but as *the* pre-eminent foundation for the exercise of the pastor's 'craft'. In the functional conception of spirituality, the latter is understood as an integral aspect alongside the other aspects of professionalism.

According to the conception of professionalism as an enhanced spirituality, the professional training of pastors is identical with their spiritual formation, whereas according to the other view we may speak of a professional training of which spiritual formation is one aspect beside others.

Both conceptions present

In our inquiry, it is especially Part 5, where the relation between spirituality and professionalism was described, which shows that both these conceptions of professionalism are attested among the pastors interviewed.

The majority of the pastors think of a professional attitude as an enhanced spirituality. These pastors are hardly, or not at all, accustomed to speaking in terms of professionalism and professional behaviour. Most of the pastors describe the content of the function, abilities and skills involved in ministry in religious terms. Formulations that typically apply to spirituality are used to describe the pastoral function as well. This applies not only to the target conceptions of ministry. Terms used to define spirituality are also employed by several pastors to describe the methods and skills involved in ministry. Few, if any, professional terms are used with reference to knowledge, insight, skills or spirituality. This first conception is found among two-thirds of the pastors.

The second conception, that of functional professionalism, according to which spirituality is one aspect beside others, is found to a greater or lesser degree among a third of the pastors interviewed. Among this group one hears more explicit statements on various aspects that are characteristic of a professional attitude: the indispensability of scientific knowledge and insight as a condition for a productive link between, for example, the traditional sources of faith and the performance of ministry within a modern cultural context; the ability to understand secular culture and to recognise opportunities for entering into a dialogue with it; the ability to deal with rituals that can establish connections; and the necessity of developing attitudes that can create space for pastoral action. What is striking here is the fact that it is mainly the pastors who are constrained in that direction by their secular environment (e.g. those in health care or forms of social ministry), for which they have freely opted themselves, who pay constant attention to the development of their professional attitude in all its aspects. There are also some parish-pastors and female pastors who show a similar concern for professionalism.

On a scale from less to more

With respect to reflection *in* and *on* spirituality we have concluded that it is possible to point to a continuum—a scale from less to more. In terms of this scale many of the pastors do exhibit reflection *in* their spirituality, but have not moved very far towards reflection *on* their spirituality. There is a small group of pastors who have developed the latter type of reflection to a high degree.

The same can be concluded with respect to conceptions of professionalism. Here, too, there is a continuum from less to more. The scale indicates that many pastors experience their professional attitude as an enhanced spirituality, but also that some are in transition from the first conception towards the second—that of functional professionalism—and finally, that there is a small group who understand professional attitude especially, or entirely, as functional professionalism.

Within the latter group one can also discern a less and a more: a limited number of them are quite articulate in speaking about functional professionalism, while the others do show an interest in professionalism, but not to the same extent. These latter ones do, however, display a development in this area.

Conclusion

An important conclusion is also that the development of pastoral professionalism is strongly tied to the extent to which pastors engage in reflection *in*, and especially *on*, their own professionalism, and therefore their pastoral spirituality. The group that shows the highest level of reflection *on* spirituality actually coincides with the group of those who most clearly think in terms of functional professionalism, and therefore of functional spirituality. It appears from this that reflection *on* spirituality goes together with the conviction that pastors have to become skilled, and that they have to train himself in spirituality as one of the aspects required for pastoral professionalism. According to our study, those who look upon spirituality as a professional attitude are also the ones who spend a lot of time on the acquisition of knowledge, insight and skills.

8. *Conclusions relating to education and training*

In the light of our conclusion that the contemporary spirituality of pastors is a pastoral spirituality, it seems important from the very beginning to incorporate this connection with the ministry into spiritual formation as an essential aspect. Spiritual formation is not a separate and isolated event. A person-oriented retreat, for example, is a good thing in itself, but insufficient for the training of pastors. It is important in every case to consider to what extent a pastor may be involved.

It is important to give spiritual formation a place within the whole structure of professionalism. Here I base myself on the idea that spirituality is an important resource or condition, which one should be able to draw on in one's quest for a professional ministry. An important element is the question whether, say, knowledge and insight constitute impediments, or whether they serve as stimuli, for spiritual formation. It is interesting to observe that the pastors who indicate most clearly the importance of functional professionalism, never suggest that the latter could constitute an impediment to spiritual development. Rather, we sense the reverse: the pastors who are in favour of an explicitly professional conception of ministry have a goal-oriented interest in reflection and practical, ethical action. With respect to prayer, a degree of differentiation is discernible. We do, however, observe a general tendency to regard a positive beginning in spiritual formation as one of the tools required for ministry. It is even possible to speak of spirituality as a basis for professional development and training, always assuming that these are not separate matters. In our judgement, the fact that we could ascertain this in what seems to us a healthy form among a number of pastors, could be an important stimulus for education and training.

In view of our conclusion that reflection plays an important role, it is clear that in the education and further training of pastors in all the relevant disciplines, attention should be given to possibilities of promoting reflection in and on professional ministry, and therefore on spirituality. Training institutes should spend more time on the interaction between reflection *in* and *on* ministry on the one hand, and spirituality on the other, and should make special arrangements for this. Knowledge and insight, for example, should be reflective knowledge and insight. The same applies to the skills and attitudes among which spirituality belongs. We should like to point here to the importance of a recent publication: J.A. van der Ven, *Reflective Ministry*, especially part IV (Van der Ven 1997).

AFTERWORD

By Frans Haarsma

I have gladly accepted Gerard Zuidberg's invitation to write this afterword. It is a welcome opportunity for me to express my appreciation for the considerable amount of work lying behind this publication: conducting the very large number of thirty extensive interviews, processing the material and, finally, writing the report which is now presented to us. It is quite an achievement, revealing a concern for the future of ministry and a fervent commitment to the well-being of the present and future generations of pastors. The way in which he, as a researcher, approached his people also deserves recognition: with an open mind, with a warm heart, with collegial confidence and respect. This is especially evident in the first part, about the context of religious development, where plenty of attention is given to the biographical aspects of religiosity and to personal identity. I shall not come back to this later on, but I do wish to highlight this explicitly at this point. Adopting the same attitude as the author's, I shall try to provide some comments on the results of this study.

1. *Design: theory and empirical research*

After the first reading of the report the question occurred to me whether the list of themes was indeed the right set of instruments for this study. It was a question to be put not only to the researcher, but also to myself. So after the event I ask myself whether we have not paid insufficient attention to the theory which is relevant to fruitful empirical research, and which should be reflected in the formulation of the themes—a theory, therefore, about the spirituality of the modern pastor. I was rightly answered by the researcher and his supervisor, Prof. J. van der Ven, that we are dealing here with a qualitative inquiry. In a qualitative inquiry, so they argued, the whole point is to discover and evolve a theory as one goes along. In this case it is impossible to proceed from a preconceived and already formulated theory.

From the perspective of the methodology of social-scientific research this answer is correct. However, it raises another question for me, namely the question of whether from a theological point of view one may, and even should, not assume an important measure of continuity in the exercise and experience of ministry within the Catholic Church. It seems that the assumption underlying this study is that present-day pastors, priests, male and female pastoral workers, married and unmarried persons, have to start from a tabula rasa in exercising their ministry. Of course we have to admit that the social, religious and spiritual climate in which the above-mentioned categories of persons exercise their ministry—their sheer variety already constituting something unprecedented—has undergone profound changes throughout. The point, then, is that there is a discontinuity, which will probably continue to affect the life and work of pastors.

It is right that this study reveals this discontinuity, but I should like to observe that discontinuity only becomes visible in its proper scope and implications against the background of continuity. If the latter is not taken into account, then one runs the risk of getting caught up in a short-term vision, and of passing over a number of components in the Christian exercise and experience of ministry which, starting from the notion of service, so fundamental to the New Testament concept of ministry, have been given concrete shape in the doctrine, practice and discipline of the Church, most recently in the documents of Vatican II and the relevant passages of the Canon Law of 1983. The fact that the whole study does not contain a single reference to these texts can perhaps be explained in two ways. Either there is too great a distance between these texts and the way in which present-day pastors in this country experience and feel about them, or the connection with the teaching and practice of the Catholic Church outside of our national boundaries has hardly any existential significance.

May I take the liberty to make another observation in this connection? Scientific research more or less reveals the actual state of affairs. However, the same research in turn influences actual developments, as well as the thinking, ideals and actions of those whom the study concerns. A certain tendency towards provincialism becomes manifest in this report, and seems to function as its presupposition, starting point and final result.

I am very well aware of the fact that these critical observations can be used for reinforcing restorative tendencies in priestly formation that are already noticeable in certain areas within the Dutch Church.

Would it not, therefore, be wiser not to bring them out into the open? From some of my other publications it will be clear that I regard any kind of return to traditional clericalism as a disaster. When I express these critical observations all the same, it is because in the long run I have more confidence in a fair discussion guided by a 'probité intellectuelle' than in caution prompted by church-political considerations.

With a view to offering the reader of this study some alternative material for comparison, I shall insert, here, a short discourse on the spirituality of the diocesan clergy during the fifties of the present century. I consider this to be justified and meaningful, because the secular priests or secular clergy are closest to the priests and male and female pastoral workers who are active in ministry today.

Now, the spirituality of the diocesan clergy went through a short period of flourishing, especially in French-speaking regions, shortly before, during, and after the Second World War. In several publications (for example *Wezen en spiritualiteit van de diocesane geestelijkheid*, Brussels-Amsterdam 1950) the Louvain theologian Gustave Thils devoted extensive studies to this. He starts from the idea that a Christian spirituality has its origin in a certain historical situation and seeks to respond to it. The Franciscan movement of poverty, for example, was an answer to the growing treasures and affluence of the Church.

As far as the spirituality of the diocesan clergy is concerned, its historical origin is supposed to lie in the appointment by the Apostles of presbyters and episcopoi for the purpose of the proclamation of the gospel. Besides, any kind of spirituality is based on certain central dogmatic truths. In this case it was believed to be the faith that the diocesan priest is an instrument of the living Christ, and continues the latter's work of mediation. What is special and distinctive about the diocesan priest is, further, that he is responsible for a visible and multifaceted ministry in the service of a certain group of believers. It is a visible service and therefore different from contemplative monastic life; it is a multifaceted service and therefore different from the—essentially specialised—missionary work of active members of the religious congregations. It is a service connected with a group of believers—for the most part, but not exclusively, a parish—and therefore focused on the local Church. As a final characteristic of this spirituality he mentioned the pastoral love with which the Church is ruled, and the awareness of a kind of fatherhood over the parish.

A comparison with this theory of the spirituality of the diocesan clergy may contribute to an even sharper contrastive picture of the spirituality of the modern pastor in the Netherlands. Perhaps this contains a suggestion for a possible approach to be adopted in further research. The procedure with respect to the place of the Holy Spirit shows how easily a distorted picture may arise when there are deficiencies in the formulation of questions. In the first round the question about the Holy Spirit was absent: the result was that the Spirit did not occur in the answers. When people were explicitly asked about it in a second round, this led to a fundamental correction.

2. *The believing subject*

For just over a third of the pastors interviewed, but also for others, faith has a strongly personal nature. It is a faith in actu, with its ups and downs, its doubts, uncertainties and varying experiences. They are believing rather than faith-ful people; the latter qualification would be too static. It is of the utmost importance to the pastors, it seems, that they can be honest, sincere and authentic in their faith.

The other side of the coin is that this may easily lead to an individualistic experience of the faith. Admittedly, one recognises a dependence on the tradition of the bible and, to a lesser extent, the tradition of the church, but the selection from these sources is determined first of all by personal experiences, personal developments and personal needs. In the few cases where pastors feel connected with a community of faith, this is limited for many of them to the group in which, and for which, they perform their pastoral duty. The ecclesial dimension in the sense of the Catholicity of the Church, both in its diachronic and synchronic sense, may be present, but remains rather latent, and obviously does not play a role in experience. The fides ecclesiae may be the sustaining ground, unconsciously, but the emphasis is still on *my* faith.

All this is intimately related to another datum, which struck me in the interviews, namely, that most of the pastors unequivocally reject a faith, which is a belief in truths. No fides obedientialis, but a *fides fiducialis*. The whole emphasis, therefore, is on faith as an attitude, as an act of faith towards God, which has to be performed again and again. What then, is the content, the *fides quae*? That seems to be something about which one hardly, if at all, expresses oneself. The more or less compelling character of certain dogmas, as they have been pronounced by councils or other bodies of ecclesiastical authority, does not seem to play any role. One gets the impression that it would be incompatible with the emancipatory creed, which is professed particularly sharply by over a third of the pastors interviewed.

This anti-intellectualist and anti-authoritarian conception of faith may be a resistance against some earlier representations of faith within Catholic theology; it may also be the product of an unintentional adaptation to certain prevailing tendencies in present-day culture. For it is impossible to pass over the cognitive content of the Christian tradition, unless the Christian faith is to be no more than an inarticulate, vague feeling of 'schlechthinnige Abhängigkeit'.

3. *Representations of God*

The interviews show a whole range of different representations and experiences of God, often varying with the same person. I think that on the basis of the statements in the text, one would be entitled to claim that this approach to God has its origin in the fear that one would detract from the divine mystery by using a language which delimits and fixates that which is profoundly unknowable. This attitude shows a certain resemblance to what the draft-report "Hedendaagse Geloofsbeleving" of the Pastoral Council of the Dutch Archdiocese describes as "believing as respect for the mystery of existence".

A characteristic tendency in this regard is the reluctance to conceive of God as a person. The latter idea is indeed encountered among several respondents. The great majority of the pastors interviewed, however, are not consistent at this point: they admit that, when presiding at the liturgy, they do address God as a person. Likewise, with the metaphor of God as a companion on the path of life, we are again dealing with a personal God. On the other hand, the fact remains that the experience of God as sustaining ground, like the faith and hope in God as destination, does seem very compatible with an impersonal representation of God.

It is striking that among the many names and images of God one looks in vain for the notion of God as the lawgiver who gives direction to life, or as the Holy One who demands from his adherents that they be holy as He is holy, and who calls upon them to perform his will on earth as it is done in heaven. Obviously, the allergic reaction to years of moralising preaching has not yet worn off. However, although these words are not used as such, that which is indicated by them is by no means absent. I am thinking, here, of that other tendency in new forms of believing, also mentioned in the aforementioned draft-report, namely "believing as dedication to one's neighbour". At the time, the report characterised this form of believing as "rather non-religious in character". As far as our pastors are concerned, this qualification seems to be out of place. After all, some of them declare that it is precisely the countenance of suffering and oppressed humanity that puts them on the track towards God.

Looking back on the chapter on faith in God and experience of God, I conclude that this is the heart of the study. It is not surprising, I think, that we find tendencies among our pastors that seem to reflect the doubts and confusions typical of present-day culture as far as the question of God is concerned. Here, one may justifiably speak of a searching faith. I am pleased about "le sens du mystère" which comes to light here. There is little reason for concern on this point when one considers that those who are looking for God have already found him/her, or—even better—have already been found by God. It is natural in this situation to take refuge in biblical stories rather than in formulated dogmas, although the two always require one another. It seems as if, for the time being, speculative theology has to give way to a narrative theology. Finally, it appears that Church documents are of little significance for the great majority of the pastors interviewed—for some they even have a negative effect. Will not this gap between the doctrine of the Church and the faith of its members, even of its pastors, lead, in the long run, to what a German philosopher has called a "horizontal schism"?

4. *Significance of Jesus*

While the pastors' experience of God shows much diversity, we find a great measure of agreement with regard to the significance accorded to Jesus in their spirituality. The focus is first of all, and not seldom exclusively, on the historical Jesus. He is experienced as an example, a guide, a challenge, a companion, and a signpost on the path of life. The pastors view the Jesus of the gospels as the ideal realisation of their own dreams and expectations. The way in which the gospels present him as a guide and a therapist of people inspires them. Typical in this regard is a statement like the following: *"I mostly speak of Jesus of Nazareth; I do not turn him into God, but I want to present him as the guide who shows you how you can deal with God in your life in a believing manner"*. We do find an affective relation to the living and risen Lord among some of the pastors, who also let themselves be inspired by the gospel of Saint John. In the case of one parish-pastor we see a surprising inversion: it is not so much Jesus as an example who takes him to the poor, but rather the poor in whose faces he discovers the countenance of Christ.

Although the historical Jesus occupies a central position for most pastors, one must not conclude from this that Christology and soteriology have given way to a pure Jesuology. Especially the metaphor of Jesus as companion, which occurs frequently, suggests more than just an example from the past. It seems clear to me that several notions from the classical theology of redemption, such as sacrifice, merit, atonement and reconciliation, no longer play any role whatsoever. In view of the prevailing embarrassment among present-day theologians, also reflected in the preaching of the church, this state of affairs is hardly surprising. An example of such embarrassment is the publication of the international theological commission entitled "Enkele vraagstukken over God als Verlosser"; this document does not give any answer to the real questions that are felt to be important by contemporary people, both inside and outside the Church.

5. *The presence of the Spirit*

Only a short time ago, "Geistvergessenheit" was a recurrent theme in theology. The starting point for this was some such critical representation of the matter as the following: the concentration of the Spirit of God in the leadership of the Church has led to a drainage of the Spirit in the rest of the people of God. This fact has in turn led to the necessity of an emanation of all grace and truth from the leadership via the bishops and the priests to the laity.

In recent years, also under the influence of Vatican II, this situation has changed. In large sections of the Catholic Church population the awareness has grown that the Spirit is not the monopoly of the hierarchy and the ministry. Hence the demand for dialogue which is heard in a variety of forms, both from a movement like the "Volksbegehren" in the German-speaking regions, and from a variety of new religious initiatives throughout the world. It is to be expected, therefore, that the majority of the pastors interviewed are aware of the presence and activity of the Spirit, not only in their own life and work, but also in the people they encounter in their ministry. Thus people become the place where God's Spirit is encountered, just as in the countenance of the same people God's Spirit and the Spirit of Jesus become manifest. For some, God's Spirit and the Spirit of Jesus is then a person to whom one can pray, while for others it is an impersonal force granted to man in the name of God.

Precisely with respect to God's Spirit, the influence of feminist theology is noticeable among these pastors; this applies, of course, not only to the female pastors. The pastors do not hesitate to speak of the Spirit in female terms and to break through a one-sided male image of God by using female metaphors and images. In this way room is created for tenderness and intimacy in one's association with God. The appearance of women adds a new dimension to the ministry. There is a clear change of perspective; women see other and new things, thus contributing to the kaleidoscopic wisdom of God which is made known in the Church (cf. Eph. 3,10). Here it becomes clear once again to what extent the Church will be depriving itself of many gifts, as long as women are allowed only a very limited scope within the ministry.

6. *Church and sacraments*

In the foregoing we noted that, among a large number of the pastors interviewed, there is a certain hesitation and reserve with respect to Jesus as the Christ, the Risen One and the Living One. This probably has to do with the way in which the church and sacraments are spoken of. In most of the interviews, to be sure, the church is presented as the institution against which one ought to react, because it oppresses people and does not give any room for the personal, individual development of people's talents and personalities. The

Church as the body of Christ, as the temple of the holy Spirit, and as the people of God which, in its long history and its world-wide dissemination, is more than the limited area of a parish, or the limited group of a particular institution: these elements apparently play no role whatsoever in the spirituality of the majority of the pastors who are allowed to speak here.

Do we not encounter here the same reserve with which God, and Christ in particular, is spoken of? If one is afraid to pin God down in words or formulas, one would be equally afraid of 'locating' God and the Spirit in the Church, its offices and its doctrine.

This becomes even clearer when we include the sacraments in our deliberations. At first sight, there is apparently little appreciation for the sacraments of baptism and confirmation. While in much of the theological literature on (male and female) pastoral workers these very sacraments are looked upon as the foundation and permanent source of inspiration for this new office, this is not reflected in the experience recorded here. This may be interpreted in two ways. It might be that, particularly as far as (male and female) pastoral workers are concerned, very little attention has been given in recent years to a thorough theological reflection on their ministry. Another possibility is that the aforementioned theology is felt to be inadequate, because the sacraments of baptism and confirmation in particular are unable to sustain what is specific about this ministry.

As shown in the answers, the Eucharist only occupies a central place in the spiritual life of ten of the thirty pastors. The ten (male and female) pastoral workers belonging to this group experience the celebrations of Holy Communion at which they preside as normal celebrations of the Eucharist. Here we touch on an unintended, but clearly negative, consequence of a church policy, which necessitates celebrations of Holy Communion, instead of the Eucharist, because of a shortage of priests. The difference between the full celebration of the Eucharist, the central sacrament of the Church, on the one hand, and Holy Communion, a purely derived ritual as far as sacramentality is concerned, on the other, is no longer taken note of. In the experience of the pastors these two have come to be seen as operating at the same level. If that is true of pastors, how much more will this misconception not take root among the rest of the church's members?

The study raises the issue of the sacrament of ordination in both a positive and a negative way. Positive, insofar as five priests affirm that their ordination is an essential fact in their spiritual life. Negative, inasmuch as, particularly among (male and female) pastoral workers, there is a resistance against, and lack of understanding of, the current criteria for the ordination of deacons and priests. The ensuing limitations with respect to liturgical qualifications are experienced by twenty of the thirty pastors, among whom are four priests, as power politics on the part of the church leadership.

Does this point to a loss of sacramental awareness, or does it contain an urgent appeal to the leadership of the Church to review its current policy on this point critically? Both these suppositions may be true. It is undeniable that a loss of sacramental awareness is at stake, when one reads that twenty of the thirty pastors attach little or no importance for their religious life to either the Eucharist or the other sacraments. As they state themselves, their spirituality lacks a sacramental dimension, certainly when sacramentality is understood as the sacraments of the Church. It seems that the 'ecclesiastical aspect', in the sense of the concrete precepts and regulations relating to the sacraments, has a negative effect on sacramental awareness. Among the (male and female) pastoral workers a similar negative effect must be attributed to the fact that, although they are allowed to prepare people for the sacraments, the actual administration of the sacraments falls outside their competence. This interpretation is confirmed by the fact that there is a growing interest among these same people in the wider meaning that symbols may have in life, and the fact that they are looking for alternative rites, like the lighting of a candle during a counselling session—a rather individualistic reduction of symbolism.

Some pastors explicitly state that, for them, the gracious proximity of God has little to do with the sacraments; rather, it is experienced in ordinary things such as a good conversation, sharing food, and sharing each other's lives. Is the traditional sacral world of the sacraments and liturgy of the church being replaced here by 'new holy things'? The accepted separation between sacred and profane, and even the very distinction between the two, seems to have been abolished. Instead of dualism, there is a search for 'holism', an all-embracing experience of unity. These tendencies are also found in process theology and philosophy, in recent theologies of creation, and in feminist theology.

7. *Prayer and reflection*

The choice of the word 'reflection' already points to a change among modern pastors compared to the previous generation. It is pointed out in the study that the pastors use the word reflection far more frequently than the term meditation. The former has a wider range of meaning than the latter. Meditation, it is said, requires a certain structure and form, whereas reflection can have a more open, unstructured form. On a par with this is the opposition, especially among the older group, to what they experienced during their upbringing, and later during their training, as coercion in the area of religious life. However, there is also a clear ambivalence on this point: on the one hand, there is a resistance against any form of 'discipline', a term that reminds them of the past and evokes associations of compulsion. On the other hand there is a need precisely for some sort of structure, which is seen to be necessary if one is not to be so absorbed by one's work that there will no longer be any time or space for personal prayer and reflection. For the great majority of the pastors interviewed there is a close connection between pastoral work on the one hand and prayer and reflection on the other; the former supports the latter and vice versa; they may even merge into one another, so that personal prayer coincides with (and is also limited to), for example, presiding at the liturgy.

The study gives little information about the content of prayer and reflection; the question remains, therefore, whether one can speak of a specific 'pastoral' piety or religiosity, distinct from that of other believers. Has the distance between ministry and the laity practically disappeared here too? Does this apply in the same measure to both the priests and the (male and female) pastoral workers? It is remarkable that the material does not contain any reference to the recitation of the daily office, and that there is no mention whatsoever of the (un)desirability of a special retreat for pastors, possibly together with the retreat for priests. Is collegiality in this respect also limited to the small group of immediate colleagues, or are the membership and activities of the Associations of Pastoral Workers to be regarded as a continuation of the esprit de corps which used to be so characteristic of the old diocesan clergy?

8. *Professional identity*

The study yielded five target conceptions of ministry. They are not intended as comprehensive definitions of ministry, but as descriptions of what the pastors experience as central aspects. It is remarkable that among those central aspects only five of the thirty pastors mention the word 'God'. The other twenty-five stick to vague descriptions that might also fit the profile of a general practitioner, a psycho-therapist, a lawyer, or a judge: creating a space in which people are done justice to, fulfilling a mediating function, liberating people, and preserving and healing people. A further reading makes it quite clear that these target conceptions have their place in the context of preaching, liturgy, prayer, reflection and pastoral counselling—in short: in the orientation on God and the neighbour. Even so, it remains a curious fact that God is absent in the direct and spontaneous formulation of target conceptions.

IIow is this fact to be interpreted? Does it arise from personal doubt and a lack of clear vision on the part of the church about ministry in the modern world? It is striking that, of the five pastors who do mention the word God, four are priests and one of is a pastoral worker. If priests and (male or female) pastoral workers are both mediators between God and people, are the priests then closer to the side of God, and the (male or female) pastoral workers closer to people? This solution is attractive in its simplicity, but it is too facile. Uncertainty and a lack of clarity are not only part of the make-up of (male and female) pastoral workers, but also of priests. The mere fact that, among the twenty-five respondents who initially do not mention God in their description of the central aspect of their ministry, there are a considerable number of priests, is an indication to this effect.

Every pastor, (male and female) pastoral worker or priest, feels the pressure of the diminishing public influence of the church, and of that which, for convenience sake, but with considerable reservations, I shall simply call the 'absence' of God in our culture. In a negative sense, this can be interpreted as alienation from the Christian tradition, also among pastors. In that case, one should consider, however, that it is not really a matter of Tradition with a capital T, but of tradition with a small t. The point at issue is then the Post-Tridentine form of the church in our region. That is why I may also draw attention to the positive side of this matter: a more acute awareness of the unspeakable mystery, which our God is, and the resulting hesitation to use the word God too quickly and too easily. These two sides are a necessary condition for working at a new form of the church.

There are two more things that I wish to point to in connection with professional identity. The first is the concern of most of the pastors to make and keep the distance between the pastor and the people with and for whom he or she works, as small as possible. It is not always said in so many words, but one does sense it in the answers. The pastor does not want to be more, higher, better, or more powerful than her or his fellow-believers. Actually, he or she does not want to be different, although professionalism does, of course, imply their being different.

The tension, arising from the democratic ethos of modernity, between solidarity and special responsibility might be clarified, theologically, by means of biblical notions like vocation and mission. However, these words do not occur in the material. A variant of this tension, which is the second point that I wish to draw attention to, is that between 'doing' and 'being'. Ministry in the view of some pastors has a culture-critical function: it is a protest against a society that is dominated by achievement and competition. These pastors consider it their primary task to be present in the world, which for some of them means being a sign of God's presence, while for others it has some vague connection to dealing with people *"tactfully and generously"* or *"bestowing on people their own, unique value"*.

It may be said, by way of summary, that the research material, especially as far as the group with the most reflective attitude to life is concerned, reflects an uncertainty, a searching with respect to Christian and, more specifically, Catholic identity, which is making itself felt both inside and outside the church. The question is asked: who am I as a pastor? But behind that question, there is another question: who am I as a Christian believer? And: who am I as a Catholic? The traditional doctrines of the Catholic Church offer little or no support in this quest; they have their origin in a different world. An open dialogue in which all the themes mentioned here can be brought up for discussion without any bias, is the only way that offers any perspective.

THEMES FOR THE IN-DEPTH INTERVIEW
WITH PASTORS

1. *Context of religious development*

1. *Biographical context*

The parental environment
  – Images of father and mother that pastors retain.
  – A good or less good relationship with him, or her or both.
  – The atmosphere at home during childhood: open or closed atmosphere, space or a lack of space for everybody, freedom, lack of freedom, rigid or lenient attitude on the part of the parents.
  – Influence exerted by parents (or one of them): strong, weak, positive, negative, how and in what areas. Development and change of this image throughout the years.
  – The religious atmosphere at home: moments of prayer, rituals, devotions, church attendance, joint reflection. The way in which pastors look back on it now and the way in which they have, or have not, distanced themselves from what their parents tried to give them for their path in life.
  – The moral aspects in education and training.
  – The images which the church of their youth calls up for the pastors: commitment to the church or not, influence resulting from it, moments which one has cherished or from which one has distanced oneself.
  – The socio-economic position of the family: economically independent, poor or rich. The way in which one dealt with it, resulting influence on further development in life and on the content given to ministry.

Further development in life
  – Important moments, persons, events—both in personal life and in socio-economic sphere—which had an influence on the development; influence of education and training, of theological developments, significance of teachers, pastors and persons in a special relation of trust, boarding-school years, association with fellow

students, significance of spiritual formation, work placement and supervision.

– Significance of places where one has worked as a pastor or in another capacity; influence exerted by colleagues and others with whom one came into contact in one's work.

– Significance and influence of moments of crisis, important choices around life and work.

2. *Personal identity*

– Experience and appreciation of the physical aspect, developments in this area and the factors that had an influence on it; experience of vulnerability and strength, weak and strong sides of the body.

– Experience and appreciation of male and female aspects in personal identity; developments and changes, factors that had an influence on it.

– Experience and appreciation of possibilities and limitations: the way in which strong and weaker sides were dealt with.

– Experience and appreciation of personal relationships, lifelong bonds; significance of enduring relationships in personal life and in work; experience and appreciation of being alone; experience of independence, dependence, space, being accepted, appreciation in the eyes of others.

– Factors connected with the development of identity: the influence of relationships with others, experience and processing of conflicts, significance of moments of resistance; influence of counselling and/or therapy.

3. *The cultural context*

– Images and conceptions of secularisation as cultural development; challenge and rejection.

– Choices demanded by the process of secularisation; facing these choices or not, developments set in motion by this.

– Positive or negative appreciation with respect to secularisation.

– New challenges or not, their influence on personal development and on the development of ministry.

4. *The context of the church*

– Positions, finding oneself at home in the institute of the church or not; reactions to this, looking for ways in situations of conflict;

especially the positions of ministry, dealing with church authority and church policy.

2. *Dimensions in spirituality*

1. *The symbolic dimension*

Significance of faith, hope and love in the relation to God
 – Preferences in the experience of faith, hope and love as a relation to God; intrinsic aspects of faith, hope and love.
 Metaphors for God
 – The use of metaphors, preferences, the reality from which the metaphors are derived, development and change in the metaphors, personal and impersonal relation to God, transcending the metaphors, interest in mystery.
 Relation to Jesus
 – Relation to Jesus, significance of the terms Christ, the Lord, Son of God, Risen Lord; central metaphors.
 Relation to the Spirit
 – The Spirit as a person and as spiritual strength; metaphors for the Spirit, preferences, the reality from which the metaphors are derived, development and change in the metaphors, personal and non-personal metaphors, transcending the metaphors, interest in the mystery.

2. *The experiential dimension*

Prayer
 – Individual and communal prayer; place, time and content of prayer; prayer connected, or unconnected, with the exercise of ministry and presiding at the liturgy; ways of addressing God, Jesus and the Spirit.
 Reflection
 – Individual and communal reflection; place, time and content of reflection; reflection connected, or unconnected, with the exercise of ministry and presiding at the liturgy.
 Commitment
 – Significance and experience of moral values and norms, content and experience of solidarity, commitment and lifestyle.
 Factors that have an influence on prayer, reflection and commitment.

– Significance and experience of discipline, time-management.
– Significance and experience of study, reading.
– Significance and experience of cultural events.
– Significance and experience of nature.
– Significance and experience of physical work.
Two special aspects of prayer, reflection and commitment
– Communal aspects: especially the significance of the church as a place for experiencing spirituality.
– Ritual aspects: especially the significance of sacraments for experiencing spirituality.

3. *Spirituality and ministry*

1. *Metaphors for ministry: metaphors used by pastors for characterising their ministry, especially in view of the goal of their ministry.*

2. *Conceptions of professional attitude: the terms used by pastors in their speaking about professionalism and competence in ministry.*

3. *Significance of spirituality with respect to ministry: spirituality as a condition for, source of, ministry.*

4. *Significance of ministry with respect to spirituality: ministry as a source for spirituality.*

A theme to wind up the interview
Perception on the part of pastors of the integral experience of spirituality, correlation, personal appropriation of separate aspects or a more fragmented experience.

BIBLIOGRAPHY

General sources

Aalders, C. (1969). *Spiritualiteit. Geestelijk leven vroeger en nu.* The Hague.

Aarnink, L., Tigcheler, J., Waaijman, K. (eds.) (1985). "Gaandeweg groeit er nieuwe spiritualiteit." *Speling Tijds. voor bezinning.* 37 (1985) 4 Tilburg.

Andriessen, H. (1994). *Spiritualiteit als modern verhaal.* Nijmegen.

——— (1996a). "Spiritualiteit, 't is toch maar gevaarlijk spul." In: *Speling, Tijds. voor bezinning* 48 (1996) 3, 53–58.

Arnold, F.X. Rahner, K., Schurr, V., Weber. L.M. (eds.). (1964–1969). *Handbuch der Pastoraltheologie. Praktische Theologie der Kirche in ihrer Gegenwart.* Vols. 1–4. Freiburg.

Beumer, J. (ed.) (1989). *Als de hemel de aarde raakt. Spiritualiteit en mystiek—Ervaringen.* Kampen.

Blommestijn, H. (ed.) (1991). *Tot op de bodem van het niets. Mystiek in tijd van oorlog en crisis.* 1920–1970. Averbode/Kampen.

Borgman, E. (1994). *Alexamenos aanbidt zijn God. Theologische essays voor sceptische lezers.* Zoetermeer.

Bruggeman, P. (1987). *Gebroken verhaal. Als je het sterven wilt door-leven.* Tielt.

Campbell, A.V. (ed.). (1990). *A Dictionary of Pastoral Care.* Edition with Supplement. London.

Deenik-Moolhuizen, J., Matti, A., Poel, C. van der, Sleegers, Fr. (ed.) (1990). *Al gaande zal je kracht vermeerderen. Teksten van en over Antoinette van Pinxteren. Zuster Francesco.* Raad van Kerken Nederland Edition.

Clinebell, H. (1984). *Basic Types of Pastoral Counseling.* Nashville, Abingdon.

Dekker, G. (1987). *Godsdienst en samenleving.* Kampen.

Donders, J. (ed.) (1994). *Spiritualiteit. Zeven inleidingen.* Han Fortmanncentrum. Nijmegen.

Drewermann, E. (1989). *Kleriker. Psychogramm eines Ideals.* Olten/Freiburg in Breisgau.

Eliade, M. (1957). *Das Heilige und das Profane. Vom Wesen des Religiösen.* Reprint 1984 Frankfurt.

Ford, M. (1999). *Wounded Prophet. A Portrait of Henri Nouwen.* London.

Gaandeweg. Opstellen aangeboden aan Dr. Herman Andriessen bij gelegenheid van zijn vijfenzestigste verjaardag. Kampen, 1992.

Gerkin, Chr. V. (1997). *An Introduction to Pastoral Care.* Nashville.

Grözinger, A. and Luther, H. (eds.) (1997). *Perspektiven zur gelebten Religion.* München.

Hoenkamp-Bisschops, A. (1991). *Celibaat: varianten van beleving. Een verkennend onderzoek rond ambtscelibaat en geestelijke gezondheid.* Baarn.

——— (1993). *Intimiteit en beschikbaarheid. Het celibaat bij priesters in het basispastoraat.* (Diss. Heerlen). Hilversum.

Höfte, B. (1990). *Bekering en bevrijding* (diss. KTU). Utrecht.

Iersel, Fr. van (1985). "De spiritualiteit van de vredesbeweger." In: *Speling, Tijds. voor bezinning* 37 (1985) 4, 70–75.

Jossutis, M. (1996). *Die Einführung in das Leben. Pastoraltheologie zwischen Phänomenologie und Spiritualität.* Gütersloh.

Kessel, R. van (1985). "Arbeiders in de wijngaard." In: Ven, J. van der (ed.). *Toekomst voor de kerk,* 202–216. Kampen.

Levinas, E. (1982). *L'au-delà du verset.* Paris. Dutch transl. (1989): *Aan gene zijde van het vers. Talmoedische studies en essays.* Hilversum.

Luijk, H. van (1975). *Pleidooi voor de ziel. Negentien schetsen voor vandaag.* Baarn.

Middelaar, P. van (1994). *Een spoor in het getij. Gedichten en gedachten, overdenkingen, verhalen en brieven.* Kampen.

———— (1996). *Reiziger in het tussenland.* Kampen.
Nouwen, H. (1976). *Reaching out. The Three Movements of the Spiritual Life.* Glasgow.
———— (1981). *Een levende heenwijzing. Dienst en gebed in aandenken aan Jezus Christus.* Serie Pastorale handreiking. Den Haag.
———— (1970). *Intimacy. Pastoral psychological essays.* Indiana.
———— (1972). *The wounded healer. Ministry in contemporary society.* New York.
Peperzak, A. (1987). *Gaandeweg.* Vught.
———— (1990) *Zoeken naar zin. Proeven van Wijsbegeerte.* Kampen/Kapellen.
Petter, D.M. de (1964). *Begrip en werkelijkheid. Aan de overzijde van het conceptualisme.* Hilversum.
Roskam Abbing, P. (ed.) (1971). *Luisterend leven. Studies over evangelische spiritualiteit.* 's-Gravenhage.
Schaeffer, H. (1988). *Geloven in niemandsland. Naar een eigen spiritualiteit.* Baarn.
Sobrino, J. (1988). *Bevrijding met Geest. Notities voor een nieuwe spiritualiteit.* Averbode/ Kampen.
Tooren, B. van den, Elderen, R. van (eds.) (1995). *Het geloofsleven van de theoloog in tekst en toelichting voor predikanten en studenten.* Zoetermeer.
Vergote, A. (1974). *Het huis is nooit af.* Antwerpen/Utrecht.
———— (1985). *Profielen van een hedendaagse spiritualiteit.* Den Haag.
———— (1987). *Het meerstemmige leven. Gedachten over mens en religie.* Kapellen/Kampen.
———— (1989). *Cultuur, religie en geloof.* Antwerpen/Amsterdam.
Voortsluis, B. (ed.) (1996). *Geïnspireerd leven. Op zoek naar een bijbels georiënteerde spiritualiteit.* Zoetermeer.
Weber, M. (1980). *Wirtschaft und Gesellschaft. Grundriss der verstehenden Soziologie.* 1 Halbb. Tübingen.
———— (1960). *Soziologische Grundbegriffe.* Tübingen.
Wegman, H. (1984). "De Geestelijke." In: *Tijds. voor Theologie* 24 (1984), no. 4, 374–388.
———— (1991). "Cosmorama. De gedichten 'Deïsme' en 'Tabor' van Gerrit Achterberg." In: Kusters, W. (ed.). *In een bezield verband. Nederlandstalige dichters op zoek naar zin.* Baarn.
Zulehner, P. (1989–1990). *Pastoraltheologie.* Vols. 1–4. Düsseldorf.

Literature used in the Introduction

Dudley, C.S. (1983). *Building Effective Ministry.* San Francisco.
Ernst, H. (1991). *De pastorale arbeid in de negentiger jaren.* Diocese Breda Edition.
Faber, J. (1994). *De spiritualiteit van de theoloog. Een protestants pleidooi.* Kampen.
Gerwen, G. van (1988) "De moeizame professionalisering van het pastorale beroep." In: Praktische Theologie 15 (1988) 5, 541–556.
Groener, G. (1993) *Professioneel pastoraat kent zijn geheim.* Bewerking inleiding jaarlijkse studiedag Raad voor klinische pastorale vorming, 29 januari 1993.
Grün, A., Dufner, M. (1996). *Spiritualiteit van beneden.* Kampen.
Haarsma, F. (ed.) (1988). *Tussen hemel en aarde. Naar nieuwe vormen van spiritualiteit.* Baarn.
———— (1994). "Kennis en kunde, maar ook deugd en devotie. De eenzijdige benadering van de pastorale professionaliteit kan leiden tot pastorale technocratie." In: *De Bazuin,* 5 augustus 1994, 5–7.
Körver, J. (1996). "Van reflectie en actie. "Reflectie in actie' als leerdoel voor de pastor." In: *Tijdschrift Geestelijke verzorging* 1 (1996) 3, 27–36.
Krogt, T.P.W.M. van der (1981). *Professionalisering en collectieve macht: een conceptueel kader.* 's-Gravenhage.
Patton, J. (1990). *From Ministry to Theology. Pastoral Action and Reflection.* Nashville.
———— (1993). *Pastoral Care in Context. An Introduction to Pastoral Care.* Westminster Kentucky.

Schilderman, J.B.A.M.; Visscher, C.A.M.; Ven, J.A. van der; Felling, A.J.A. (1993). *Professionalisering van het pastorale ambt. Onderzoeksverslag voor de Federatie van Pastoraal Werkenden Nederland.* Intern VPW-rapport, november 1993.

——— (1994). *Pastores en het ambt. Verslag van een onderzoek onder R.K. pastores.* Federatie VPW Nederland Edition.

Steggink, O., Waaijman, K. (1985). *Spiritualiteit en mystiek, I. Inleiding.* Nijmegen.

Ven, J.A. van der (1990). *Entwurf einer empirischen Theologie.* Kampen/Weinheim.

——— (1991a). "Religieuze variaties: religie in een geseculariseerde en multiculturele samenleving." In: *Tijds. v. Theol.* 31 (1991) 2, 163–182.

——— (1991b). "De identiteit van pastorale counseling." In: *Prakt. Theol.* 18 (1991) 2, 230–256.

——— (1992a). "God in Nijmegen. Een theologisch perspektief." In: *Tijds. v. Theol.* 32 (1992) 3, 225–249.

Ven, J.A. van der, Biemans, B. (1992b). *Pastorale professionalisering.* Intern rapport vakgroep praktische theologie. KU Nijmegen.

Ven, J.A. van der, Ziebertz, H.G. (Eds.) (1993b). *Paradigmenentwicklung in der praktischen Theologie.* Kampen/Weinheim.

Ven, J.A. van der (1993–1994). "Pastorale protocolanalyse I." In: Prakt. Theol. 20 (1993) 5, 467–474; "Pastorale Protocolanalyse II." In: *Prakt. Theol.* 21 (1994) 1, 7–20; Pastorale protocolanalyse III. In: *Prakt. Theol.* 21 (1994) 1, 21–42.

——— (1994). "Nogmaals: Pastoraat in maat en getal." In: *Prakt. Theol.* 21 (1994) 5, 489–496.

——— (1997). *Education for reflective ministry.* Louvain.

Waaijman, K. (1992). *Wat is spiritualiteit?* (TBI-studies 1), Nijmegen.

——— (ed.) (1996). *Kansen voor spiritualiteit. Kwetsbaarheid, meerstemmig zelf, differentiedenken.* Baarn/Nijmegen.

——— *Spiritualiteit, dynamisch—structureel benaderd.* (TBI Studies 2). Nijmegen.

Winquist, C. (1987). "Re-visioning Ministry: Postmodern Reflections." In: Mudge, L., Poling, J., (eds). *Formation and Reflection. The Promise of Practical Theology.* pp. 27–35. Philadelphia.

Wissink, J.B.M., Zweerman, Th. (ed.) (1989). *Ruimte van de Geest. Over ascese, spiritualiteit en geestelijk leiderschap.* Kampen.

Zegveld, A. (1993). *Een plaats om te wonen. Over spiritualiteit en menswording.* Hilversum.

——— (1994). *Tot vrijheid bestemd. Spiritualiteit en geloofsbelijdenis.* Hilversum.

Zuidberg, G. (1984). *Zeven is voldoende. Krachtlijnen in de spiritualiteit van pastores in Nederland.* Hilversum.

Literature used in Chapters 1 and 2

Aden, L. and Ellens, J.H. (1990). *Turning Points in Pastoral Care. The Legacy of Anton Boisen and Sewart Hiltner.* Michigan.

Andriessen, H. (1970). *Groei en grens in de volwassenheid. Inleiding in de psychologie van de volwassen levensloop.* Nijmegen.

——— (1979). *Verlangen en volwassenheid. Beschouwingen over levensloop, zinsbeleving en pastoraal handelen.* Den Haag.

——— (1984). *Spiritualiteit en levensloop.* Averbode.

Buytendijk, F. (1980). *Bezinning over de levensloop.* Baarn.

Clinebell, H. (1992). *Well being, a Personal Plan for Exploring and Enriching the seven Dimensions of Life: Mind, Body, Spirit, Love, Work, Play, Earth.* San Francisco.

——— (1995). *Counseling for a spiritually empowered Wholeness. A Hope—centered Approach* (Originally published as *Growth Counseling*). New York, London.

Erikson, E. (1968). *Identity, youth and crisis.* New York. Dutch transl. (1972): *Identiteit, Jeugd en crisis.* Utrecht, Antwerpen.

Fowler, J., Nipkow, K. and Schweitzer, F. (1991). *Stages of Faith and Religion Development. Implications for Church, Education and Society.* London.

Fowler, J. (1992). *Weaving the new creation. Stages of faith and the public church.* London.
Imbens-Fransen, A. (1995). *God in de beleving van vrouwen.* Kampen.
Janssen, M.J. (1988). *Naar een kerk op twee benen. Studie over de Pastoraal Werkster in de R.K. Kerk.* Aalsmeer.
Lifton, R. (1971). *Grenzen. De mens op zoek naar onsterfelijkheid.* Bilthoven.
Nauta, R. (1993a). "Personal identity and pastoral communication." *Journal of Empirical Theology,* 6.
———— (1993b). *Pastoral and personal identity of protestant ministers and catholic pastors.* Paper Society for the Scientific Study of Religion. Annual Meeting. Raleigh, NC.
Noordzij, J. (1994). *Religieus concept en religieuze ervaring in de christelijke traditie. Proeve van een psychologie van de spirituele ontwikkeling.* Kampen.
Nouwen, H. (1991). *Open uw hart. De weg naar onszelf, de ander en God.* Tielt.
Otto, H. (ed.). (1968). *Human potentialities: the challenge and the Promise.* St. Louis.
Parsons, T. and Bales, R.F. (1955). *Family, Sozialisation and Interaction Process.* Glencoe.
Pruyser, P. (1992). *Geloof en verbeelding. Essays over levensbeschouwing en geestelijke gezondheid.* Baarn.
Schaupp, Kl. (1995). Persönlichkeit und pastorale Beruf. In: Baumgart (Hrsg.). *Handbuch Pastoralpsychologie.* Regensburg.
Schüssler Fiorenza, E. (1983). *In Memory of Her.* New York. Dutch transl. (1987): *Ter herinnering aan haar.* Hilversum.
Sheldrake, Ph. (1991). *Spirituality and History. Questions of Interpretation and Method.* London.
Stewart, Ch. W. (1967). *Adolescent Religion. A Developmental Study of the Religion of Youth.* Nashville, New York.
Tigcheler, J. (1985). *Vrouw en spiritualiteit in het Nieuwe testament.* Kampen.
Uleijn, A. (1993). *Zelfbeeld en godsbeeld.* Baarn.
Wit, H. de (1993). *De verborgen bloei. Over de psychologische achtergronden van spiritualiteit.* Kampen.
Wolski Conn, J. (1989). *Spirituality ans Personal Maturity.* New York, London.

Literature used in chapter 3

Berger, P., Luckmann, Th. (1966). "Secularisation and Pluralism" In: *Intern. Yearbook for the Sociology of Religion II*, 73–86. Köln, Opladen.
Borgman, E. (1995). "Na de grote verhalen. Theologiseren vanuit de postmoderne ervaring" In: Kalsky, M., Borgman, E., Merkx, M. (eds.), *Herfsttij van de moderne tijd. Theologische visies op het postmodernisme.* Nijmegen, Zoetermeer, 13–27.
Bouritius, G., Claessens, P., Slik, F. van der (eds.) (1988). *Religieuze ervaring; een veelvormig perspektief op de zin van bestaan.* Tilburg.
Bulhof, I.N. (1990). "Het postmodernisme als uitdaging." In: *Postmodernisme als uitdaging*, 11–50. Baarn.
———— (1992). *Naar een postmoderne spiritualiteit?* Rede uitgesproken bij de aanvaarding van het ambt van bijzonder hoogleraar in de Fac. der Wijsbegeerte op 30 okt. 1992 R.U. Leiden.
Gerkin, Chr. V. (1986). *Widening the Horizons. Pastoral Responses to a fragmented Society.* Philadelphia.
Habermas, J. (1988). *Nachmetaphysisches Denken.* Frankfurt a. M. Dutch transl. (1990): *Na-metafysisch denken.* Kampen/Kapellen.
Harskamp, A. van (ed.) (1991). *Verborgen God of lege kerk. Theologen en sociologen over secularisatie.* Kampen.
Hartt, J., Hart, R. and Scharlemann (1986). *The critique of modernity. Theological reflections on contemporary culture.* Virginia.
Houdijk, R. (ed.) (1992). *Theologie en marginalisering.* Baarn.
Houtepen, A. (1985). *In God is geen geweld. Theologie als geloofsverantwoording in een natheïstische cultuur.* Vught.

Kaufmann, F.X. (1989). *Religion und Modernität. Sozialwissenschaftliche Perspektiven.* Tübingen.

Kessel, R. van (1986). "De crisis van de christelijke identiteit." In: *Tijds. v. Theol.* 26 (1986) 4, 329–350.

Mette, N. (1990). "Vom Säkularisierungs- zum Evangelisierungsparadigma." In: *Diakonia* 21, 1990, 420–429.

Metz, J.B. (1981). *Jenseits bürgerlicher Religion.* München' Mainz.

Schaller, L. (1987). *It's a Different World: The Challenge for Today's Pastor.* New York.

Stange, O. (ed). (1992). *Pastoral Care and Context.* Amsterdam.

Tieleman, D. (1995). *Geloofscrisis als gezichtsbedrog. Spiritualiteit en pastoraat in een postmoderne cultuur.* Kampen.

———— (1996). "De pastor als grensganger. Pastoraat in een postmoderne context voorbij restauratie en secularisatie," In: *Praktische Theologie* 23 (1996) 1, 3–23.

Weima, J. (1989). *De Religie, de mens en de geseculariseerde samenleving.* Kampen.

Ziebertz, H. (1996). *Religie in een tijd zonder religie?* Inaugurele rede van 24 april 1996 aan de Kath. Theol. Universiteit Utrecht, Utrecht.

Zuidberg, G. (1996). "Toegewijd aan de aardse werkelijkheid." In: *Speling, Tijds. voor bezinning* 48 (1996) 2, 63–68.

Literature used in chapter 4

Besluiten van de Particuliere Synode van de Bisschoppen van Nederland. In: *Archief van de kerken 35* (1980).

Dijk, B. van, Salemink, Th. (ed.) (1986). *Van beroep: pastor. De arbeidsverhoudingen van pastores in de r.k. kerk van Nederland.* Hilversum.

Ernst, H., Ven, J.A. van der (1987). *Bisschoppen in dialoog.* Verslag van gesprekken over de funktie van pastoraal werk(st)er, in een werkgroep samengesteld vanuit kerkelijk beleid en theologie. Kampen.

Gerwen, G. van (1983). "Privatisering als thema in de ecclesiologie." In: *Tijds. v. Theol.* 23 (1983), 125–146.

Haarsma, F. (1981). *Morren tegen Mozes. Pastoraaltheologische beschouwingen over het kerkelijk leven.* Kampen.

———— (1983). "Partiële identificatie met de kerk." In: Häring, H., Schoof, T., Willems, A. (eds.). *Meedenken met Edward Schillebeeckx.* Baarn.

———— (1991). *Kandelaar en korenmaat, pastoraaltheologische studies over kerk en pastoraat.* Kampen.

Howe, E. (1982). *Women and Church Leadership.* Michigan.

Oomen-van der Vegt, R. (1995). *Vrouwen in het pastoraal werk. Een onderzoek naar de positie van vrouwelijke pastores in de katholieke kerk.* M.th. Tilburg.

Sobrino, J. (1989). *The True Church and the Poor.* New York.

Ven, J.A. van der (ed.) (1985a). *Toekomst voor de kerk? Studies voor Frans Haarsma.* Kampen.

———— (1993a). *Ecclesiologie in context.* Kampen.

Zulehner, P. (1988). "Ecclesiastical Atheism." In: *Journal of Emp. Theol.* 1 (1988) 2, 5–20.

Literature used in chapter 5

Guardini, R. (1979–2de). *Religiöse Erfahrung und Glaube.* Mainz.

Hiltner, S. (1972). *Theological Dynamics.* New York.

Moltmann, J. (1980). *Trinität und Reich Gottes. Zur Gotteslehre.* München.

Peursen, C. van (1992). *Verhaal en werkelijkheid. Een deiktische ontologie.* Kampen/Kapellen.

Literature used in chapter 6

Baest, M. van (1989). "Dat alles is God niet." In: *Geest en Leven* 66 (1989) 2, 81–87.

Bernard, Ch. A. (1994). *Le Dieu des Mystiques. Les voies de l'intériorité.* Paris.

Borgman, E. (1990). *Sporen van de bevrijdende God. Universitaire theologie in aansluiting op latijnsamerikaanse bevrijdingstheologie, zwarte theologie en feministische theologie.* (diss.) Kampen.

Brady, J. (1995). *God on a Harley.* Dutch transl. *(1995): God op een Harley. Een eigentijdse parabel waarin God de mensen 'persoonlijk' begeleidt.* Utrecht.

Daly, M. (1986). Glory to God the Verb. In: Aman, K. *Border Religions of Faith. An Anthology of Religion ans Social Change.* New York.

Fox, M. (1993). *Schepping en spiritualiteit. Gaven tot bevrijding.* Zoetermeer.

Gerven, H. van (1992). *'God is altijd voortvluchtig'. Gesprekken over godsbeelden.* Baarn.

Glock, Ch., Ringer, B., Babbie, E. (1967). *To Comfort and to Challenge. A Dilemma of the Contemporary Church.* Berkeley.

Guttierez, G. (1974). *Theologie van de bevrijding.* Baarn.

———— (1987). *On Job.* New York.

Häring, H. (1995a). *De vele gezichten van God.* Concilium 1995-2. Hilversum.

———— (1995b). "Opnieuw leren wat zij zijn vergeten: de vele kanten van het spreken over God in een seculiere samenleving." In: *Tijds. v. Theol.* 35 (1995) 148-170.

———— (1996). "Op zoek naar de religieuze wortels van het gewone leven. Over het verlies van het sacrale en het profane." In: Speling, *Tijds. voor bezinning* 48 (1996) 3, 4-10.

Harmsen, H., Keyzer, R. de, Vilsteren, E. van (eds.) (1997). *Mijn God. Bedrijfspastores en God.* Disk Studiereeks nr 22. Amsterdam.

Harskamp, A. van (1991). "Behoefte aan religie of verlangen naar God?" In: *Tijds. v. Theol.* 31 (1991) 3, 223-245.

Houtepen, A. (1997). *God, een open vraag. Theologische perspectieven in een cultuur van agnosme.* Zoetermeer.

James, W. (1902). *The Varieties of Religious Experience.* Dutch transl. (1963) *Varianten van religieuze beleving. Een onderzoek naar de menselijke aard.* Zeist/Antwerpen.

Kuitert, H. (1997). *Aan God doen. Een vingerwijzing.* Baarn.

Laeyendecker, L. (1992). "Het vervagend Godsbeeld. Enkele sociologische opmerkingen." In: Arts, W.A. et al. (eds.). *Tempora mutantur,* 28-50. Baarn.

Leenhouwers, P., Logister, W., Maas, F., Meewus, H., Peeters, R.J. (1991). *Godsverduistering—Godsontmoeting. Beschouwingen over Gods openbaring onder ons.* Aalsmeer.

Maas, F. (1975). *Van God houden als van niemand. Preken van Meester Eckhart.* Haarlem.

———— (1989). *Er is meer God dan we denken. Essays over spiritualiteit.* Averbode/Kampen.

Mouw, R.J. (1990). *The God who commands.* Notre Dame.

Neven, G. (ed.) (1988). *Levenslang wachten op U. Teksten over de Godsvraag in deze tijd.* Kampen.

Nieuwenhove, J. van (1991). *Bronnen van bevrijding. Varianten in de theologie van Gustavo Guttierez.* Kampen.

Pagels, E.H. (1986). "What became of God the Mother? Conflicting Images of God in Early Christianity." In: Aman, K. Border *Religions of Faith. An Anthology of Religion and Social Change.* New York.

Pattison, St. (1994). *Pastoral care and liberation theology.* Cambridge.

Peters, J., Jacobs, J. (eds.) (1974). *Het donker is mij licht genoeg. Bloemlezing uit de werken van Johannes van het Kruis.* Bilthoven.

Peursen, C. van (1993). *De verborgen aanwezige. Godservaringen in bijbelse verhalen.* Kampen.

Pohier, J. (1985). *Dieu fractures.* Dutch transl. (1986): *God in fragmenten.* Hilversum.

Sandt, H. van de, Tongeren, L. van (eds.) (1989). *Naar mijn daden word Ik genoemd. Over de betekenis en het gebruik van de Godsnaam.* Boxtel/Brugge.

Schillebeeckx, E. (ed.) (1990). *Mystiek en politiek. Studies bij de zestigste verjaardag van Johann Baptist Metz.* Baarn.

Siemerink, J. (1989). "Prayer and our image of God." In: *Journal of Empirical Theology* 2 (1989) 1,27-44.

Simonis, Adr. Kard. (1986). *God: 'Iets' of 'Iemand'?* Brief bij gelegenheid van de Veertigdagentijd 1986. Utrecht.
Sölle, D. (1984). *God heeft mensen nodig. Een theologie van de schepping.* Baarn.
——— (1997). Droom mij, *God. Bijbelse thema's met lastige politieke vragen.* Baarn.
Tongeren, P. van (1992). *Schepping, verlossing en het kwaad. Wijsgerige en theologische reflecties.* Baarn.
Veldhuis, W. (1994). *De taal van God. Een theologische reflectie op de wijze waarop God zich openbaart.* Baarn.
Waaijman, K. (1984). *Betekenis van de Naam Jahwe.* Kampen.

Literature used in chapter 7

Boff, L. (1987a). *Passion of Christ, Passion of the World.* New York.
Dillmann, R. and Hochstaffl, J. (1991). *Jesus als Modell. Heilende Seelsorge. Praxisbegleitung in einem Gemeindebesuchsdienst.* Mainz.
Drewermann, E. (1990). *Beelden van verlossing. Toelichtingen op het evangelie van Marcus.* The Hague.
Groot, M. de (1986). *Messiaanse ikonen. Een vrouwenstudie van het evangelie naar Johannes.* Kampen.
God met ons (1997). Herderlijk schrijven over Jezus Christus. Bisschoppelijke brieven 35. Utrecht.
Harris, M.J. (1992). *Jesus as God: The New Testament use of Theos in reference to Jesus.* Michigan.
Heyer, C. den (1996). *Opnieuw: Wie is jezus? Balans van 150 jaar onderzoek naar Jezus.* Zoetermeer.
Lindijer, C., Baneke, J., Cornelissen, E. (1992). *Jezus ter sprake. Op zoek naar de plaats van Jezus Christus in pastorale praktijk en pastorale psychologie.* Zoetermeer.
Lohfink, G. (1986). "Jesus und die Kirche." In: *Hb. der Fundamental-theologie* 3, Traktat "Kirche," 49–97. Freiburg, Basel, Wien.
Nouwen, H. (1986). "Christ of the Americas." In: Aman, K. (ed.) Border Religions of Faith. An Anthology of Religion and Social Change. New York.
Rietveld, J., Stap, D.H., Duinstra, Tj. Fr., Oyen, G. van, Vloet, J. van der. (1996). *Essays over Jezus.* Kampen.
Schillebeeckx, E. (1974). *Jezus, het verhaal van een levende.* Bloemendaal.
Sobrino, J. (1986). Christology and Discipleship. In: Aman, K. (ed). *Border Religions of Faith. Aan Anthology of Religion and Social Change.* New York.
Veldhuis, W. (1974). *Over Jezus gesproken. Een oud verhaal dat verder gaat.* Hilversum.

Literature used in chapter 8

Schoonenberg, P. (1991). *De Geest, het Woord en de Zoon. Theologische overdenkingen over Geest-christologie, Logos-christologie en drieëenheidsleer.* Kampen.
Wegman, H. (1994). "Achtmaal de Geest gedenken. Schriftlezingen in de paastijd volgens recente leesroosters." In: *Tijds. voor theologie* 34 (1994) nr 2, 145–168.

Literature used in chapter 9

Bloom, A. (1973). *Tijd voor gebed.* Antwerpen/Utrecht.
Fafié, A., Renes, P. (eds.) (1995). *Mantel van gebed. Ervaringen met bidden.* Zoetermeer.

Literature used in chapter 10

Bloom, A. (1974). *De weg naar binnen.* Nijmegen.
Hammarskjöld, D. (1968). *Merkstenen.* Brugge.
Hartensveld, F. (1995). *De dynamiek van de stilte. Een spirituele zoektocht in het licht van grote denkers.* Hilversum.

Literature used in chapter 11

McCormick, R.A. (1989). *The critical Calling. Reflections on Moral Dilemmas since Vatican II.* Washington.

Engelen, J. (1985). *Het gelaat: Jij die mij aanziet. Een eerste inleiding in de filosofie van Emmanuel Levinas.* Hilversum.

Fuchs, J. (1988). *Für eine menschliche Moral. Grundfragen der theologischen Ethik.* Vols. 1–3. Freiburg i. Br.

Mc. Intyre, A. (1998). "Virtue, Tradition and God." In: Fergusson, D. (ed.). *Community, Liberalism and Christian Ethics.* Cambridge.

Izard, C.E. a.o. (ed.). (1984). *Emotions, Cognitions and Behaviour.* Cambridge.

Ricoeur, P. (1995). *Het probleem van de grondslagen van de moraal.* Kampen—Kapellen.

Schillebeeckx, E. (1977), *Gerechtigheid en liefde, genade en bevrijding.* Bloemendaal.

Schindler, Th. (1989). *Ethics: the Social Dimension. Individualism and the Catholic Tradition.* Wilmington Delaware.

Simonis, Adr. Kard. (1993). *Priesterschap en Celibaat.* Pastorale brief bij gelegenheid van Advent 1993. Utrecht.

Tigcheler, J. (1987–2de). *De Bergrede. Mattheus 5–7.* Kampen.

Zuidberg, G. (1979). "De mystiek van de alledaagse dienstbaarheid: Dag Hammarskjöld." In: *Tijds.v. Geest. Leven* 35 (1979) 3, 295–309.

Literature used in chapter 13

Boff, L. (1987b). *Und die Kirche ist Volk geworden.* Düsseldorf.

Bras, K. (1995). "Als de Heer het huis niet bouwt. Mystiek en kerkopbouw." In: *Prakt. Theologie* 1995, 3, 287–302.

Callahan. K.L. (1990) *Effective Church-leadership: Building of the twelve keys.* New York.

Derksen, N. (1989). *Eigenlijk wisten we het wel, maar we waren het vergeten. Een onderzoek naar parochie-ontwikkeling en geloofscommunicatie in de parochies van het aartsbisdom Utrecht.* (Th.D. thesis Heerlen). Kampen.

Dietterich, I.T. (1991). *An Evaluation of Approaches to Church Transformation.* The Center for Parish Development. Chicago.

Dolan, J.P., Appleby, R.S., Byrne, P., Campbell, D. (1990). *Transforming Parish Ministry. The changing Roles of Catholic Clergy, Laity and Woman Religious.* New York.

Firet, J. (1987). "Spiritualiteit als structuurprincipe van kerk en theologie." In: *Spreken als leerling,* 167–176. Kampen.

Gaudium et spes. Vaticanum II. Katholiek Archief. Amersfoort.

Greinacher, N. (1990). "Demokratisierung in der Kirche." In: *Theologische Quartalschrift* 170 (1990), 253–260.

——— (1992). Das Heil des Menschen Oberstes Gesetz in der Kirche. *Theol. Quartalschrift* 172 (1992), 1.2–15.

Gremillion, J., Castelli, J. (1987). *The Emerging Parish. The Notre Dame Study of Catholic LIfe since Vatican II.* San Francisco.

Groener, G. (1989) "Spiritualiteit en parochie-opbouw". In: J. Wissink en Th. Zweerman, *Ruimte van de Geest; over ascese, spiritualiteit en geestelijk leiderschap.* Kampen 1989, 128–143.

Hendriks, J. (1990). *Een vitale en aantrekkelijke gemeente. Model en methode van gemeenteopbouw.* Kampen.

Kessel, R. van (1989). *Zes kruiken water. Enkele theologische bijdragen voor kerkopbouw.* Hilversum.

Luijckx, M. (1981). "Leken als kerkelijke ambtsdragers: het probleem van de wijding." In: *Tijds. v. Theol.* 21 (1981) 2, 147–159.

Rikhof, H. (1981). *The Concept of Church. A Methodological Inquiry into the Use of Metaphors in Ecclesiology.* (Th.D. thesis KU Nijmegen) London.

Schillebeeckx, E. (1982). "De sociale context van de verschuivingen in het kerkelijk ambt." In: *Tijds. v. Theol.* 22 (1982), 1, 24–59.

————— (1985). *Pleidooi voor mensen in de kerk.* Baarn.
Siemerink, J. (1992). *Voorgaan in de liturgie.* Kampen.
Tigcheler, J. (1987). *Gemeenschappen in het Nieuwe Testament.* Kampen.
Zuidberg, G. (1985). *Ranken aan de wijnstok. Een briefwisseling in een parochie.* Hilversum.
————— (1996). "Parochiegemeenschap op basis van ieders eigenheid." In: *Speling, Tijds. voor bezinning* 48 (1996) 3, 27–33.

Literature used in chapter 14

Ramshaw, E. (1987). "Ritual and Pastoral Care." In: *Theology and Pastoral Care* (ed. Browning, D.S.). Philadelphia.
Wegman, H. (1995). "Het drama van de oorsprong." In: *Katholiek in de moderne tijd. Een onderzoek van de Acht mei beweging.* Zoetermeer, 152–162.

Literature used in chapter 15

Andriessen, H. (1996b). *Oorspronkelijk bestaan. Geestelijke begeleiding in onze tijd.* Baarn.
Firet, J. (1983). "Het krachtveld van de pastorale dienst." In: *Praktische Theologie* 1983, 461–480.
Ford, M. (1999). *Wounded Prophet. A Portrait of Henri J.M. Nouwen.* London.
Gerkin, Ch.V. (1997). *An Introduction to Pastoral Care.* Nashville.
Gerwen, G. van (1992). "Geestelijke verzorging in instellingen van gezondheidszorg." In: *Praktische Theologie* 19 (1992) 5, 467–482.
Grün, A. (1991). *Bilder von Seelsorge. Heilende Seelsorge. Biblische Modelle einer therapeutischen Pastoral.* Mainz.
Heeswijk, A. van (1996). *Pastoraat en geestelijke gezondheidszorg.* Baarn.
Heitink, G., Vossen, H. (eds.) (1995). "De toekomst van het pastorale beroep. Hoe blijf ik als pastor overeind?" *Praktische.* In: *Theologie* 2 (1995). Zwolle.
Heitink, G., Körver, J., van den Berg, M., Dullaert, H. (1996). *Pastoraat en geestelijke gezondheidszorg.* Baarn.
Hiltner, S. (1949). *Pastoral Counseling.* New York.
Hoeben, G. (1996). *De pastor, herder en manager? Pleidooi voor het herderschap.* Inleiding voor pastores bisdom Rotterdam, 24 april 1996. DPC Diocese Rotterdam Edition.
Koot, A-M., Zuidberg, G. (1995). *Acht vragen aan de pastor. Een handleiding voor gesprek.* Federatie VPW Nederland Edition. Utrecht.
Korsten, H., Meertens, H. Reijnen, A. (1973). *Werken aan de basis. Opbouwwerk en pastoraat.* Wegen tot pastoraat, deel 12. Nijmegen.
Lyall, D. (1995). *Counseling in the Pastoral and Spiritual Context.* London.
Mooren, J. (1989). Geestelijke verzorging en psychotherapie. Baarn.
Nouwen, H., Mc Neill, D.P., Morrison, D.A. (1982). *Compassion. A Reflection on the Christian Life.* London.
Oden, Th. (1982). *Pastoral theology. Essentials of ministry.* San Francisco.
Peters, J. (1984). *Al was het maar je schaduw: een spiritualiteit voor de hulpverlening.* Hilversum.
Peterson, E. (z.j.). *Dragende delen. Pastor zijn op authentieke wijze.* Ekklesia. Gorinchem.
Sapp, G.L. (ed.) (1993). *Compassionate Ministry.* Birmingham, Alabama.
Schillebeeckx, E. (1980). *Kerkelijk ambt, voorgangers in de gemeente van Jezus Christus.* Bloemendaal.
Schippers, K. et al. (1990). *Kerkelijke presentie in een oude stadswijk. Onderzoek naar buurtpastoraat vanuit behoeften en belangen van bewoners.* Kampen.
Schreuder, O. (1964). *Het professioneel karakter van het geestelijk ambt.* Openbare les, gegeven bij de aanvaarding van het ambt van lector in de godsdienst- en pastoraalsociologie aan de Katholieke Universiteit van Nijmegen op vrijdag 13 november 1964. Nijmegen—Utrecht.
UTP-teksten nrs. 24, 25 en 26 over 'Spiritualiteit en Pastoraat': I *De plaatselijke gemeente—een heilige ruimte; II De plaatselijke gemeente—een weg naar de bron; III*

De plaatselijke gemeente—een bron van heil; esp. B. Wolbers, "Spiritualiteit en Pastoraat" in deel II, blz. 65–73. Heerlen.

Ven, J.A. van der (ed.) (1985b). *Pastoraal tussen ideaal en werkelijkheid*. Kampen.

Witte, H. (1989). Professionalisering en kerkelijke binding van het pastoraal handelen. In: *Pastor: professional of gezondene!?* Inleidingen van de jaarlijkse landdag van de katholieke sector VGVZ. Leidschendam 1989, 13–25.

Zegveld, A. (1996). Spiritualiteit en pastoraat. In: Analecta Aartsbisdom Utrecht mei/juni 1996, 150–164.

Zuidberg, G. (1990). *Zachtmoedigheid en integriteit in het pastoraat. Notities voor een spiritualiteit van de weerbaarheid*. Hilversum.

———— (1992). *Barmhartigheid en trouw in het pastoraat. Notities voor een spiritualiteit van de volharding*. Hilversum.

———— (1993). "Ruimte in het pastoraat." Inleiding bij het afscheid van Jo Nibbelke van het DPC Zeist. DPC Zeist Edition.

INDEX